SEX AND ENLIGHTENMENT

Sex and Enlightenment

Women in Richardson and Diderot

RITA GOLDBERG

Trinity Hall, Cambridge

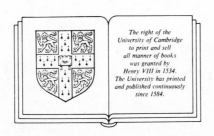

The right of the
University of Cambridge
to print and sell
all manner of books
was granted by
Henry VIII in 1534.
The University has printed
and published continuously
since 1584.

CAMBRIDGE UNIVERSITY PRESS

Cambridge

London   New York   New Rochelle
Melbourne   Sydney

Published by the Press Syndicate of the University of Cambridge
The Pitt Building, Trumpington Street, Cambridge CB2 1RP
32 East 57th Street, New York, NY 10022, USA
296 Beaconsfield Parade, Middle Park, Melbourne 3206, Australia

First published 1984

Printed in Great Britain at
the University Press, Cambridge

Library of Congress catalogue card number: 83–23210

British Library Cataloguing in Publication Data
Goldberg, Rita
Sex and enlightenment.
1. Richardson, Samuel, *Clarissa*
2. Diderot, Denis, *Religieuse, La*
I. Title
823'.6 PR3664.C34

ISBN 0 521 26069 8

For Max and Hilde Goldberg

CONTENTS

Contents

PREFACE

When I began work on the thesis that eventually became this book, Samuel Richardson was a name known to few and one often mocked even where known. *Clarissa* was grudgingly acknowledged as important, but it was not often read. Its prodigious length was thought to be a formidable deterrent to any closer acquaintance. Richardson was the sort of author duly mentioned in History of the Novel courses as taught in American universities, but rarely prescribed on reading lists. In the last few years, however, his reputation has risen so rapidly that Richardson scholarship could be called a growth industry. I have tried to explore the reasons for this Richardson revival in my Introduction, which has itself grown as new works appeared. Most of these recent books and articles have been inspired by the feminist movement, and especially by the general reappraisal of our literary traditions by feminist critics. Since my own work is no exception, first thanks must go to my feminist colleagues, who have made it possible to ask new questions. Diderot, on the other hand, has always been a source of speculation and delight for his readers, though his works too have benefited from the current interest in writers who manipulate language and literary expectation. The conjunction of Richardson and Diderot in this study has been rewarding for me, and I hope will do neither an injury.

I have many friends and colleagues to thank for their help in this project. Professor Ralph Freedman of Princeton University supervised the fledgling dissertation. He remained enthusiastic no matter where in the world we both found ourselves. A Research Fellowship at Trinity Hall, Cambridge, allowed me to turn the dissertation into a book. I am most grateful to the Master and Fellows of the College for giving me such an opportunity. More specific intellectual help came from Gillian Beer and Marian Jeanneret, who generously read the book at several stages and offered sensitive and helpful comments. Jonathan Steinberg, my colleague at Trinity Hall, went through the manuscript with his blue pen and helped push it finally into the light of day. Ian Jack pointed out some errors in the course of his sympathetic reading. Christine King, my meticulous subeditor, filled me with admiration during our exchanges over the telephone and in writing. Andrew Brown of Cambridge University Press has been a patient editor.

The most basic help of all has come on the domestic front. I should like to thank Betty Wisbey for the warm and responsible care she has given to my two sons, Daniel and Benjamin. Daniel and Benjamin themselves have been a constant source of joy, even during the hours they have made complicated. My husband, Oliver Hart, supported me as actively with his help in our domestic arrangements as he did in every other way. I am deeply grateful to him for his loving endurance.

A NOTE ON THE TEXTS

There has been much controversy recently over the versions of *Clarissa*. Most scholars rely either on the third edition of 1751, or on the Shakespeare Head edition (Oxford: 1929–30). Neither of these editions is always readily available, especially to the student or general reader. I have therefore chosen to refer to the Everyman edition, edited by John Butt (London, Melbourne and Toronto: repr. 1978). The differences between editions can be quite considerable, and the reader is alerted to this fact.

In the Diderot section I have been more fortunate, since many of the *philosophe*'s works are easy to find. These are published in paperback by Garnier Frères, and are authoritatively edited. Other works may be found in the new edition of Diderot's *Oeuvres* which has been coming out since 1975 under the supervision of H. Dieckmann, J. Proust and J. Varloot (Paris: Hermann, Éditeurs des Sciences et des Arts). Whenever possible, I have used this new edition, abbreviated as DPV in the references. Otherwise I have used the older edition of the *Oeuvres* edited by Assézat and Tourneux (Paris: Garnier Frères, 1875–7). References to this collection are abbreviated as A–T in the text.

INTRODUCTION

Clarissa and European culture

Samuel Richardson (1689–1761), a self-made printer who happened also to write three major novels towards the end of a long and successful professional life, has been and still is a source of controversy. *La querelle Richardson* began in the eighteenth century itself, when readers were divided about his morality and the elegance of his style. For every preacher who cried up the virtues of his first novel, *Pamela* (1740), from the pulpit, there was another to denounce the lubriciousness and moral ambiguity of the novel in the press.[1] His third book, *Sir Charles Grandison* (1754), has been generally dismissed as his least successful, though it has exerted an enormous influence over English writers in particular. But his second novel, *Clarissa* (1748), had had a profound impact on European culture. *Clarissa* has never been quite so much the object of public debate as *Pamela*, but its effects have been deeper for all that. Certainly the literate world has spent much time debating the qualities of Richardson's masterpiece.

The extent to which *Clarissa* has become a European novel, despite its obvious and specific Englishness, comes as a surprise even to scholars who are used to thinking about the connections between national literatures. In the study which follows, I have attempted to understand Richardson's originality in terms of this European reception. There was hardly a writer, major or minor, working in the decade or two after the publication of this novel who did not attempt something on the Richardsonian model; and of course the influence did not end with the eighteenth century. But it is always useful to begin at the beginning. I have chosen to focus on Denis Diderot (1713–84), the French *philosophe*, not only because he attempted a novel which shows clear Richardsonian origins (*La Religieuse*, 1760), but because he became, and remains, the most sympathetic and perceptive reader of Richardson's works ever to have written. Unlike Richardson himself, Diderot was immensely cultivated, and self-conscious in a way which today's Paris intellectuals would find congenial. It seems at the outset mysterious that a reader of Diderot's sophistication would find much to admire in the tribulations of an apparently rather prim low-church English maiden. But Diderot's *Éloge de Richardson* (1762) is a subtle appreciation of Richardson's method and success as well as of his social impact. When we study it along with other works of Diderot's – his sentimental comedies, which are concerned with sex and class and even make reference to Richardson's novels; his essays on English writers concerned with the life of feeling (Shaftesbury in particular); and most of all his works on sexuality (some of the *contes*, the pornographic novel *Les Bijoux indiscrets*, the essay 'Sur les femmes' and the philosophical fantasy *Supplément au voyage de Bougainville*) – we are given a unique chance to observe one genius reacting self-consciously to another. We are allowed to watch the effect of Clarissa's unlikely story on the creative life of Diderot and his gifted circle of friends. And we are given extended commentaries on the significance of the literary experience as it develops. Even the quarrel between Diderot and Rousseau is filtered through a reading of Richardson: Diderot has made *Clarissa*, and to a lesser extent *Grandison*, his personal touchstone for social and sentimental behaviour. He attacks Rousseau in several of his works for his inadequacy as a friend, as a writer, and as a sensitive being. Occasionally, as in the *Éloge*, he is compared directly and unfavourably to Richardson. Rousseau, meanwhile, manages to publish his highly Richardsonian love-story, *Julie, ou La Nouvelle Héloïse* (1761), perhaps the most important French novel of the century and certainly one of the most popular, without acknowledging that he owes anything to the object of Diderot's veneration.

From the start, Richardson was viewed with some suspicion because he took the advice of women seriously. Particularly during the composition of the last novel, *Sir Charles Grandison*, he surrounded himself with clever ladies, some old and most young. He frequently solicited their views, and they in turn offered extensive commentaries and criticism. Their remarks were scrupulously ignored, of course (Richardson never altered his books to accommodate the comments of any of his friends, of whatever sex), but that has not prevented critics ever since from worrying about the integrity of Richardson's creative impulses. It was exactly because Richardson's novels were offered up as educational material, more likely to be read by young ladies than conduct books or Bibles, that the guardians of youthful morals worried. And there is no question that sexuality is dealt with candidly in the novels, especially in the first two. The religious and moral wholesomeness of the enterprise might sometimes be hard for the

simple of heart to see. The women who wrote in the decades following
Richardson's death were acutely conscious of this problem. Mme Le
Prince de Beaumont, an interesting if uninspired author of eighty
pedagogical novels in addition to her best-remembered fairy tale,
'Beauty and the Beast', had this to say about Richardson in 1774:

> Le bon & l'honnête M. Ritcharson, auteur de Pamela, Clarice, &c. a donné
> dans cet écueil, & tout en voulant donner l'amour de la vertu a porté dans plus
> d'un coeur la connoissance du vice; lumière toujours funeste. J'entrerois bien
> dans un plus grand détail, & je prouverois ce que je dis par des exemples, mais
> ce seroit tomber dans le défaut que je reprends, &, quoiquil soit rare aux jeunes
> personnes de lire des préfaces, il s'en pourroit trou᾿er qui sortiroient de la règle,
> & elles m'imposent silence.[2]

Despite her own prodigious output (she was translated into many
languages and was considered proper reading for young girls well into
the nineteenth century), her concern about the moral contamination
in fiction of the Richardsonian sort was typical. Nonetheless, she was
the author of two novels which were direct reworkings of *Clarissa*. *La
Nouvelle Clarice* (1768) owes as much to Rousseau as to Richardson. *Le
Vrai Point d'honneur* (1774) is slightly more English in orientation than
the earlier novel. But both try to soften the sexual openness and the
moral despair of the original.

We may compare Mme de Beaumont's comments with those of
Rousseau in the 'Préface' to *La Nouvelle Héloïse*. A fundamental
suspicion of art and literature is combined with the sexual austerity his
readers would have come to expect from the author of *Émile* and *Sophie*:

> Il faut des spectacles dans les grandes villes, et des romans aux peuples
> corrompus. J'ai vu les moeurs de mon temps, et j'ai publié ces lettres. Que n'ai-
> je vécu dans un siècle où je dusse les jeter au feu! . . .
> . . . Ce recueil avec son gothique ton convient mieux aux femmes que les
> livres de philosophie. Il peut même être utile à celles qui, dans une vie déréglée,
> ont conservé quelque amour pour l'honnêteté. Quant aux filles, c'est autre
> chose. Jamais fille chaste n'a lu de romans, . . . Celle qui, malgré ce titre, en
> osera lire une seule page est une fille perdue; mais qu'elle n'impute point sa
> perte à ce livre, le mal était fait d'avance.[3]

This view is such a common one in all the countries of Europe
throughout the eighteenth and nineteenth centuries that it hardly
needs elaboration. The most interesting thing about it is that Rousseau
himself doesn't choose to recognize the origins of the notion. It is
essentially a Puritan (or, in Rousseau's case, Calvinist) world-view
that makes women so terribly responsible for sexual misdeeds and their
social effects. Rousseau is writing very consciously for Catholic France,

or worse, for atheist Paris; and he is too angry to see that a popularization of this Puritan view about female sexuality has already begun. His book could hardly have been a best-seller had it not been for Richardson.

It is the popularization on the one hand, and the tremendous appeal which *Clarissa* had for the intellectuals of Europe on the other, that make this kind of cross-cultural study so rewarding. If Rousseau was suspicious, Diderot was totally trusting. He compared *Clarissa* to the Bible and measured friends (not only the lapsed Rousseau) by its standard. If they laughed when they should have cried, he could never look them in the eye again. Because he was a feminist in many ways (and certainly so in comparison with Rousseau), he used Richardson to extend his own lifelong study of women and their sexuality. His friend Mme Riccoboni, who had married into an acting family and was herself the author of several novels *à l'anglaise*, including most notably the Richardsonian *Lettres de Mistriss Fanni Butlerd* (1757), was another member of his circle who took the morality of Richardson's novels seriously. But they debated the aesthetics of feelings as well, and both wrote consciously with an eye on what they saw as a new literary method.

From the beginning, then, fiction has raised special problems; and fiction of the kind which Richardson produced, which pretended to some sort[4] of absolute truth to experience, raised the most difficult problems of all. On the one hand, it offered the new and challenging methodology which Diderot and his friends recognized early on (Vivienne Mylne points out, for example, that the letter-novel, one variation of the form, reached its fashionable height, both in France and in England, in the decade 1780–90, even though few plots were really appropriate for such treatment).[5] It filled the gap left by the decline of the major forms of poetry and tragedy, but substituted unlikely characters – women in domestic struggles – for kings and angels and knights. Letters, journals and conversation became the favoured means of approaching this truth. On the other hand, truth itself became absolutely personal, something to be sought in private and not on the stage of public life. This was a challenge indeed. It demanded an active readership, but not an educated one: the reading itself was meant to be an education. And it was left to this relatively ill-equipped readership (as some writers at the time thought), consisting mostly of young girls and eager matrons, to form moral judgments on the basis of their imaginative identification with people like themselves. The accessibility of all this easy self-made morality must have seemed frightening at the time.

In France, indeed, an interest in *Clarissa* seems to have been linked, on the whole, to an interest in feminism. The novel of feeling appears always to have been recognized as a form peculiarly suited to the predicament of women. While we may observe a general feminization of point of view in Europe at this time, there are no writers in Germany, for instance, who take quite so active an interest in female sexuality as do Diderot and his successors, Laclos and Stendhal. Laclos's *Liaisons dangereuses* (1782) makes such devastating use of the epistolary technique that it may well be seen as the last major work possible in the letter form. There is no question that the controlling consciousness in the novel is a woman's. But there is no spiritual redemption in sight. Instead, Mme de Merteuil is a terrifyingly intelligent strategist who uses her sexuality as a powerful weapon in a world that respects convention, but not much else. The only woman who makes any attempt to make moral sense of her world, Mme de Tourvel, is seen as weak and defeated, and she eventually dies of shame.

The letters are masterpieces of literary sophistication: they are recognized as fictional devices by the characters themselves. But though they are skilfully manipulated by Mme de Merteuil and her sometime lover, the Comte de Valmont, they are truth-telling in the end. The written word has been shown to be highly dangerous; and in a way the tut-tutting matrons of the mid-eighteenth century are vindicated. Nonetheless, *Les Liaisons dangereuses* is an assessment of what is seen as a frank declaration of war between the sexes, and it was written by a soldier who also wrote a passionate treatise (composed in 1784 but unpublished until 1904)[6] urging women to take up the struggle for their own equality and freedom. As Tony Tanner has pointed out in his book entitled *Adultery in the Novel*,[7] the European tendency is to focus on sexuality outside marriage. There is a marked turning away from these explorations of female sexuality which we see in England. Perhaps the large number of women authors writing in English has something to do with the interest in virgins rather than in adulteresses. The Gothic novel, for example, defines sexual terror in terms of the prenuptial unknown. Laclos was an admirer of Richardson. Stendhal, another student of women's sexuality, admired Laclos, and both authors could hardly escape being Rousseauvians. Interestingly enough, Vivienne Mylne tells us that Stendhal was moved by the novels of Mme Riccoboni.[8] In any case, the studies of desire which he produced, and his own treatises on sex and love, put him firmly in the Richardsonian line, sinuous though the family tree may have become by the time Napoleon overran Europe.

Had it been possible, I should have liked to have discussed Richardson's impact in Germany. The moral plays of Lessing, the novels of Goethe, Sophie von la Roche, Jean Paul and Gellert, and even the tempestuous poems of Klopstock could all be considered in the light of interrelations both with England and with France. But there are limits as well as beginnings; and perhaps it is time now to turn to the critical debate in England. It has been consistent over the years. There is little doubt that the skirmishes have lasted longest on Richardson's home ground, though in recent years the battlefield has shifted to include America as well. A closer look at the history of these controversies may help to illuminate the general predicament in Europe as a whole; for in the English-speaking world critics have felt strongly that they had to engage with Richardson to make sense of the development of the novel.

Clarissa and the critics

Because Fielding was an exact contemporary, and perhaps also because *Shamela*, his attack on *Pamela*, was so amusing as well as so devastating, English and American critics have tended to polarize over their favourite authors. It is only a relatively recent development that the tiresome quest for the paternity of the English novel has been more or less abandoned: until after the Second World War, to be for Fielding was to be against Richardson. And to be for either was to declare one's favourite the Homer of the field: the first, the most original, and also the best. But it is not necessary, nor even particularly useful, to approach the *querelle* in this way; and these days it is certainly very much out of favour to impose such values on any body of literary material.

The reason for this critical split is apparent from the eighteenth century on. Fielding is seen as the champion of an aristocratic, cultivated and decidedly 'masculine' approach to matters of taste, whether these are questions of style or questions of correct social behaviour. The mistrust of Puritan values both enlivens and distorts *Shamela*, and is typical for his class. Even though he later became a generous admirer of Richardson, and wrote his *Amelia* (1751) almost as a direct answer to the Richardsonian challenge set forth in *Clarissa* and *Grandison*, it is the Fielding of *Shamela* and *Joseph Andrews* whom Richardson himself never forgave, and whom critics of a certain cast have ever since held up as their standard-bearer. In *Joseph Andrews* and *Tom Jones* there is plenty of earthiness and knockabout comedy, but it doesn't take much to see that Fielding is playing basically with *literary* conventions. As in drama, we learn about human nature in the mass: that it is susceptible to fleshly weakness, that it doesn't practise what it preaches, and so on. But wenches are wenches, ladies are ladies, and good-hearted foundlings are high-born in the end. There is no challenge to society in his books, though plenty of calls to the individual reader to remember that feeling hearts are the only alternative to cruelty and exploitation. It is odd to reflect that one can pull these kinds of generalization – maxims, if one likes – out of Fielding's novels, when it was indeed Richardson and not Fielding who drove subsequent generations of readers mad with his moralizing and sentence-abstracting tendencies. Perhaps there are two important points to remember about Fielding which help to explain his popularity with the male critical establishment, in the nineteenth century especially. First, he challenged neither class and social boundaries on the one hand, nor sexual categories on the other. Secondly, his upper-class narrators in *Joseph Andrews* and *Tom Jones* are themselves ideal critics: learned, worldly masters of linguistic manipulation. This second part of the 'masculinist' point of view has become prominent in our own century (it once depended on an education available only to men, and there is still a certain residual effect in the critical world), and I shall discuss it shortly.

Any society which itself values an ideology of individualism but depends on rigid social structures to achieve its aims will admire the call to the development of an individual morality. Such a view would have suited the Victorians, for whom repression was such a powerful and creative force. Despite Fielding's earthiness, and his hard-headed approach to sex, it is not seen as dark or subversive. It is merely a sign of right feeling, though it occasionally makes a nuisance of itself. Even in *Amelia*, where the challenge to domesticity in the person of Miss Matthews is more direct than in any other of Fielding's writings, we are given an essentially masculine view of the problem: it doesn't really *matter*, even though an affair is bound to cause some pain. In some ways, such a view must have reassured the Victorians, whose own uneasy feelings about such matters were susceptible to volcanic explosions now and then. There is the late-Victorian view of Leslie Stephen, for example, who was, after all, the editor of Richardson's collected works and the father of Virginia Woolf, a novelist very much in the Richardsonian tradition:

I will confess that the last time I read *Clarissa Harlowe* it affected me with a kind of disgust. We wonder sometimes at the coarse nerves of our ancestors, who could see on the stage any quantity of murders and ghosts and miscellaneous horrors. Richardson gave me the same shock from the elaborate detail in which he tells the story of Clarissa; rubbing our noses, if I may say so, in all her agony, and squeezing the last drop of bitterness out of every incident. I should have liked some symptom that he was anxious to turn his eyes from the tragedy instead of giving it so minutely as to suggest that he enjoys the spectacle. Books sometimes owe part of their success, as I fear we must admit, to the very fact that they are in bad taste. They attract the contemporary audience by exaggerating and overweighting the new vein of sentiment which they have discovered.[9]

Even Romantics like Coleridge, who were great admirers of Richardson's explorations of forbidden subjects, had some difficulty with the murkier parts of Richardson's world (of course, like Fielding, they were usually defining themselves as anti-Pamelists, rather than as opponents of subsequent novels). Here is the learned Coleridge, irritated and wondering together: 'I confess that it has cost, and still costs, my philosophy some exertion not to be vexed that I must admire, aye, greatly admire, Richardson. His mind is so very vile a mind, so oozy, so hypocritical, praise-mad, canting, envious, concupiscent!'[10]

The linked charges of what might be termed prurience, on the one hand, and of 'unmanliness', on the other, have until recently persisted in the criticism, and seem to be beginning a revival under the sting of more feminist readings, if I may so term them. Even a little mistake by Ian Watt, who focuses with sympathy on Richardson – and on Defoe and Fielding, the two other writers with whom he is inevitably compared – has something to say about Richardson's identification with women. 'Indeed', says Watt, 'there is much in his letters to suggest that he had a deep personal identification with the opposite sex which went far beyond social preference and cultural rapport. Such, certainly, is the implication of the fact that he was afraid of mice, or at least confessed to the future Mrs Chapone, that he had "ever had a kind of natural aversion to that species of animal".'[11]

The strangeness of this piece of evidence, and the use to which it is put, are quite arresting enough on their own. But the genesis of this excursion into psycho-criticism is even more interesting. Watt has completely misread an exchange of letters between Richardson and a friend. Richardson was actually writing to a much older lady than Watt thinks: to the mother-in-law of the future Mrs Chapone, in fact. She had told him that her youngest son, aged twelve, had written a sermon on a text from Parson Williams in *Pamela*, 'The liberal soul shall be fat', but before the child could show Richardson his creation it had been eaten by rats. Richardson replied, not unnaturally, 'Vile Vermin – I ever had a kind of natural Aversion to that Species of Animals – I shall now hate them worse than ever.'[12] Even such a lighthearted example is revealing, because we can see how easily distortions occur. Straight biographical details may be manipulated so that they suit our beliefs and prejudices.

And this question of 'beliefs and prejudices' is a thorny one indeed. Until quite recently, interpretations of *Clarissa* have more or less been revisions of each other. Pro-Fieldingites and pro-Richardsonians did battle over the relative merits and nastinesses of the world which Richardson produced in his massive novel. Any modern critic will provide a summary of these positions somewhere in the footnotes (see, for example, Mark Kinkead-Weekes's introduction to his book of 1973, and William Beatty Warner in his of 1979). Critics have never stopped being appalled at the sexuality in Richardson's novels, however much they disguised their horror; and debates have tended to centre around the 'realism' of the technique and the strangeness of Richardson's psychological makeup. There is no question that much anxiety has been caused because heroines carry so much of the religious and moral freight of Richardson's novels. They are taken seriously in Richardson as they are not in any other early novelist. The most striking reinterpretations of Richardson until the late 1970s have been those produced by feminists, who have reassessed almost every aspect of the critical orthodoxy. No longer is Clarissa seen as frigid because she doesn't enjoy the rape, nor as 'over-punctilious' because she will not submit to marriage. Even though some readings have been as primitive as the ones which they have attacked, showing an unfortunate lack of literary sophistication in their eagerness to revise and readmit their heroine into the canon of critical acceptability, on the whole they have been crucial to the more balanced view of the novel and its impact which we enjoy today.[13]

The most recent wave of criticism, however, which sometimes overlaps with the feminist wave, doesn't escape controversy either. It sees most of what has preceded it as work in the service of unexamined ideology, and comes along with the reassessment of the eighteenth century under the influence of French structuralists and post-structuralists. The work of Michel Foucault on the structures of power and sexuality which have governed the development of our culture from the eighteenth century to our own has been part of this reassessment.[14] But some literary critics, especially in America, have been influenced most recently by the work of Jacques Derrida. There has been considerable confusion about the nature of this influence. In general, they have been concerned to show how the authority of canonical texts has been established through conventions of interpretation which do not fundamentally challenge the supremacy of the author and of prevailing ideologies. For them, previous readings have been 'humanist', well-intended but ultimately authoritarian. The traditional terms of literary criticism – 'theme', 'character', 'meaning' – assume an ultimate text which some but not all qualified readers are able to recognize. I shall dwell at greater length on some of the challenges offered to 'humanist' readings, and point out some of the paradoxes inherent in this sort of critical radicalism.

Who are the major exponents of the humanist line? I suppose that all readings until the late 1970s have been humanist ones, because they have not been able to take account of contemporary critical theory. But the three best-known and moderately recent treatments of Richardson have been those by Ian Watt in *The Rise of the Novel*, a work now too well known to need discussion here; Mark Kinkead-Weekes's *Samuel Richardson: Dramatic Novelist*;[15] and Margaret Doody's *A Natural Passion: A Study of the Novels of Samuel Richardson*.[16] Despite some flaws, Watt's book is still a basic critical text. It is essentially a sociology of the novel, and therefore an important document. Current theory is often contemptuous of societal connections, because it hasn't developed a proper historiography or sociology which could incorporate its methods and outlook (and perhaps, indeed, it is not possible to do so).

Mark Kinkead-Weekes's own work is a model of humanist criticism at its best. He is both attacked and given due credit by William Beatty Warner, the angry young man of the Derridean line (who appears to owe much to Roland Barthes as well), and for good reason. It would be hard to fault his respect for the text, and his literary sensitivity. Richardson, of course, lies at the centre of his study, as his title suggests. He shirks neither the task of interpretation, which as a good humanist critic he sees as the purpose of his enterprise, nor the obligation of respect for the creative power of the artist. I suppose it could be said that this does reflect a certain world-view, but it is sometimes difficult to see how even his critics overcome the realities of literary practice when they seek to depose the author and the validity of the search for meaning from their own writings. Kinkead-Weekes's central point, which is again suggested in his title, is that Richardson 'formally banishes himself, and creates by becoming each of his characters'.[17] In this way, he is more of a 'dramatic' writer, despite his use of the epistolary form, than is Laclos, for example, whose mastery of the personal letter is seen by Kinkead-Weekes as considerably superior to Richardson's. There is much more recorded dialogue than there is in *Les Liaisons dangereuses*. In *Pamela*, this has the effect of making some parts of letters into 'scenes' linked only by stage directions ('I said', 'he said' and so on). In *Clarissa*, dialogue and gesture are rendered almost entirely directly. Kinkead-Weekes gives the quarrelsome scenes between Clarissa and Arabella as examples.[18]

Kinkead-Weekes makes a particularly interesting distinction between History, Fable and Myth as dominant modes of story-telling; and he applies his categories to eighteenth-century fiction in order to make certain points about Richardson. His definitions owe little to contemporary theory, but are useful just the same:

> In Myth, an author presents a lifelike world, but does so in order to discover and reveal behind it, a hidden structure of 'truth', in a different and deeper dimension. In Fable the author constructs an artefact, a confessedly 'made-up' world, in order to be able to analyse certain features of 'reality' more freely and more precisely. But in History the author explores the contingent and phenomenal for its own sake, and is most concerned to create a world which can imitate 'reality' as fully as possible; refusing to impose shape or authorial vision on multifarious experience.[19]

In his view, novelists tend towards one or another of these imaginative modes, even though we always find a mixture in any given work. He calls Defoe an essentially mythic writer, Fielding a fabulist, and Richardson a historian. Richardson's skill at 'dramatic narrative' doesn't contradict the overall historical emphasis, because both of these modes are particularly concerned with character, not with plot or hidden abstract meaning.[20] I was interested in these distinctions, because I should not have used such categories and I think Richardson in particular suffers from them. I shall be discussing my own view of Richardson's importance later in this chapter. The point here is that Kinkead-Weekes has made the author absolutely central to the work of art, and that, to some extent, influences what he can see. If we are most interested in the novel as a work received by a community, then we must ask ourselves other sorts of questions. How does a novel acquire meaning and significance? Why do people read it? There is quite a different aesthetic problem to be contemplated when we consider the relation of any work of art to its contemporary readers and to its posterity from the ones which are raised when we think about the author alone.

Kinkead-Weekes suffers from the same problem as most other Richardsonians: the organization of this vast edifice into some sort of critical whole. Similar difficulties assail Margaret Doody, another major critic in the 'humanist' line, whose work *A Natural Passion* was published in 1974. There is always the desire to include everything, and Doody's study of the three novels does just that. Much attention is given to literary antecedents, and close readings of the texts themselves. The book is gracefully written, and is certainly necessary reading for anyone embarking on a study of Richardson, but one can see why more recent critics have felt that a core is missing. Perhaps most humanist critics (and I include myself in their number, at least in this respect) accept the novel as a world on its own, but few of us have very closely examined the implications of such an assumption for criticism. Are we to treat the novel on its own terms, accepting as our limits those arranged for us by its author? In that case, we are bound to give the author prominence. He or she is like God, presiding over the creation which we, like good natural scientists, examine for laws, flaws and regularities, giving credit all the while, of course, to the one who has made it all possible. Or do we puzzle about how such a world came to be? In that case, we are like creationists and cosmologists, depending on our critical orientation; but we are interested in origins, raw materials, antecedents. The religious and scientific comparisons can hardly be inappropriate when we consider how similar are the questions which the various human disciplines ask of themselves. I suppose that most traditional criticism relies on the categories which it has been given, assuming that it is the servant and not the spy of art.[21]

As I have hinted already, however, radical questions have been raised about these matters in the past decade or so. I should like to devote a few moments to William Beatty Warner,[22] because he is so aggressive in his attack on what he sees as the authoritarianism of the old humanist line. He continues to admire Kinkead-Weekes, he says, as the best of a benighted lot. Warner's is a skilfully written book, and contains the fiercest use of inverted commas that I have ever seen: all the humanist terms, such as 'character', 'theme', 'self', 'integrity' and other such messy but in their limited and clouded way useful words are dispensed with two blows from Warner's electric typewriter. The book has many merits. It emphasizes the fictional elements of the novel, and the rhetorical devices; and indeed it is quite scholarly. But one has to be impressed all the same by the observation that we have not advanced very far across the battlefield of sexual criticism. There was a time when Fielding was seen as masculine, breezy and healthy and Richardson was seen as feminine, confined and sick, as I've already suggested. And now, in the late 1970s, we find that Warner is absolutely furious because Clarissa wins over Lovelace, and dominates the text that bears her name. It is probably he, and not most of Richardson's ordinary readers, who needs to be reminded that this novel is *fiction*, and not an autonomous world. On the other hand, the power of his response reminds us that novels have actually formed consciousness and expectations, literary and extra-literary. This is a point that much modern criticism both recognizes and shies from; and it has led Warner into some interesting difficulties. It is hard to guess at the cause of all this anxiety, though we can see some immediate connections in the reaction against the feminist criticism of the last fifteen years or so. In every generation, it seems, there are academic Don Juans wishing that the rake's brilliance would show some *result*. In every generation, someone is furious with Clarissa. Warner calls Clarissa a con-artist, and says that 'by contrast with Lovelace's feelings for Clarissa, Clarissa seems irreducibly self-centred, and her friendship with Anna Howe chill and uninteresting . . .'.[23] He cites the French critic Gaston Bachelard, whose *Psychoanalysis of Fire* includes the following gem of insight: 'Feminine heat attacks things from without. The masculine heat attacks things from within at the very heart of the essential being.' Armed with this assertion, Warner says that Lovelace is 'like fire' while Clarissa is 'like light'.[24] This is curious, because that very quality of essentiality which Warner sees, indeed with much reason, as a fictional construct in Clarissa's case is merely transferred by him to the male impulse in the book. What really disturbs him is the indisputable fact that Lovelace's main literary and sexual skills, his talents for parody, subversion and the creation of plots, are dependent on Clarissa's great design, the book of virtue. Lovelace is by nature a reactor, an interpreter, and Warner is irritated that so many generations of readers have been duped into accepting Clarissa's version of the story as engineered by Richardson. But his only defence against this state of things seems to be the exclusion of the female reader. 'Each reader', he says oddly, 'acts out the disturbing and pleasurable desire to penetrate the Lady . . .' and he continues elsewhere: 'The Lady is the text; the serpent is the reader.' The rape, for him, is also the moment of completion, the moment when Clarissa 'will be undressed, seen, penetrated and known. These are activities which engage every reader, like Lovelace, who wishes to win authority for his interpretation.'[25] Since *Clarissa* had from its inception a large female readership, and still seems to attract women perhaps rather more than men (if recent scholarship is any criterion), one can only call this sort of criticism defensive – and that is strange in so self-conscious a writer as Warner.

Winning authority seems to be a general problem for some modern critics. Terry Eagleton, whose book *The Rape of Clarissa* (Oxford: Basil Blackwell, 1982) is perhaps the shortest monograph on Richardson ever produced, enlists the help of various approaches: feminism, Marxism, psychoanalysis and neo-structuralist literary theory. This lively eclecticism has done much to popularize Richardson in unlikely circles. But it has its dangers. It seems to me that Eagleton occasionally confuses authority with authoritarianism. He thinks himself more subversive than he is. Clarissa and her rape, after all, have received a great deal of attention in recent years from a number of feminist critics. Perhaps he becomes unnecessarily combative as a result. A remark like the following is not challenging to anything in particular, but it proposes its own rather unpleasant set of dogmas: 'Deeply ambiguous though Richardson's novels are, he would have found the modern liberal's complacent cult of confusion simply obnoxious. And though he preached a good many obnoxious doctrines himself, he would surely have been right' (p. 24). These 'would haves' loaded onto the shoulders of a writer long dead are a bad sign in a critic who has strong views of his own. There are passages with which I strongly disagree (if I understand them correctly, and I may misread).

One example will serve. Lovelace begins his campaign early in the novel by luring Clarissa into corresponding with him. He reassures her of the innocence of their exchange by telling her (as he gloats to Belford later) that letters contain 'nothing of body'. Eagleton reflects at length on Lovelace's remark:

'Nothing of body': if this is unintentionally ironic (for Lovelace's whole aim in writing is of course to possess Clarissa's body), it is also self-undoing, for it shows how language does indeed have a 'body', a material weight of connotations, which outstrips authorial meaning. If it is meant as ironic it is equally self-undoing, for as we shall see Clarissa's body is indeed a sort of 'nothing', a sheer resistance to symbolization which signals the death of script. That the body finally escapes language is the subversive truth which this most remorselessly representational of texts will have finally to confront. 'Nothing of body': blandly desexualized, writing cuts free from the carnal only the more ably to wield dominance over it: 'the mind impelling sovereignly the vassal-fingers', male *écriture* subduing the female flesh to its pleasures. If 'body' means substance, law, constraint, there must indeed be none of it in the scriptive congress between the pair; such bodily resistance must be dissolved into the free play of the letter, so that Lovelace may finally come to inscribe Clarissa with his penis rather than his pen. (p. 48)

Here again it is difficult to see what is 'subversive' about the acknowledgment of the fact that in the end all writing is bodiless. Surely this must be evident to all but the most credulous. Eagleton makes very strange assumptions about the nature of 'body' on the one hand, and 'script' on the other. If we were to read this passage without having read the novel upon which it is a commentary, we would be surprised to learn that Clarissa herself writes voluminously. Even after her death, it is her words and not Lovelace's which take us through the final rewards and punishments meted out to the other characters.

Clarissa's will and her posthumous letters assure her presence in the consciousness of her survivors and of her readers. What, then, is male 'script' as opposed to female 'script'? And why *should* 'body' mean 'substance, law, constraint'? That is Eagleton's assumption. In fact the law itself in all its more conventional interpretations is a highly male institution in *Clarissa*. It is unlikely that Lovelace would set out to convince Clarissa of the propriety of correspondence by asserting that letter-writing had 'nothing of substance, law, constraint' in it; but that is where the argument leads us, if Eagleton's definition is substituted for the word 'body' in the original passage. There are a few pages like this one which have confused me. Eagleton's book has been a colourful addition, however, to the feminist reappraisal of Richardson's importance.

A genuinely eccentric interpretation of the rape comes from Judith Wilt in her article 'He Could Go No Farther: A Modest Proposal about Lovelace and Clarissa', *PMLA*, 92, no. 1 (January 1977), 19–32. One could not accuse *her* of seeking authority for her view of the matter. She suggests that it is Mother Sinclair, the harlot and 'man–woman', who did the dirty work in the nightmarish scene of the rape. Lovelace, on the contrary, is himself 'feminine'. He and Clarissa 'struggle together for the position of victim/tyrant inside a rape relationship'. Lovelace, though he is an overreacher, is an instrument in the hands of women; indeed, his 'crazed servitude to obsession' (p. 22) is seen as somehow feminine. It is quite true that the debate about identity in this novel centres around notions of *sexual* identity. All four letter-writers devote a number of pages to the subject. Lovelace and Clarissa share the opinion that men and women are not so much opposites as bands on a spectrum of sexual character. Borderline figures like the prostitutes are seen as disturbing by everyone. But we are back in the land of Eagleton's 'would haves'. If the rape scene is ambiguous, it will always be ambiguous. It is fiction, after all. It is no good assuming that some Sherlock Holmes of the card catalogues is going to come along with a fresh piece of evidence and clear up the mystery. And it is downright bizarre to assume that Lovelace is consistently impotent because he is troubled by conflict. Even in life, spiritual and sexual identity do not always mirror each other quite so crudely. We are bound to be far more cautious when we are trying to understand literary constructions.

A highly intelligent study of *Pamela* and *Clarissa* by Terry Castle ('The Insistence of the Letter: Fiction and Experience in the Novels of Samuel Richardson', Diss. University of Minnesota, 1980)[26] is based on the same premises as Warner's. It must be said, however, that

Castle attacks Warner on the same grounds as I do (p. 221). She suggests that his denial of the reality of what she calls 'sexual politics' has very much blurred the sharpness of his remarks. Castle's work focuses on the act, or acts, of interpretation which the novels press us into. There is no ultimate meaning in the text itself, she says, but rather a series of interpretations, or misreadings. Her skill with literary theory and with the techniques of semiotics allows her to show very cogently how characters, especially Clarissa herself, of course, become texts for other characters or 'readers' in the novels themselves; and she sees Clarissa's predicament (a fundamentally female one, at that) as one of constant interruption and misreading. She tries to resist what she feels is the strong pull of the novel to make us draw a single set of meanings from the text, or, as she puts it, to 'naturalize' one interpretation, Clarissa's, above all others. To fall into the trap of meaning is to become too rigid, to assume that the novel has only one thing to tell us. Even though none of us escapes interpretation entirely, because we are all to varying degrees passionately involved in what is before us, we must be aware of our own role in constructing and deconstructing what the text offers. Or as Castle puts it in her usual clear way, 'Readers, the structuralists point out, tend to naturalize meaning in texts. That is, even though the reader produces meaning actively, in the moment of reading, this significance seems to take on immediately a quality of immanence. It seems to have been present "in" the text all along' (p. 72).

At this point, I find myself in rather a dilemma. I admire greatly the intelligence and insight of Castle's work, and share many of her assumptions about the importance of misreading as a principle of development, both for characters and for 'real' readers (as she puts it). But it is still difficult to regard a book as historically isolated, or to pretend that it has not functioned *as if* it had certain meanings on the larger stage of culture. In any work of art, as in any human activity, we are confronted with more than epistemological problems, however basic these may be. There is always a Platonic unease about the notion of 'misreading', creative and productive though it is; after all, it implies that there is a reading of which the others could be a distortion, and that seems directly contradictory to the strenuously anti-Platonic efforts of deconstructionists. Similarly, in this passage, the reader can't help feeling that there is a 'real' Clarissa whom the Harlowe family are not seeing properly; and that deposits us squarely back in the humanist world, where no one much minded about such things.

There are reasons for the ease with which we fall into contradictions. Novels, after all, are artefacts. It is clearly difficult to maintain our balance when it comes to fiction. The vehemence, even bitterness, of modern controversies only confirms our anxieties. If we abandon ourselves and allow the characters in a novel too much autonomy, we err in forgetting that they are creatures of a single imagination and its language. But if we are too interested in the author and questions of intention and historical circumstance, we risk the abandonment of the novel as a work of art with its own rules and peculiarities. Up to a point, novel-readers resemble the innocent maidens of eighteenth-century fiction. They must be strenuously vigilant, always aware of the malleability of their own receptive imaginations. We are easily seduced into a fictional world, abandoning all as-ifs at the threshold of the narrative. But our precautions can be carried too far. As Samuel Johnson wrote in his defence of Shakespeare's 'irregularities' against the attacks of eighteenth-century neoclassical critics:

> The objection arising from the impossibility of passing the first hour at Alexandria and the next at Rome, supposes that when the play opens the spectator really imagines himself at Alexandria and believes that his walk to the theatre has been a voyage to Egypt and that he lives in the days of Antony and Cleopatra. Surely he that imagines this may imagine more. . . . Delusion, if delusion be admitted, has no certain limitation; if the spectator can be once persuaded that his old acquaintance are Alexander and Caesar, that a room illuminated with candles is the plain of Pharsalia or the bank of Granicus, he is in a state of elevation above the reach of reason or of truth, and from the heights of empyrean poetry may despise the circumscriptions of terrestrial nature.[27]

If Johnson is sometimes rather four-square and commonsensical (he was notoriously intolerant of speculation on certain subjects), he does raise a basic problem. For the purposes of discussion, we must occasionally pretend that the world of the novel has autonomy. Otherwise we cannot speak at all. All questions about mimesis and value have their beginnings and ends in language. But when I suggest that the Harlowes' misunderstandings of their daughter are a matter of belief as well as of knowledge, I am quite aware that all of these characters have been made by Richardson and his readers. The Freudian principle of projection, for example, operates powerfully both within the novel and within its readership. The Harlowes undermine Clarissa's authority by detaching words from the meanings she gives them, but they also project. It is the *projection* which creates misreading – of a person of his or her own motivation, and of people by one another. There are countless examples of projection among the characters in the novel. Clarissa's unwillingness to admit the degree of her attraction to Lovelace is a famous one which has given much smug satisfaction to some critics of the masculinist school. But certain points are presented as fixed for Clarissa, fixed both for her and for us as readers. She recognizes the psychological truth of running off with Lovelace by inscribing it on her coffin and steadfastly refusing to make excuses for herself because of Lovelace's trickery. For her, there is such a truth: certain words and gestures cannot be wrung loose from one another, no matter who assails her. And the novel as a whole, for all its epistemological complexity, has functioned as a kind of standard, even though this has meant constant misreading of the kind chronicled in an amusing book like *Pamela's Daughters*,[28] as well as the kind more sophisticated critics have told us about since.

The fact that Richardson's novels introduced the sexual dilemmas of young girls into fiction, with strong religious connections, meant that a Christian set of beliefs was undergoing re-examination. *Clarissa* particularly was used by the educated to measure behaviour, and as such cannot merely be seen as a series of ruptures of meaning, true and seductive though such a view may be within its limits. Of course we can read many things into the text, and indeed are invited to do so by the characters themselves. But it is still profitable to remember that *Clarissa* has also served as a *model*, with all the ambiguities and breadth of possibility of any model; but with the fixed sticking-places of some sort of systematic point of view as well. It is this aspect of *Clarissa* which ⁘ should like to consider in the study which follows.

Clarissa as a sexual myth or model

I should like to show that there is indeed a powerful sexual myth articulated in *Clarissa*, one which has had an enormous effect on European and American culture. I can only emphasize once more that one need not read *only* in terms of such a myth. But I am interested in the importance that Richardson had for the cultivated and not-so-cultivated of his own time and after: and one needs more than a model of individual sensibility to help explore that sort of problem. On the other hand, I pay a great deal of attention to language and its distortions. Like Terry Castle and William Warner, I have great respect for the Bloomian notion of misreading, though I should democratize the principle a little. It is not only great (and male) poets who creatively misinterpret the literature of their parents.

The definition of myth is a difficult task indeed. The writers who have addressed themselves to the subject, especially since the Romantic period, are numerous and illustrious. It is not my purpose to set myself up next to Cassirer or Freud, or to propose to challenge the sophistication of anthropologists like Lévi-Strauss, Edmund Leach or Roy Wagner.[29] Theories of myth involve us in fascinating debates about the structure of consciousness itself. We would be going rather far afield if we moved from Clarissa and her readers to arguments about the fundamental principles of human knowing. I should only like to say something briefly about the common fallacies to which literary critics are prey when they discuss myth. Since they tend on the whole to be less interested in the functionalist or social aspect of the problem, which is what largely interests anthropologists, they tend also to lack the anthropologist's tolerance for the existence of ideologies, the ' as-ifs' of culture.

Anthropologists may be helpful to literary critics because they are interested in how the products of a culture, from its food to its pottery to its stories and songs, shape that culture, conserve it even while allowing for change, and generally help to keep the community going. If we think that our works of art, unique and complex as they undoubtedly are, escape those obligations, then we are allowing our ideology, our western individualism, to blind us. Ideology in itself, however, is not a bad or lying thing. Ideologies are necessary, the constructs of thought and belief upon which our societies are built. But we can always strive to understand them, to make them work for us rather than against us. We can learn to appreciate the opacities of our limited historical moment, but to make our views transparent where that is possible.

There is one other important way in which anthropologists can help students of literature, at this moment in our intellectual history at least. The best of them, such as Roy Wagner or Edmund Leach, are sophisticated critics of the structuralist methods developed by Lévi-Strauss and his followers. Today's anthropologists use structuralist methods and theories as givens, just as psychoanalysts make use of Freud, if only by reaction. These thinkers have provided the groundwork for their disciplines. But just because those who have done their work in the wake of Lévi-Strauss have thought about their fields of study in great depth, they can provide a refreshing counter-stimulant to the attitudes towards myth which we find in some structuralist literary critics. Roland Barthes, for example, uses myth in quite a primitive way compared to the anthropologists and psycho-analysts, who are much more used to dealing with them.

Even in *Mythologies*,[30] Barthes describes myth as something *wrong*, a conveyor of oppressive 'ideology' against which we must be forever vigilant. His most famous example is a cover from the popular magazine *Paris-Match*, which appeared during the Franco-Algerian war of the mid- to late 1950s. This cover showed a grinning black soldier, obviously a Berber, in French uniform, saluting a French tricolour waving gloriously in a blue sky.[31] We may all agree that this is a nasty piece of imperialist work. But is it a 'mytheme', as Lévi-Strauss would put it? It is a visual metaphor, and an inversion, of course, of the real social order. That is what makes it so particularly unpleasant. It may even be a symbol, or a cluster of symbols. But what does it mean to say that it is a basic unit of myth? Does it really keep us from right thinking and critical inquiry, even if we could give it such a name?

Many followers of Barthes have since clung to this surprisingly unthought-out view of myth. After all, what is the difference between the usage of this vastly intelligent literary critic and the television commentator who talks about the 'myth' of British tolerance, for instance? In ordinary popular usage, a myth is always a lie, a concealment, a view which must be destroyed. Paul Ricoeur, a French psychoanalytic critic and philosopher, makes a simple but very useful distinction about the way we think in western culture when he discusses the implications of the opposition 'univocal/equivocal'.[32] Our 'culture of science', as Roy Wagner calls it,[33] likes words or signs to be 'univocal', to have only one precise meaning, to be nailed down. The very connotations of the word 'equivocal' are negative. If you equivocate, you are lying. You are beating around the bush. Things that are equivocal are (in the popular imagination, at least) sleazy and unclean. They speak with forked tongue, because they give out two messages at the same time. And yet we all know that we equivocate: indeed, perhaps that is the reason for our profound mistrust of anything obviously ambiguous. Art is equivocal by its nature. All the richness of our dreams, and even of our conversation (we can think of cockney rhyming slang as an obvious example) comes exactly from the fact that they are equivocal. We live by symbols, those most equivocal of relationships. We are torn in our own culture; and perhaps the lack of sophistication of much structuralist myth criticism (on the literary side) comes out of the same split. On the one hand, the semioticians have tried to develop a science of literature and art. That means searching for the univocal, the taxonomies and definitions.[34] On the other hand, all the material they work with is hopelessly messy and equivocal.

It is still the case, however, that in much literary criticism appearing in journals the term 'myth' is bandied about in just this loose and disapproving way. The most that people will attempt is an exposure. They try to show how a work is 'mythic' if some ideology contained in it has been manoeuvered into axiom (or 'naturalized', as Terry Castle, among others, puts it) when it should not have been. By this they mean that the characters in the book (it is usually fiction to which these categories are applied) and we, the audience, are taken in. We are made to believe that something quite strange and extraordinary, or at least something that we don't have to accept, has been made acceptable.

Such a suspicious attitude towards myth must eventually lead to unhappy paradox, and to ultimate dissatisfaction. We cannot always see texts as so many criminals on the run, escapees from justice whom we must jump up on from behind and expose for what they really are. Clarissa has many powers, but it is a little hard to rape her more than once for her sins of eloquence. Nor do most other characters in books need to be assaulted for the crime of being fictional and therefore dangerous. It is worth reflecting for a moment on the motivation which might possibly lie behind such a fascination with what is wrong in symbolic thinking and, by extension, in ideology in general. There is an almost touching Puritanism in the mistrust of all the products of culture. Selves and persons are also constructions or products, of course, but if we evade their role in culture we are simply pushing the burdens of intention and meaning further along the chain of artefacts, from the animate, as it were, to the less animate. In some of the work of Barthes, there is occasionally an assumption that any fiction, indeed any symbol, can be seen as so potentially corrupting, so much a possible hoodwinker of the unsuspecting public, that we need literary police to expose its hypocrisy and clarify its baleful intentions. The symbol, character or myth seems to take on an identity and purpose of its own, since authorial intention is currently such a contested matter. The unmasking involves something murkier than simple intention: perhaps the unspeakable depths in us all that allow us to be uncritical and visceral. In short, the demythologists imply, it is the task of the critic to enlighten an audience so that it may always be on guard against a symbol, a myth, or a fiction of any sort.

Those, then, are the fallacies. But there have been many literary critics who have tried to go beyond this rather unexamined view of the subject. Indeed, most critics have at some time or another given some consideration to the problem of myth. But as K. K. Ruthven points out in his dense little introduction to the subject,[35] they have tended to look for archetypes, great themes lurking behind the ostensibly low mimetic forms of novels and stories. Fiction can, of course, offer an obvious and highly conscious reworking of old *topoi* (as in *Ulysses* or *Moby Dick*). A more radical point of view would be one which proposed myth as an organizing principle of all literature. That is the general suggestion which Northrop Frye makes in his *Anatomy of Criticism*:[36] he applies himself particularly to the structure of narrative. Jonathan Culler laments in his most recent book, *The Pursuit of Signs*,[37] that Frye's work has become simply another contribution to archetypal myth-criticism, a 'set of labeling devices' (p. 9). And indeed, such theories are difficult to assimilate, though Culler may be a little stern in his criticism of Frye. They are first of all irrefutable, because they are unproveable, though like a strong herb they have a useful effect when taken judiciously.

Where does all this leave us? Despite the extensive work which has been done on myth and metaphorical language by literary critics; linguists, anthropologists and even philosophers of science, it still seems to be surpassingly difficult to demonstrate the interrelation between belief and mimetic naturalism in modern fiction. Even if we agree with Frye that narrative produces its own necessity (and once more, we see how easy it is to end up discussing basic problems of perception and cognition, even in the simplest attempt to separate literary categories from one another), it is difficult to apply his definition to a work which is as clearly immersed in a specific set of cultural problems as is *Clarissa*.

In the end, we end up rather lamely casting about for a working definition, one which could at least serve for a single project. The simplest definitions have to do with the place of myth in a community. For anthropologists, this would be a living community in which myth and ritual are intertwined in daily practice. For literary historians or critics, the community would of course be one of readers – not only those contemporary with the work in question, but those who make up its posterity. We could, I suppose, settle for the 'horizon of expectations' postulated by Karl Popper and Hans Robert Jauss. The *Rezeptionsästhetik* of the latter offers a complex set of approaches to the historical understanding of a work of literature and its impact, even though it does not address itself specifically to the larger structures of belief.[38]

Perhaps we could just make a flat statement about the whole matter. Diderot was right in comparing *Clarissa* to the works of Homer, if only because both works reinterpret the past and its beliefs in an entirely new form. Even in the eighteenth century, which admired Virgil as much as Homer, there was a long critical tradition, hoary even then, which claimed that no one after Homer could write a true epic. We would be on shaky ground indeed if we made a parallel claim for Richardson, and suggested that no one had really written a novel since 1748. But perhaps we could say that Homer and Richardson shared an opportunity: both wrote at times when their cultures were at a turning-point. In the case of Richardson, the work which was supposed to support a rigorous Christian code of conduct turned out instead to contribute materially to its decline. The questions raised in this new form were too profound to be overlooked. The history of misreadings of *Clarissa* is one clue that it was regarded as a test of beliefs about both religion and sexuality. It could be seen on the one hand as a model for docile behaviour in young women, and on the other as a frightening relocation of the notion of Christian trial in the sexual combat of this world. As such, it became a model for behaviour and also a lens through which to perceive both actual and fictional events, in the world and in books. In this very simple way, *Clarissa* could be called mythic. The transformation of a language which had been universally recognized as spiritual into a treacherous rhetoric of daily life might be seen as a poetic *rite de passage*. Suddenly old categories lose their meaning, and the adolescent heroine must work hard to recover a sense of herself in the spiritual and social hierarchy. In the process, of course, she is transformed, and so is her world. Both the characters in the novel and we, its readers, must strive to understand the implications of hazy and ill-understood events. And the way in which we interpret this basic story tells us as much about our place in our own culture as it does about its origins in certain literary traditions. Few anthropologists would disagree that myths, especially in primitive cultures, serve exactly such a function. If there are horizons of expectation for prospective readers of a novel, there are also structures within it which direct and sometimes muddle belief about a variety of matters. That is all that I claim for *Clarissa*. In the following pages, I hope to show precisely how such transformations occur.

I

CLARISSA AND THE PURITAN CONDUCT BOOKS

A preliminary account of Richardson's writings

Richardson began his novel-writing career during the composition of *Familiar Letters on Important Occasions* (1741), a handbook which advised those unfortunates less competent with their pens than the prolix author on how to deal with all sorts of epistolary situations. It was his work on this collection which inspired him to write *Pamela* (1740), the story of a fifteen-year-old servant girl who preserves her virtue from the persistent attacks of her master, the country squire Mr B. In the end she wins out, and marries him. Not surprisingly, she has been subject to another sort of attack ever since Fielding pointed out the mercenary side of her steadfastness in his mordant and hilarious satire, *Shamela* (1741).

Indeed, Richardson's very originality may have worked against him in *Pamela*. The roots of his novel in what was really meant to be a manual for the moderately literate, rather than a conduct book for the godly, made the question of exemplariness, always crucial to his work, rather ambiguous. Even in the *Familiar Letters*, Richardson did not merely fulfil his duties and offer correct epistolary models for his young travellers. His teenaged ladies fought off madams, rakes and other urbanized incarnations of the devil with more energy than was usual even then in a simple exchange of letters. Similarly, Richardson gave his readers a form of thinking to emulate in *Pamela* – the state of high self-consciousness which only an obsessive awareness of language could bring. If Pamela herself, however, was also offered as a model of behaviour for other girls in her class, there could be no doubt that she was subversive of both generic and social expectations. There had been courtship novels before, but the parties united either were or proved eventually to be high-born. The servant classes, as in Shakespeare, could provide comic relief, but there was no serious crossing of social boundaries. The sexual union of upper- and lower-class partners was a subject for pornographers, and then the question of marriage did not arise.

Whatever its faults, *Pamela* was probably the first novel which attempted to give a really detailed account of a character's inmost thoughts and feelings. The astonishing literacy of its lower-class heroine, for all its ambiguities, was instrumental in attracting an upper-class husband, as well as a cult following all over Europe. It was as if social mobility had received its *cachet* (however limited in practice): Richardson's spiritual egalitarianism shone through his own tiresome defences of rank and social position. There can be no doubt that he gave lower-class women a new dignity. Formally, of course, *Pamela* is not altogether successful. The letters are written almost entirely from the heroine's point of view, and during her captivity at the hands of Mr B. they turn into a journal. The second part of *Pamela*, after her marriage, is a disappointing sequel. Despite some moments of drama, it is a dry collection of the perpetually pregnant Pamela's views about everything from Locke's treatises on education to adultery. Her native pedantry finally takes over, without the charm of youth to relieve it. The second part of *Pamela* is a mine of information about eighteenth-century mores, but as literature it must be seen as a failure.

Sir Charles Grandison (1754), Richardson's last novel, suffers from similar weaknesses, though it has recently acquired some new admirers. Sir Charles's integrity has led him into a distressful situation. He must make a choice between two admirable ladies: the English-woman Harriet Byron, and the aristocratic Clementina Porretta, who, despite the disadvantages of being Italian and Catholic, is possessed of a sensibility which would do any Englishwoman credit. The conflict between her love for Sir Charles and her loyalty to church and family drives her temporarily mad, and she remains unbalanced even after a typically uneasy Richardsonian solution is achieved. Sir Charles marries Harriet in the end, having spent most of the novel abroad in Italy attending the distraught but consistently narcissistic Clementina; but there are pages and pages of unexampled priggishness on the way to conjugal felicity. Despite its title, the interesting characters in the book are all women (just as in Fielding's weakest novel, *Amelia*, the most dynamic figure is Captain Booth, Amelia's husband). During the composition of *Grandison* Richardson began gathering a coterie of young ladies around him at his suburban house in Fulham. The novel was much admired in its time, especially by intellectual women like the ones who became his protégées. The character of Clementina charmed the same contemporaries who praised Clarissa, and even delighted the Romantics. It is common knowledge, of course, that *Grandison* was Jane Austen's favourite novel. But the lack of dramatic energy in the novel was obvious, then as now. A young nobleman with nearly infinite resources at his command cannot enlist much sympathy when we learn that he is saving his virginity for marriage. *Grandison* is a novel of manners, and still has some appeal as such, but it lacks the immense and mysterious passion of *Clarissa*. The most interesting parts of it, indeed, are those which take up some of the concerns of the earlier work: the initial attempt at a rape, Clementina's mad scenes, Harriet Byron's internal struggle as she awaits the outcome of Sir Charles's foreign adventure. Whenever social and sexual pressure are Richardson's subjects (and they can be so only when women occupy the centre of the stage), the sweep of epistolary days and months acquires a proper tension; but when Sir Charles holds forth to his awestruck household after dinner, it is likely to be irritation, and not reverence, which will keep his readers awake through the long, talkative eighteenth-century evening.

Clarissa (1748), unlike the works which preceded and followed it, is consistently masterful, though sometimes intimidating in its mixture of intensity of emotion and long static stretches. Its plot is relatively simple by the standards of its time, though the novel runs to over a million words. Clarissa Harlowe is the youngest child of a rich country family whose wealth was originally amassed in trade. The Harlowes, particularly Clarissa's brother James, are ambitious for a baronetcy and have decided to concentrate their energies on achieving this end. James's only obstacle is Clarissa. She is beautiful, well educated – that is, she can spell, do simple arithmetic and read some Latin – and perfectly virtuous. Her best friend, Anna Howe, with whom she corresponds clandestinely, helps the reader to appreciate her many outstanding qualities. But her charms are problematic for James.

Because Clarissa was the favourite of her grandfather, she has already inherited his estate (though she has given it over to the guardianship of her father), and this has put one piece of property out of the Harlowes' reach from the start. Clarissa's uncles also dote on her, and the jealous James fears that their benevolence upon her marriage might further damage his own claims. In order, therefore, to prevent any further attrition of land or money, James and his malicious sister, Arabella, manage to persuade the family that Clarissa should marry Solmes, a repulsive, uneducated, middle-aged man of lowly birth who has nothing to recommend him but wealth and estates that border on the Harlowes' own. Clarissa adamantly refuses to consider such a match. She has been receiving the attentions of Robert Lovelace, a notorious but brilliantly attractive rake who has been an enemy of James's since they fought at Cambridge as students. The story opens with an account of a duel between the two men when James returns from a visit to the family's Scottish estates to find his fondest dreams on the point of being thwarted. Solmes is thrust forward, and Clarissa's tragedy begins. The family tries to coerce its daughter into marriage: eventually she becomes a prisoner in her own house, and the family subjects her to all the tortures of deprivation and psychological brutality. The Harlowes believe that she loves Lovelace, and that she would not otherwise refuse Solmes. Her repeated suggestions that she never marry at all therefore carry no weight with them.

Out of desperation, Clarissa continues to correspond with Lovelace, for whom she admits (to Anna Howe alone) 'a conditional kind of liking' (I, 203). She agrees finally to meet him in the garden, though she intends only to break off contact with him; but he frightens her into fleeing by making her think that the enraged family is about to burst in upon them. Eventually, he takes her to a brothel run by the terrible Mrs Sinclair and her 'nymphs', but they are given respectable parts to play and Clarissa is led to believe that she is lodging with gentlewomen.

By skilful manoeuvring, Lovelace makes it impossible for her to accept his offers of marriage, and now he uses all his wiles to seduce her and break her will. Clarissa's communication with her family is cut off after Arabella writes that her father has cursed her for ever; Lovelace begins intercepting letters from Anna Howe and writing his own replies on both sides; he invents many plots, all of which enmesh Clarissa ever more deeply in a world of deception. Finally she attempts an escape to Hampstead. He disguises himself as a wronged husband and the prostitutes as women relatives, and brings her back to the brothel. Lovelace drugs her immediately upon their return, and rapes her while she is unconscious, in the presence of Mrs Sinclair and the prostitutes. Clarissa goes temporarily mad, tries to get away, nearly commits suicide, and at last succeeds in escaping. But Mrs Sinclair's whores have her arrested on a pretext, and she is put first into a sponging-house and then into a room at a glover's, where, after seven hundred agonizing pages, she dies a saint's death. The rest of the novel is an account of other people's reactions to her death and of their own fates. Lovelace leaves the country and is killed in a duel (against Clarissa's dying wishes) by her cousin Morden.

Far more than *Pamela* and *Sir Charles Grandison*, *Clarissa* is the expression of a unified but complex vision. Modern readers probably perceive its difficulties differently from eighteenth-century readers, but we can liberate some of its old power, and come to terms with much that remains, by remembering that Richardson began work on this novel with a clearly moralistic intention. 'Religion', he told Lady

Bradshaigh in his first letter to her in 1748, 'never was at so low an ebb as at present. And if my work must be supposed of the moral kind, I was willing to try if a religious novel would do good.'[1] The religious content of the work was immediately recognized by his contemporaries. Edward Young, a close friend of Richardson's, hailed it as 'The Whole Duty of WOMAN', while other clerical friends, such as Philip Skelton, praised it for distinguishing itself from other novels by teaching morality and religion. One Miss Frances Cotterell, who was in her youth when Richardson's novels appeared and who never much liked them, recalled with considerably less enthusiasm that 'when she was a young woman one might as well have said one had not read the Bible as Clarissa Harlowe'.[2]

As Young's comment suggests, however, the chief antecedent for a 'religious' novel would have been the Puritan tradition of conduct books, or manuals of spiritual guidance for practical life, which were written mostly in the seventeenth century but continued to circulate throughout the eighteenth. There is a fairly clear distinction to be made between the 'courtesy books', or simple manuals of correct behaviour (some of which appeared in the seventeenth century and many in the eighteenth), and those conduct books with a solidly religious basis. The list of eighteenth-century conduct books in the *CBEL*, for example, is dominated by fundamentally secular works. In my brief discussion of some conduct books, on the other hand, I have used only those referred to by Richardson and which appear in *Clarissa*. Even then I have not exhausted the category, but have chosen rather to offer a representative selection of texts.[3] On the whole, they are concerned with practical piety; and one, the *Meditations* of Thomas à Kempis, is originally the work of a medieval mystic. One could, in fact, regard all of Richardson's novels as versions of the conduct book: they were written with the purpose of illustrating virtuous behaviour in the various stations of social life. In all three, of course, art got the better of moral instruction, though not always, as we have seen, with equal success. It is important, however, to understand the basic text, the code of humble and active Christian piety, upon which all the distortions, projections, interpretations and flights of fancy eventually are built.

Structure and moral content in *Clarissa*

At Harlowe Place, before the persecutions begin in earnest, Clarissa can lead a Christian life comparatively undisturbed; but it becomes quickly apparent to her that the very language of buying and selling which she uses to keep her moral accounts can be used by the Harlowes for quite different purposes. The books that she and her family read are, after all, identical. Arabella asks her during her imprisonment, for example, if she can borrow Nelson's edition of the medieval mystic Thomas à Kempis (an irony on Richardson's part, perhaps, since of all such manuals it is the least concerned with practical morality).[4] The reader also learns that Bayly's *Practice of Piety* and Allestree's *Whole Duty of Man* were given to Clarissa by her family, and is later told the contents of Mrs Sinclair's library.[5] Better examples may be selected from such works, written in the seventeenth and eighteenth centuries, than from reprints of very early Christian meditations; for here the imagery is often mercantile or political, and the virtues extolled are those of the merchant: frugality, temperance, sobriety. Writers such as Allestree, William Gouge, Fleetwood and Taylor list their reasons for performing virtuous actions. They argue in terms of benefit versus cost, profit versus loss. In the authors who write in the years after the publication of Locke's works, and particularly in the treatise of William Fleetwood (1705), who has been touched by secular philosophy, these arguments are even more rationalized and less crass than the earlier weighings of advantage and disadvantage in the matter of personal grace.[6] There is no escaping the utilitarianism of much of the language, however, in works both early and late.[7]

We can again take Jeremy Taylor as an example: he was in his tenth edition by 1674. His introduction to the definition of Christian sobriety, the cornerstone, in his argument, of a virtuous personal life, is founded on the notion that it is both unreasonable and unnatural not to follow the Christian path. Reason is still, for him, the organizing principle of nature, which is itself the divinely appointed order. The individual who does not submit him- or herself to the order is denying participation in that universality, and is thus working against self-interest:

Christian Religion in all its moral parts is nothing else but the Law of Nature, and great Reason, complying with the great necessities of all the world; and promoting the great profit of all relations, and carrying us through all accidents of variety of chances to that end which God hath from eternal ages purposed for all that live according to it, and which he hath revealed in *Jesus* Christ; and according to the Apostles Arithmetick hath but these three parts of it; 1. Sobriety, 2. Justice, 3. Religion. . . . The first contains all our deportment in our personal and private capacities, the fair treating of our bodies and our spirits. The second enlarges our duty in all relations to our Neighbour. The third contains the offices of direct Religion and entercourse [*sic*] with God.[8]

All of the aspects of human life are neatly laid out into three compartments and, if the devout reader will only learn how to attend to the order around him, he (or she) will doubtless benefit from 'the great profit of all relations'. In the chapter entitled 'On exercising Charity during our whole life', Taylor writes that 'Charity with its Twin daughters, *Alms* and *Forgiveness*, is especially effectual for the procuring God's mercies in the day and manner of our death' (Taylor, *HD*, p. 52).

It is hardly startling that people of little discernment might read these manuals as a means towards ensuring earthly rewards. Even heavenly rewards may take on a distinctly earthly character if one does not already possess grace. Clarissa might interpret his passage on 'Purity of Intention' in quite a different way from James or Arabella: 'In every action reflect upon the *end*; and in your undertaking it, consider *why* you do it, and what you propound *to your self for a reward*, and *to your action as its end*' (Taylor, *HL*, p. 15). The sentence can stand on its own and, while it might encourage introspection, it can also be interpreted as a convenient means of being frank about one's motivations, however unsavoury. Such directness seems to have the sanction of spiritual authority, and one detects this kind of apparent honesty in the Harlowes' candour about the reasons for trying to marry Clarissa off to Solmes. The family's financial motivations for a forced wedding with Solmes, for instance, are candidly described to Clarissa by her Aunt Hervey (I, 53ff). Another even more striking example is Clarissa's mother's attitude (I, 87). The admonition that follows is certainly not heeded by any member of her family, save Clarissa herself: 'a man's *heart may deceive him* . . . and he may not well know what is in his own spirit; therefore by these following signs shall we best make a judgment *whether our intentions be pure, and our purposes holy*'. Taylor then offers a list of ways in which one can separate one's motivations (for example, whether one performs charities for glory or for grace), and suggests that one pay attention to one's feelings about one's duties (Taylor, *HL*, p. 18).

Richard Allestree, too, uses mercantile language in his discussion of how to lead the good life in *The Whole Duty of Man*.[9] Like Taylor, he suggests an accounting for sins; one should repent daily, at set times, and also at times of calamity and affliction. He makes the point again, like Taylor, that this eases the burden of full repentance on the deathbed; and he goes on to list the disadvantages of a belated repentance. For each virtue enumerated he lists and describes the contrary vice, so that the reader may at all times be guided through the

internal wilderness. In his account of the sin of pride he lists the ways in
which one can transgress. One can be proud of the 'goods of nature'
(physical appearance, talents), the 'goods of fortune' (wealth,
honour), and the 'goods of grace' (our own virtues). We possess
worldly goods 'but as stewards to lay out for our Master's use; and
therefore we should rather think how to make our accounts, than pride
ourselves in our receipts'.

The vocabulary of stewardship is used, of course, by James (I, 54).
The same vocabulary, used by Clarissa in a letter to Anna, points – as
her language so often does – to an afterworld. Unlike James, who sees
stewardship as a temporal condition which applies to others but not to
himself (since his family will have eventually to defer to him), Clarissa
generalizes and thinks of herself *primarily* as a steward. This gives quite
a different cast to the matter, since transience itself, rather than
accumulated wealth, is emphasized. The latter is for her only a means
to increased charities: 'It is true, thought I, that I have formed
agreeable schemes of making others as happy as myself, by the proper
discharge of the stewardship intrusted to me. [*Are not all estates
stewardships, my dear?*]' (I, 92). To have pride in the goods of grace 'is of
all the rest the greatest folly . . . The being proud of grace is the sure
way to lose it', and one will certainly receive eternal punishment for
abusing this gift (Allestree, pp. 87–9).

In the various areas of human relationship covered by the manuals,
the language of property is sometimes even more direct: it is no longer
necessary to confine it to the subtlety of imagery. William Gouge, one
of the earliest and sternest of the Puritan writers, announces in his
Domesticall Duties that

children are as the Goods of their Parents, wholly in their power, to be ordered
and disposed by them. On this ground Satan having all that *Job* had, put into
his hand, took liberty over his children, as well as over his goods and chattell. –
Children while they be under government, (even the eldest that are heires)
differ nothing from servants.[10]

Children should disobey their parents, he adds, only if obeying would
be a sin against the Ten Commandments or any other injunction in the
Bible, or against their own religion (W. Gouge, p. 474). Allestree
expresses similar sentiments in *The Whole Duty of Man*:

of all the acts of disobedience, that of marrying against the consent of the
parent is one of the highest. Children are so much the goods, the possessions of
their parents, that they cannot, without a kind of theft, give away themselves
without the allowance of those that have the right in them . . . it belongs to

children to perform duty, not only to the kind and virtuous, but even to the harshest and wickedest parent.   (Allestree, pp. 182–3)

Here one can still observe the original force of Nonconformist patriarchy: the male heir is under the authority of his father. Most of the conduct books were not quite so blunt. While they demand complete filial obedience, they assume a certain amount of free will in the child, wife or servant. Taylor, for example, tries to persuade rather than to lay down the law. In fact, it is the spirit rather than the letter of the law that interests him:

the charity of the Law is to be preferred before its discipline, and the reason of it before the letter . . . Obedience to humane laws must be for *conscience sake*: that is, because in such obedience publick order and charity and benefit is concerned, and because the Law of God commands us, therefore we must make a conscience in keeping the just Laws of Superiors . . . Lift not up thy hand against thy Prince or Parent upon what pretence soever: but bear all personal affronts and inconveniences at their hands, and seek no remedy but by patience and piety, yielding and praying, or absenting thyself.

(Taylor, *HL*, pp. 148, 150)

By the time we arrive at Fleetwood's *Relative Duties of Parents and Children* (1705), the influence of secular philosophy on Nonconformist thought has become obvious: ' I see no reason to think that Parents are by Nature, Masters of the Liberty and Life of the Children; and if the Laws of any Kingdom make them so, they had their reasons probably for so doing, and ought to be obeyed; but there is no inferring that the children of other Kingdoms, where no such Laws have being, are oblig'd to the same obedience . . .' (Fleetwood, pp. 46–7). Fleetwood is the first to introduce some new standards of behaviour in these conduct books. One of these is public opinion. He sees it as a means of measuring the justice of a child's cause against a parent, since he refuses to generalize any longer about filial relationships:

Children have a great duty, but they are not tied like Slaves in all cases, and with bonds that will last forever; but when they do not obey, they must do it with reluctance; and it must be in cases of great and lasting moment and concern, and such, as when represented to fair and equal, wise and understanding People, they may find themselves both pittied for their Trials, and approv'd for their Resolution . . .   (Fleetwood, pp. 53–4)

Even if a child chooses to bring suit against a parent, Fleetwood does not disapprove, as long as public opinion favours the child (pp. 68, 70–1).

What are we to conclude from these extensive quotations from the manuals of religious behaviour? First, it might be suggested that the language of Nonconformist spirituality was an ambiguous code, even in its earliest and purest forms. By using the imagery of the marketplace, and on occasion by referring to persons or spiritual qualities as goods, it may have blunted the sensibilities of those pious folk in the middle station of life who, until Richardson's time read little else besides such material.[11]

Because they were usually practical guides, these books attempted to eliminate the distinction between the spiritual and the daily lives of their readers. For example Thomas Gouge, a London minister, suggests that even the most overburdened businessman has time for short ejaculatory prayers in the intervals between tasks.[12] Laudable as this enterprise may have seemed – after all, it was meant to serve as a contrast to what was perceived as the papist hypocrisy of the high Anglican church, which clogged up the direct relation to God with elaborate and specialized ritual – it was clearly difficult to make language serve so subtle a cause. At least, however, the obsessive weighing up of moral worth required the centrality of a conscience, or inner light, to serve as both a discriminating and an organizing power. Presumably the devout reader, blessed with such judgment, would not be misled into reading the language of buying and selling too literally; in fact, however, Puritan divines did attribute worldly success to God's favour. It would have been a small step for the businessman to assume that God might sanction some of his unholier methods: one can understand the elaborate detailing of pro and con, the categorizing of motive and recommendation of perpetual spiritual self-mortification when the pitfalls of practical morality are clearly seen.

The early Puritans had emphasized faith above works, so that worldly success was a possible affirmation of one's election to the community of Saints, rather than a goal in itself. With increasing Latitudinarian influence after about 1660, and increasing influence from secular philosophers in the last decades of the century, the fragility of this moral system was increased as well. We find in Taylor and Fleetwood a more social view of virtue and far greater tolerance for individuals than in the earlier writers. Taylor tells his readers, as we have seen, to obey the reason of the law above the letter; Fleetwood goes further and separates the laws of God from the laws of man by no more than a comma (Fleetwood, pp. 27–8). It would be wrong to say that the earlier conduct books are not concerned with the secular world: that would be a most glaring contradiction of their purpose. Nor, as we shall see, are they rigid in all matters. But the earlier books see the world order as hierarchized from above: they urge quietism in politics as they urge obedience in the home, because both are aspects of obedience to God. Fleetwood, on the other hand, is the first of this group of writers to cite cultural differences between countries to account for what might seem unreasonable laws to his readers; and he no longer supports the notion of a universal law, applicable in all cases. Public opinion for its own sake becomes a moral force: the standards of the conduct books have become relative.

Let us now turn back to *Clarissa*. We can soon see that it is organized as much in terms of the difficult religious and moral problems it has set itself as it is along conventional literary lines. This superposition of structures may be one reason for the strain – and complexity – in the narrative. The most obvious shape of the novel is that described by Mark Kinkead-Weekes: it becomes the basis for his subsequent analysis. He divides it into three parts. The first is set at Harlowe Place and ends with Clarissa's flight from home; the second is the long imprisonment in London; the third – or 'religious' – part continues from Clarissa's last escape from Lovelace through to her death. This is a convenient and obvious way to deal with such a long work; any reader must refer to these three parts.[13] But there is a deeper if looser organization which offers us a glimpse beneath narrative, as it were. We can see the moral, religious and sexual struggle gnarled up in the language itself, before and after events sweep Clarissa on their larger course.

The central part of the novel, in terms of both organization and meaning, is the relationship between Clarissa and Lovelace. It is quite possible to argue that the very idea of individualism undergoes a broadening of definition in this section. Richardson's 'new species of writing' develops along with his explorations into values personal and religious; for the conflicts raised lie far beyond the scope both of the moral treatises that helped shape them and of previous fiction. Seen from this perspective, the book may be organized on another principle. We might say that the beginning and end function as a cradle or framework for this central part. The beginning and end are, of course, no less skilled or 'novelistic' than this core, but they serve a different function. They give the reader a notion of Clarissa's view of herself before she is troubled by crisis, and they establish the values of moral convention – the values of the conduct books – and of the society immediately around her, against which her internal struggles must be seen.[14]

Anna Howe writes two letters at the beginning and end which serve as a bracket upon which this framework depends (the language of carpentry must occasionally be pressed into unusual service). The first opens the novel; the second, a kind of saint's life written at the request of John Belford after Clarissa's death, in effect closes Clarissa's story, since all that is left after it is the chronicle of Lovelace's travels and death, and Richardson's conclusion in which his rewards and punishments are judiciously meted out. In each letter Anna's language is not conversational and lively, as in the rest of the novel, but grave and formal. And each, upon closer examination, creates ambiguity even as it outlines an established moral code.

In the following pages, I shall be reading these letters in some detail. A close analysis of the two framework letters leads naturally into a discussion of the relationship between text and context. I shall try to give some account of cultural circumstances, as well as of literary ones. Out of this mosaic of literary and social analysis, I hope that I can develop a clear if necessarily limited picture of a religious society in decadence. The Puritan code of practical morality had become treacherous by the mid-eighteenth century, so that Clarissa's venture into new realms of moral (and literary) experience is even more radically innovative than has been generally recognized. This is an exercise, I suppose, in the recovery of a past which may exist only in works of the imagination. It may be partial, but it cannot lack interest, since *Clarissa* has done as much to form literary – and social – expectations as any work we possess.

Unusually enough, I shall begin my close readings with a look at the second of Anna Howe's 'framework' letters. There is a reason for starting off with what is really the end of the book. In this second letter, Anna gives a detailed account of how Clarissa ordered her life. It is an attempt to show that Clarissa met the standards set in the spiritual manuals and conduct books, and it therefore offers us the first full and relatively dispassionate description of an exemplary life to be met with in the novel, though of course we are given hints of it throughout. With this letter and its moral history in mind, we can turn to Anna's letter in the first part of *Clarissa*, where the standards are implied but not stated; and to their travesty during the imprisonment at Harlowe Place.

Anna Howe's testimonial letter: conduct books, *The Ladies Library* and 'Heroick Virtue'

At the crux of the differences in consciousness between the characters at Harlowe Place are different interpretations of Christian belief and practice. Clarissa, who is well read in the conduct books, leads her life according to their precepts, whether these apply to the externals of life or to the great and small crises of the soul. For the Nonconformist authors of such works the world is of a piece: the good Christian strives to imitate Christ in all the aspects of his or her life, and God offers guidance through an inner light. According to the affiliations of the writer, this inner light may be conscience, individual reason or, later, the feeling heart; but in all of these works what is required of the pious reader is *attention*. The inner light can be perceived and interpreted only by those who are fit to give it pride of place in their lives.

Jeremy Taylor, for example, one of the most widely read of these authors, begins his *Holy Living and Holy Dying* (as it was popularly called) with the heading 'The first general instrument of holy Living, Care of our Time', in which he suggests that the pious reader sleep the minimum, rise early, waste no time, and spend moments of leisure thinking about God. Taylor's proposals for a godly life, like those of his fellow authors, present the inner life not only as an informing essence but as an organizing principle. A powerful notion of order binds the spiritual life firmly into daily routine; and nowhere is this clearer than in his words on the duties of high-born ladies:

Let the *women of noble birth* and great fortunes do the same things in their proportions and capacities, nurse their children, look to the affairs of the house, visit poor-cottages, and relieve their necessities, be courteous to the neighbourhood, learn in silence of their husbands or their spiritual Guides, read good books, pray often and speak little, and *learn to do good works for necessary uses*; for by that phrase S. *Paul* expresses the obligation of Christian women to good huswifery, and charitable provisions for their family and neighbourhood.

(Taylor, *HL*, p. 9)

Richardson had already given his readers the portrait of the married woman 'in high life' who performs these Christian duties in the second part of *Pamela*, when his heroine, now Lady B., describes her good works in her journal.[15] Clarissa, on the other hand, is a single woman. Her only 'spiritual guides' are Dr Lewen, her old minister (who is mentioned peripherally in the first sections of the novel, and dies before he can intervene at the end), and Mrs Norton, her nurse, who becomes a visible character only in Clarissa's correspondence with her near the end of the book (in volumes IV and V, though she, too, tries to help Clarissa ineffectually at Harlowe Place). Mrs Norton, indeed, is a nearly powerless figure: though she certainly possesses the virtue of piety, she is no cleric. She is portrayed almost as a type of suffering Christian womanhood, whose forbearance is matched only by her desire to serve. It is a little odd, then, that Mrs Norton has a particular affection for the *Iliad*, that model of pagan heroism. The letter in which Richardson mentions this taste (to Frances Grainger, 22 January 1749/50) makes us aware of the importance of these two

fictional figures, however limited their appearances in the novel may
be. Typically, he writes about Mrs Norton as if she were a member of
their circle rather than his own creature:

You are exceedingly just in your Observation, that for a young Lady to
become a Clarissa the Foundations of Goodness must be laid early. They *were*
laid early with her; So early as from her Cradle, by means of her excellent
Norton, a woman of Reading and fine Observation, whose chief Attention was
to the Beauties of the *Iliad*; and afterwards, when her sweet Pupil was able to
write, in ye Correspondence and Visits that passed between herself and Dr
Lewen, and other divines whom she mentions in her Will.[16]

Perhaps there are hints of Clarissa's early self-sufficiency in this
somewhat skimpy account of her moral education. The two 'spiritual
guides' are influential, but they seem to play rather an indirect role. In
any case, the reader does not learn of the actual structure of Clarissa's
daily life – which, as it turns out, follows the conduct books in almost
every detail – until Anna Howe describes it in the long testimonial
letter at the end of volume V, well after Clarissa's death. It is as clear in
this letter as in Anna's first, which opens the novel, that Anna has great
confidence in her friend's ability to find her own way in the world. In
that first letter, Anna had written: 'I wish to heaven you were at
liberty to pursue your own methods: all would then, I daresay, be easy
and honourably ended' (I, 3). Despite Clarissa's careful obedience to
all the maxims of the conduct books (whose advice for women relies
heavily on the teachings of St Paul, the most deeply misogynistic of the
New Testament writers), there is one important qualification. She has
faith in her own powers of judgment, however modestly she offers her
respect to her teachers and mentors. She cherishes the freedom to
structure her own life and sees it as the source of her strength. Were
Clarissa not a woman, there would be nothing unusual about this
emphasis on Puritan self-reliance; but the conduct books are distinctly
uneasy about spiritual independence in the female sex.

In the second or testimonial letter, Anna gives an account of an
exchange between the two friends. When Clarissa is chided by Anna
for not waking the servants to light her fire (because she rises so early
that she thinks it unfair to disturb them), she replies: 'I have my
choice: *who* can wish for more? Why should I oppress others to gratify
myself? You see what *free-will* enables one to do; while *imposition* would
make a light burden heavy' (IV, 506). Clarissa loses no opportunity to
assert her judgment. Like her ancestors in Bunyan and Defoe, she
exercises her spiritual rights in matters great and small, showing a
proper consciousness of the role of Providence in doing so. The

imitation of Christ does not appear entirely to preclude imitation of the creative, or at least the ordering, power of the Deity: in some ways Clarissa has an almost authorial freedom over her own life (recent critics have made much of this *aperçu*, though it is difficult to see what basic literary problems can be resolved by defictionalizing a fictional character). The exercising of choice might well serve as a definition of freedom; and indeed, one of the central confusions of the novel arises from Clarissa's flight with Lovelace, which is construed by her as a fatal misuse of this right. The penalty, it appears, is death; but the gentler reading public has on the whole seen Clarissa as a victim of Lovelace's machinations. Out of this essential ambiguity have arisen many of the readings and misreadings that have made *Clarissa* such an important document in the literary (and indeed moral) history of women. Modern readers might say that Clarissa strives for total control, through repression or sublimation, of her unconscious. If terror betrays her, or if she recognizes even the glimmer of a wish, however mixed, surfacing briefly, she has failed in her own estimation. Victorians, on the whole, seem to have admired, and indeed to have perceived only, the repressive history; while modern readers, fresh from their own therapies, tend rather to seize on the moments when darkness makes itself known. In general, Clarissa uses her freedom of choice to achieve rigorous conformity to a tradition. She is on the side of the *anciens* in a bourgeois and religious way, even though, in literary terms, the telling of her story is most decidedly a blow for the *modernes*.

We should remember, however, that we are given this portrait through the eyes of Anna Howe, who has not seen Clarissa nor received proper letters from her for some months. The reader by now knows (having read the novel) of Clarissa's extensive self-doubt, and her breakdown in the course of her relationship with Lovelace. The 'character' that Anna gives of Clarissa at the request of John Belford (IV, 490) is a portrait of Clarissa before she goes off with Lovelace, and in that respect the reader is again made aware of the ambiguity of the moral code against which Clarissa is being measured for sainthood. The whole thrust of the novel has been to sanctify Clarissa, not only in spite of but *because* of her error in seeing Lovelace in the garden house, and her subsequent violation. But here is Anna Howe, her closest friend and, at times, her most useful (because loving) critic, giving a testimonial, a saint's life, which omits nearly the whole span of the novel behind it.

There have, of course, been crucial moments at other times when Anna has simply not kept faith, which is perhaps another way of saying that she, unlike her friend, has been inattentive. She has let Lovelace trick her into anger at Clarissa, and has thus, like St Peter denying Christ, failed to support her correspondent at the moment when support was most needed. At one point late in the novel, Anna scolds her friend sharply for not having answered her last three letters and shows little sympathy for Clarissa's present plight. When she comes to realize her error, her apology reflects the lapse in attentiveness and patience which have made her fail when tested: 'Once more forgive me, my dearest creature, for my barbarous tauntings in mine of the 5th! Yet I can hardly forgive myself. I to be so cruel, yet to know you so well! whence, whence, had I this vile impatiency of spirit!' (III, 381). In Anna, the potential freedom to become completely conscious (and to make choices with total knowledge) cannot be recognized and seized. We might say that the unconscious, with its wishes and angers, makes itself felt in her as in all ordinary mortals.

Richardson's letter to Sarah Chapone, 2 March 1752, gives us some insight into his own view of Anna:

> Lovelace could frighten Miss Howe, cowardly girl, as she shewed herself, wanting a Guard to protect her from him, when she thought he had got at her letters. But could he appall, could he intimidate Clarissa, when she had her Duty or Honour in View? Miss Howe, in short, tho' I love her, is a blustering bullying Girl; soon terrified . . . But Clarissa is a Heroine: And by her Meekness, where neither her Virtue nor Honour, nor her Friendships, nor her Piety were concerned; and her Courage where they were: she shewed *that* Magnanimity, which ever will be the Distinction of a true Spirit.
>
> (Carroll, 204)[17]

As I have already remarked, on the other hand, Anna has been asked by Belford to paint Clarissa's portrait as she knew her; and Anna has not had a direct glimpse of her friend living for many months by the time she comes to write this letter. One might expect her, therefore, to focus on that period of her subject's life when Anna knew her best.

The effect of the inevitable omission of the space of the novel itself, however, is to recall the heroine's profound isolation during her crisis – an isolation so deep that the distance between her and those formerly closest to her cannot be made good. It has become an epistemological distance: the 'character' which Anna gives is not only incomplete but, coming as it does at the end of the novel, also a painful irony. No one person, except Lovelace, who is never allowed to understand Clarissa, has been witness to the whole process of which this work is the chronicle. The process has been one of integration out of destruction, but the social world which Clarissa leaves behind never really absorbs her lesson. Her death throws her family and friends into temporary chaos; but her cousin Morden, against Clarissa's dying wishes, still kills Lovelace in a duel (IV, 526ff). In Richardson's 'Conclusion', her friends profit by her example and flourish, while her persecutors suffer. But the reader knows that this is mere poetic justice, a decorous curtain of moralization to be drawn over the novel's final scenes (IV, 532–51). The restored order is more precarious than ever, because it has become a defence against the questions raised by Clarissa's tragedy.

The contrast between these different sorts of confusion and the little cosmos which Clarissa in happier days had created for herself is thus, by its placement, made particularly sharp. The order described in Anna's letter is a return to the unified Christian world of daily life outlined in the works of Jeremy Taylor and the other practical moralists. 'She was of opinion', Anna tells Belford, 'that no one could spend their time properly, who did not live by some rule: who did not appropriate the hours, as near as might be, to particular purposes and employments . . . For Rest', we learn,

she allotted SIX *hours only . . . her first* THREE *morning hours* were generally passed in her study, and in her closet duties: and were occasionally augmented by those she saved from rest: and in these passed her epistolary amusements.

TWO *hours she generally allotted to domestic management.* These at different times of the day, as occasions required; all the housekeeper's bills, in ease of her mother, passing through her hands. For she was a perfect mistress of the four principal rules of arithmetic.

FIVE *hours to her needle, drawings, music, etc . . .* TWO *hours she allotted to her two first meals.* But if conversation, or the desire of friends, or the falling-in of company or guests, required it to be otherwise, she never scrupled to oblige; and would, on such occasions, *borrow*, as she called it, from other distributions. And as she found it very hard not to exceed in this appropriation, she put down

ONE *hour more to dinner-time conversation*, to be added or subtracted, as occasions offered, or the desire of her friends required: and yet found it difficult, as she often said, to keep this account even . . .

ONE *hour to visits to the neighbouring poor*; to a select number of whom, and to their children, she used to give brief instructions, and good books: and as this happened not every day, and seldom above twice a week, she had two or three hours at a time to bestow in this benevolent employment.

The remaining FOUR *hours* were occasionally allotted to supper, to conversation, or to reading after supper to the family. This allotment she called *her fund*, upon which she used to draw to satisfy her other debits: and in this she included visits received and returned, shows, spectacles, etc., which, in a *country life*, not occurring every day, she used to think a great allowance, no less than *two* days in *six*, for amusements only . . .   (IV, 506–8)

Anna goes on at length with this recollection, detailing Clarissa's activities on Sundays, and how she managed her 'accounts' when she visited away from home. The reader learns from it that Clarissa possessed a superhuman self-discipline, as incredible in its way as Lovelace's. She led a life of monastic rigour (and vigour) in the midst of luxury and potential distraction. She was given a considerable amount of freedom, but she also knew how to use it: the right to choose was exercised almost without remission. The habit of keeping accounts to oneself and God, so meticulously observed by Clarissa, is suggested in Taylor, where it is part of the preparation for deathbed repentance (*HD*, p. 44).

The mercantilism of the imagery, which is omnipresent in works such as Taylor's and in the writers – Bunyan, Defoe and Richardson – who owe most to their influence, is a reliable indication of the class affiliations both of Nonconformist authors and their readers. A successful businessman – Richardson himself, for example – would perhaps not have found it difficult to structure his spiritual life much as he did his business day. One must remember that the seventeenth-century Puritan divines who wrote these works had a very active awareness of the possible consequences of not performing one's duty before God, and their congregations, of whose commitment to church and doctrine much was demanded, would presumably have shared some of that lively consciousness of incipient damnation: 'So soon as thou art up', writes Thomas Gouge in 1661, 'goe into thy closet, or into some private place, and there offer up unto God a Morning Sacrifice of prayer and thanksgiving, let any thing be omitted rather than that; if thy business be urgent and great, rise the sooner, dare not attempt any thing, till thou hast commended thy self, and thine affairs to God by prayer.'[18]

We are given hints of the viciousness of Clarissa's brother and sister, conversely, because both are guilty of the most unpleasant sorts of petty sloppiness, according to their sex. We know from the beginning of the book, of course, that James is intemperate and hasty in his judgments and actions: his violence, though lamented, does not surprise anyone. 'There are people', Anna writes in the first letter, 'who love not your brother, because of his natural imperiousness and fierce and uncontrollable temper . . .' (I, 1). In the testimonial letter at the end of volume IV, when Anna discusses Clarissa's views on learning in men and women, she points to James as an example of male snobbery in educational matters:

Nor were the little slights she would now and then (following, as I must own, my lead) put upon such *mere* scholars [and her stupid and pedantic brother was one of those who deserved these slights] as despised not only *our sex*, but all such as had not had their opportunities of being acquainted with the *parts of speech* [I cannot speak low enough of such] and with the dead languages, owing to that contempt which some affect for what they have not been able to master . . .

(IV, 496)

Indeed, one would not expect Clarissa, the mistress of a rhetoric which is whole and graceful because it has spiritual meaning for her, to feel any envy of James, who seems to have knowledge only of what is dead and dismembered in language. There is an exchange of letters between James and Clarissa at the beginning of the novel, when his pedantry becomes the subject of some acrimonious passages (I, 257, 259–60). James, then, is disorderly, proud and insensitive. He certainly misuses his opportunities, in contrast to his prudent younger sister. We detect an odour of corruption in his pedantry. Even in these two 'bracket' letters by Anna Howe we can surmise that he will come to no good end. His persecution of Clarissa is only an affirmation of what the reader already knows about him from the beginning.

Similar contrasts are offered between Clarissa and her sister Arabella in the testimonial letter, this time in the appropriately feminine areas of home economy and dress. Clarissa, we are told, took an active part in her dairy house, on her grandfather's estate, and she was often visited by her family:

Her mother and Aunt Hervey generally admired her in silence, that they might not give uneasiness to her sister; a spiteful, perverse, unimitating thing, who usually looked upon her all the time with speechless envy. Now and then, however, the pouting creature would suffer extorted and sparing praise to burst open her lips; though looking at the same time like Saul meditating the pointed javelin at the heart of David, the glory of his kingdom. And now, methinks, I see my angel-friend (too superior to take notice of her gloom) courting her acceptance of the milk-white curd from hands more pure than that.

In the matter of dress poor Arabella is again hopelessly out of the running:

It was usual with one sister, when company was expected, to be half the morning dressing; while the other would give directions for the whole business and entertainment of the day; and then go up to her dressing room, and before she could well be missed [*having all her things in admirable order*], come down fit to receive company, and with all that graceful ease and tranquillity as if she had had nothing else to think of. Long after *her* [hours perhaps of previous preparation having passed], down would come rustling and bustling the tawdry and awkward Bella, disordering more her native disorderliness at the sight of her serene sister, by her sullen envy, to see herself so much surpassed with such little pains, and in a sixth part of the time. (IV, 497–8)

In this last passage, Arabella even has the language weighted against her. Crammed into a few lines are clumsy rhymes and half rhymes: 'rustling and bustling', 'tawdry and awkward'; repetitions and frequent alliterations: 'disordering her disorderliness', 'sight of her serene sister', and so on. In both descriptions it is obvious that Arabella's guiding passion is envy. This is hardly surprising, under the circumstances, but it gets short shrift from Richardson, who gives Anna full linguistic rein.

Clarissa tries to be kind towards her brother and sister, whatever the reader may think of her feelings towards them. She is instructed to make this effort in Allestree's *Whole Duty of Man* (1659). Arabella, in contrast, because she does not look into herself as Clarissa does, is not only envious but 'unimitating'. A good Christian tries to lead a Christlike life and can recognize those exemplary souls around him or her who are imitating Christ with greater success, even if one of those souls happens to be a member of one's own family. The important eighteenth-century trade in such spiritual autobiographies as Bunyan's *Grace Abounding* (1666) and testimonials of Christian death as Foxe's *Book of Martyrs* (1563) is an indication of the seriousness with which the notion of exemplariness was taken.[19] Arabella's envy, like James's ambition, blinds her to the real merit of her sister: she sees only an image distorted through her own emotion. She is compared (after the fact of Clarissa's death, it must be remembered, and by no impartial witness) to Saul on the verge of slaying David. This strangely masculine image suggests the real power struggle that underlies the rather saccharine scene in the dairy house. Anna Howe, who is always clear-sighted, if occasionally misled by her own strong feelings, has caught the darkness of emotion behind the orderly little world of dairy house and poultry-yard. We have another example, to put it in psychoanalytic terms, of projection at work. Arabella distorts the picture of Clarissa, and Anna, though she may perceive Arabella's envy correctly, makes the scene the basis for quite a wild flight of biblical reference, if one considers the context. In the middle of it all is Clarissa, pure white cheese in hand, all charity, the perfect picture of innocence. Indeed, she invites interpretation. The gulf between Clarissa's carefully structured Christian life and the blindly emotional life of her brother and sister has been yawning before Lovelace ever appears. The central portions of the book teach Clarissa that the gulf lies also in herself.

If we were to give a name to this 'gulf', perhaps we could call it Clarissa's image-making capacity, graceless though this phrase may be. In Richardson generally, the recognition of feeling is a central problem. Curiously, each of his three novels places a different emphasis on the way in which the central figures educate themselves in emotional matters. Pamela, for example, does occasionally project. Most strikingly, she mistakes a cow for a bull, so filled is she with sexual terror; and although she is being persecuted in earnest, she also reads her terror into everything. In *Sir Charles Grandison*, on the other hand, almost no distortion of feeling, and hence no fantasizing, occurs. The only character with any imagination at all, Clementina, is mad; and indeed, the very weakness of the novel comes from the relative paucity of emotional texture. In all three novels there is a great deal of emphasis on disguise, as critics have ceaselessly pointed out; masquerades, in particular, are condemned in all Richardson's books. But if we reflect on disguises for a moment, we can see that a distrust of them is based on an uncertainty of their place in a rationalistic world. If you whip off a disguise, after all, you will find truth underneath. The truth must clearly be unpalatable or ugly, or there would be no need for spangles; but it is there to be perceived.

Clarissa, on the other hand, is particularly austere in this respect. The heroine in this novel is curiously free of fantasy, though she is ceaselessly the object of it. Distortions, dreams, speculations and projections swirl around her: Lovelace, who prides himself on his freethinking, is freethinking in exactly this way. He is blind to denotation, as it were, but all alive to images. Clarissa herself is blind where Lovelace is particularly perceptive. She cannot recognize the projective and fantasizing capacities of the people around her. She has rationalistic expectations, both in language and in behaviour. In the dairy house scene with Arabella, she does not *see* her sister's envy, because she has successfully repressed the sight; but the obviousness and energy of it rebound, as it were, in Anna's extended and startling biblical comparison. When Clarissa is educated, it is to proper perception, but no scales drop from her eyes. She has been tricked, but not by her own feelings. To be modern about it, it is not primarily the mechanism of individual repression which is challenged, but the fundamental irrationality of social arrangements. When Mrs Sinclair assumes her monstrous proportions, for example, it is only in the moments before the rape. Until then, Clarissa shows no particular fear or loathing of her 'landlady'. Clarissa's delusions are a function of the manipulation of reality around her. They are not created by her, and she recognizes the true state of things when they are clarified by revelation or explanation. When she learns about the brothel, the prostitutes and the rewritten letters, she is like any audience in a mystery novel. This is the way in which she remains virginal. She is, and remains, free of the imagery which could have ensnared and seduced her. She has been give no vocabulary for expressing erotic feelings, for example (a favourite eighteenth-century fear for young girls who read novels): she has never been a reader of romances, but she knows her Bible, her Milton and her Homer. She is saved by her mental purity.

The fragments which Clarissa writes during her breakdown are particularly significant, on the other hand, because they give us that rush of darkness, the pressure of unconscious energy on the limited language which Clarissa has at her disposal. She has to make do with scraps of biblical and parabolic language. There is nothing erotic or *nameable* to rise up and surprise her. But she does learn from the rape and its subsequent burst of distracted language that she has had a blind spot all along. She has been blind, not to truth, but to untruth, to the possibility that the passions – envy, lust, ambition and so on – can actually distort and transform language and behaviour in difficult and unexpected ways. Until that moment, the one knowledge which Clarissa has not had is of other people's image-making (projective) capacities; nor has she been aware of her own. But having learned her lesson, she is able to rise like a phoenix from her despair (and, curiously, to write her only letter with a double meaning in it, that about 'her father's house'). Perhaps it is impossible to acquire total knowledge and survive: that is surely the lesson of *Faust*. What a blow this would be for the constant hope of a perfect psychoanalysis! We are still left with grave doubts about knowledge and its power; but not, perhaps, about its goodness.

The recovery of meaning from the past and its literature is itself the subject of much discussion. But we cannot live without making meanings, even if we use the past only to expose the ways in which ideology becomes 'naturalized', made to seem part of the order of things. There are few more troubled and productive territories for study than the border country between sex and religion. In the eighteenth century, in particular, the counterpoint between general secularizing trends and the complicated position of women is par-ticularly fascinating. Important religious events, such as the Great Awakening, the rise of Methodism, and the Evangelical Revival towards the end of the century, had much to do with the role which women and the powerless in general played in English culture. Ian Watt, among others, discusses secularization and the reactions to it in his *Rise of the Novel* (Watt, p. 82). Ann Douglas, in *The Feminization of*

American Culture, gives a brilliant and thorough picture of the relationship between religion, sex and ideology in nineteenth-century America;[20] but there is much still to be done on this subject. We may still expect many insights into the origins of such a 'feminization' in the peculiarly hybrid piety of the eighteenth century.[21]

A remarkable example of the range of possible opinions on women and religion in the first part of the eighteenth century is Defoe's *Good Advice to the Ladies* (London, 1702). This pamphlet, written in doggerel, is full of sympathy for mistreated women: 'O *Eve*! black was the Guilt that thou wast in!/Or else the Curse is greater than the Sin', he writes on page 7. On page 11, he becomes even more explicit:

> Fly then, Dear *Lesbia*, shun the Crocodile,
> Fierce to Devour, and subtile to beguile;
> Keep, dearest Saint, your Freedom while you may,
> Nor, for a triffle, sell you Joys away:
> Just like fall'n Spirits, to whom they'r near a kin,
> They'll tempt, and they'll plague you for the Sin.
> This Legion shall contrive to run you down,
> And make you guilty, tho' the crime's their own.

And to complete the provocative inversion of the usual picture of original sin, he concludes: 'I hate Mankind, and were it not for shame,/I'll swear I'd Publickly disown the Name:/To be call'd *Man*, with me doth sound no more/Than if you call'd an honest Woman Whore.'

The Marquis of Halifax, on the other hand, certainly thinks of women as dangerously weak-minded, and looks upon intellectual curiosity as a hindrance to a woman in her domestic life. In his *Lady's New-years Gift: or, Advice to a Daughter* (London, 1688), he advises his daughter to keep to her religion, even though many men do not:

As to your particular *Faith*, keep to the *Religion* that is grown up with you, both as it is the best in it self, and that the reason of staying in it upon that Ground is somewhat stronger for your *Sex*, than it will perhaps be allow'd to be for ours; in respect that the Voluminous Enquiries into the *Truth*, by Reading; are less expected of you. The *Best* of *Books* will be direction enough to you not to change; and whilst you are fix'd and sufficiently confirm'd in your own *Mind*, you'll do best to keep vain *Doubts* and *Scruples* at such a distance, that they may give you no disquiet. (pp. 22–3)

It is interesting to observe this contrast between a seventeenth-century aristocrat and an eighteenth-century Dissenter. Defoe is, of course, a writer with many voices. But it is still quite startling to discover *this* voice: that of a man who turns from his own sex in disgust and advises women against marriage because it pollutes an idealized, though anti-erotic, female spirit.

These examples, among thousands, indicate that there was an unusual interest in the relationship between women and religion at this time, perhaps under the pressure of social change. There is indeed some evidence of an evolution of attitude in the last decades of the seventeenth century and early years of the eighteenth. One sign of a possible change is the publication of an anthology called *The Ladies Library* under the auspices of the *Spectator* in 1714. While the Christian conduct books were widely reprinted and read by members of both sexes, like the *Spectators* themselves, there is some significance in the fact that this particular collection of reprints was specifically aimed at women, even though the obvious references to men in the excerpts have been left unchanged.

The manuals of the earlier seventeenth century offered, as we have seen, a sturdy, practical Christianity in which belief and practice were thoroughly intertwined. The separation of a Christian code from the ordinary business of marketplace and workshop gave the notion of spirituality a new apartness. It took a lower and perhaps less distinct place in the Protestant system of values after the more integrated view of the years before the Revolution: it may be possible to date the 'spiritualization' and idealization of women from this period, as well as the decline of the church's position in society. Raymond Williams describes the increasing separation of traditional virtues from practical life, and uses *Clarissa* as an example. It is not a great step from his analysis to noting that women have become the main preservers of the old virtues.[22]

But how did these texts, originally written for a broad readership, come to be directed at women only? We can see changes in the conduct books themselves over the course of the seventeenth century. Chastity and obedience, for example, were clearly expected of both sexes in the earlier conduct books.[23] And while St Paul's words on the subjection of wives to husbands were taken quite literally by clergymen early in the period, they were often qualified. Thomas Gouge writes in 1661, for example, that ' as the main duty on the Husbands part was *love*, so the main duty on the wives part is *subjection* . . .' but goes on to add: ' I grant indeed there is but a very little disparity, and small inequality between Husband and Wife, being both governours of the same Family, Parents of the same Children, and *heirs together of the grace of life*, yet God having so expressly appointed subjection on the Wives part, it ought to be acknowledged' (T. Gouge, under section XXV, ' Of the Duties of Wives', p. 137 – the pagination is unreliable). The high value that seventeenth-century Puritans placed on the institution of marriage has been often discussed in social and literary histories: it is obvious in such a passage.[24] Taken together with an economic flexibility which did not exist for the well-born of the eighteenth century, this point of view put women into a relatively favourable position: the justification for wifely submission from the teachings of St Paul sounds rather lame.

Even earlier and more striking passages may be found in the writings of William Gouge, who was in his third edition by 1632. He is the stern upholder of patriarchy who asserts that 'the *authoritie* of parents requireth *feare* in children: and their *affection, love* . . . so supreme and absolute is their *authority* over them, as it would make children like slaves to dread their parents, if a fatherly *affection* were not tempered therewith to breed *love*' (W. Gouge, p. 433). But even he defends the equality of parents: 'The first point then to be noted is, that children beare an equall respect to both their naturall parents, and performe duty to both alike. The law expressly mentioneth both, Honour thy Father and thy Mother' (W. Gouge, p. 491). He offers a great deal of specific advice on the husband's obligation towards his wife, especially during pregnancy. The assumption of moral equality throughout undoubtedly reflects Gouge's esteem for the institution of marriage.[25] Most impressive of all is the passage in which he offers his opinion 'of the difference of adultery in a man, and in a wife':

Though the ancient Romans and Canonists have aggravated the womans fault in this kinde farre above the mans, and given the man more priviledges than the woman, yet I see not how that difference in the sinne can stand with the tenour of Gods Word. I deny not but that more inconveniences may follow upon the woman's default than upon the mans . . . Yet in regard of the breach of wedlocke, and transgression against God, the sinne of either party is alike. Gods Word maketh no disparity betwixt them. At the beginning God said of them both, *they two shall be one flesh*: not the woman onely with the man, but the man also with the woman is made *one flesh*. Their power also over one another in this respect is alike. If on just occasion they abstaine, it must be with mutuall consent. If the husband leave his wife, she is as free, as he should be if she left him. (W. Gouge, p. 221)

We may compare these sentiments to those expressed by Bishop Fleetwood on the same subject in 1705. He is the (unacknowledged) source of the section on the duty of wives to husbands in *The Ladies Library*:

There is no need of saying much in commendation of this great virtue, [that is, chastity] to Wives; they cannot choose but know, that without it, they are Wives no longer, the band of Wedlock is immediately dissolv'd before God;

and before Man, as soon as the Husband pleases to ask the assistance of the Law; but this is not without the breach of the most solemn and tremendous Vow and Promise that can be thought on; the guilt of such a Perjury, as cannot ever be atton'd for in this World, and of such horrible injustice as can never be repair'd, either to Husband or to Children. In other cases, a Perjury may take away a Mans good Name, or his Estate, but there may be some amends made him for both of them, by Repentance; his good Estate may come again, by force of Law, or voluntary Surrender . . . but the Perjury and Injustice of an adulterous Wife, are such offences as can receive no reparation or amendment . . .   (Fleetwood, pp. 179–80)

In general, Fleetwood seems to think that women need more instruction in marriage than men. He devotes 126 pages to their duties, while husbands' duties to wives are dealt with in forty-six pages. Husbands are also enjoined to be faithful to their wives, but Fleetwood's language when he addresses the men is not nearly as severe (Fleetwood, p. 323). It is significant that Fleetwood demands the most abject submission of wives, even though the wording is moderate and full of typically Latitudinarian appeals to nature and reason: 'the next enquiry is to be, whether this Superiority, that is so unavoidably necessary to the Support of Rule and Order, is well and rightly plac'd in *Husbands*, rather than in *Wives*; and for this, they are to consider, 1. Where Nature has design'd this Sovereignty; *2ly*, Where Use and Custom have plac'd it; and *lastly*, what the Laws of God say to the matter' (Fleetwood, p. 108).

Jeremy Taylor, in 1650, is direct on the question. Though he thinks the wife 'is of a more pliant and easie spirit, and weaker understanding, and hath nothing to supply the unequal strengthe of men, but the defensative of a passive nature and armour of modesty', he objects to the double standard and considers the crime of adultery equally heinous in both sexes. Unlike Fleetwood, he is also candid, and magnificently thunderous, about the reasons for finding the wife's adultery worse: '*In respect of the effects and evil consequences*, the adultery of the woman is worse, as bringing bastardy into a family, and dis-inheritons or great injuries to the lawful children, and infinite violations of peace, and murthers, and divorces, and all the effects of rage and madness' (Taylor, p. 71). On this matter, at least, the earlier writers are somewhat more egalitarian, and certainly a good deal more practical, than the apparently more worldly Bishop Fleetwood.

While an awareness of the implications of adultery for the conduct-book writers helps us to recognize the family tensions in *Clarissa* in a rather simple way, the passages I have just cited are most useful because they give us an ear for Puritan language. Joanna C. Dales has written about the attempt at 'plain speech' on the part of some of the writers whom we have been discussing; they were reacting to the elaborate language of Metaphysical poets and preachers. But in fact their prose is rich with imagery, rhetorical figures and emblematic references.[26] It is important for us to hear the intensity of this language if we are to understand the tone and emotional power of the conflicts – *linguistic* conflicts, first of all – in Richardson's novel. Strictly speaking, of course, the attitude towards virginity taken by the writers is of obvious interest for any reader of *Clarissa*. One example, as striking for its rhetoric as for its passion, will be sufficient.

The anthologist of *The Ladies Library* uses Jeremy Taylor's *Holy Living*, that most widely circulated of all conduct books, for the selection on 'Chastity'. Once again, it is perfectly clear that in the original source the passage in question was directed more at men than at women. Women, in fact, are nowhere singled out for disapproval. Some paragraphs, which instruct the reader to refrain from 'private Society with strange Women, gazing upon a beauteous Face, from singing Women',[27] are specifically for men. The following passage ends also with an obviously male reference. 'Virginity', writes Taylor in prose exuberant with conviction,

is a life of Angels, the enamel of the Soul, the huge advantage of Religion, the great opportunity for the retirements of devotion: and being empty of cares it is full of prayers; being unmingled with the world, it is apt to converse with God; and by not feeling the warmth of a too forward and indulgent nature, flames out with holy fires, till it be burning like the Cherubim and the most extasied order of holy and unpolluted Spirits . . . it containeth in it a victory over lusts, and greater desires of Religion, and self-denial, and therefore is more excellent than the married life, . . . and just so is to expect that little coronet or special reward which God hath prepared (extraordinary and besides the great Crown of all faithful Souls) for those *who have not defiled themselves with women, but follow the Virgin Lamb for ever.*   (Taylor, pp. 66–7)

By the time the *Spectator* publishes *The Ladies Library* in 1714, however, the question of sexual continence, whether before or during marriage, seems no longer to be as important an issue for men as for women. The Introduction to the first volume of *The Ladies Library* by 'A Lady' (perhaps Lady Mary Wray, but perhaps Steele himself) cites passages hostile to women from Milton, Dryden and Otway, but dismisses them by asserting that 'it is the Business of ingenious debauch'd Men, who regard us only as such, to give us those Ideas of ourselves, that we may become their more easy Prey'. Instead of acknowledging the views of such authors by allowing them a place in the selections that follow, the editor decides to stick to pious works: 'I resolve therefore to confine my little Studies, which are to lead to the

Conduct of my Life, to the Writings of the most eminent of our Divines, and from thence . . . make for my own private Use a Common-Place, that may direct me in all the relations of Life, that do now, or possibly may, concern me as a Woman . . .'[28]

While it is difficult to envision Milton as 'debauch'd' (though he may certainly be called 'ingenious'), it remains clear that the lady of the Introduction has made a distinction between an apparently misogynistic secular sphere of 'polite letters' and a Christian one more favourable to women. Indeed, Otway and Dryden, both Restoration dramatists, offer an aristocratic and therefore contemptuous view of women in comparison with which the religious writers appear almost feminist. Otway's *Venice Preserv'd* (1682), for example, is the play to which Lovelace takes Clarissa during her captivity with him (II, 342, 372). The heroine of the play, Belvidera, has shown nothing but the most flawless devotion and love towards her husband, Jaffeir, who promptly ransoms her to a group of co-conspirators as a token of his loyalty to their cause. He kills himself to avoid punishment, and his wife dies immediately of grief. She can be at the most a pathetic, but not a tragic, figure, since her destiny is completely fortuituous and dependent on the wills of other characters. She is much more object than subject; but her self-immolation is nonetheless held up as exemplary in the drama..

It is not unusual, however, that Lady Mary – or Sir Richard – makes such a distinction between Christian and secular literature. But it is surprising that a basic rhetorical fact has been completely overlooked by the editor of *The Ladies Library*: these Christian selections were not originally directed at women. At some point in this period, sexual purity has become an exclusively female matter. Furthermore, female chastity in marriage has increased in importance while the status of virginity has declined,[29] perhaps in accordance with changing marriage patterns. Richard Allestree, whose *Ladies Calling* is incorporated into *The Ladies Library*, has already observed the change as early as 1673: 'Women are so little transported with this zeal of voluntary Virginity, that there are but few can find patience with it when necessary. An old Maid is now thought such a Curse, as no Poetic fury can exceed, look'd on as the most calamitous Creature in Nature.'[30]

Social life: some controversies about marriage in the eighteenth century

Perhaps it is not entirely becoming to a scholar to admit to some scepticism about the enterprise of studying the past; but it is clear from the evidence that we are unlikely ever to know exactly what *did* happen to the institution of marriage among the privileged and moderately privileged classes in the England of this period. Two eminent historians disagree on the matter. A generation ago, H.J. Habakkuk wrote a much cited article called 'Marriage Settlements in the Eighteenth Century'[31] which has remained a standard reference ever since. It has been used in support of all sorts of hypotheses, including those advanced by Christopher Hill in his even more famous article called 'Clarissa Harlowe and her Times' (*Essays in Criticism*, 5 (1955), 315–40). Rather more recently, Lawrence Stone published a massive volume called *The Family, Sex and Marriage in England, 1500–1800* (London, Weidenfeld & Nicolson, 1977) which was full of contentious claims made in highly readable prose. Among other things, he flatly contradicted Habakkuk.

In his article, Habakkuk argues that there was in effect a rise in the price of husbands in the late seventeenth century and particularly in the eighteenth. He documents the complex of factors which led to this circumstance quite thoroughly. They were, of course, mostly economic, and revolved around the ratio of dowry (the sum the bride's father paid a prospective husband) to jointure (the annual income agreed upon in the marriage contract as the sum which the prospective husband would settle on the wife if she survived him). This in turn arose out of the necessity of maintaining a succession and amalgamating landed wealth. In the seventeenth century the portion or dowry was about three times the jointure, and the jointure itself was often a one-third share in the estate. In the early eighteenth century it rose to ten times the jointure, which had by then become a fixed fee, rather than a share in the land.

The change in marriage patterns, as I have hinted, was closely linked (according to Habakkuk) with a change in the laws of inheritance. While in the seventeenth century estates were often divided equally among the sons, in the eighteenth the eldest son became sole heir. So powerful was this tendency that the terms for the son's future children were drawn up upon his birth, whereas in the sixteenth and seventeenth centuries arrangements were made when the son came of age or became betrothed. The father, upon the birth of a son, automatically became a life tenant upon his estate, with administrative rights, but none which could have any effect beyond his own lifetime. Habakkuk explains this trend as being a response to the changing sources of political power at the time. In the sixteenth and seventeenth centuries, political importance was measured not by wealth but by royal favour; in the eighteenth century, wealth had become the road to success. But wealth in the early to mid-eighteenth century was not yet the mercantile accumulation of money and investments which came in at the turn of the nineteenth century; above all, it consisted of land, though in the battle during Queen Anne's reign and after between the largely mercantile Whigs and the largely landowning Tories we see the patterns changing. The greatest landowners were often politically the most powerful men, and therefore aspiring families tended to consolidate their possessions, and to concentrate them on one heir instead of on many. It was, as will easily be recalled, the age when the enclosure of public lands was greatly accelerated. This threw small tenant farmers and independent yeomen off their claims and into the cities, reduced drastically the extent of common lands, and created the pool of urban poor depicted by Hogarth and exploited by the industrialists of later generations.[32]

Habakkuk's reading of his documents supports the prevailing ideology in the eighteenth century – that of a decadence in the status of the affectionate marriage – though here, as always in matters of opinion and current prejudice, we are on rather thin ice. Even Sir William Temple, for example, who died a year before the seventeenth century turned into the eighteenth, could be cited in support of the view that less attention than ever (especially among the upper classes) was paid to the emotional side of marriage. In Temple's essay 'On Popular Discontents' (*Works*, London: 1750, 4th edn, I, 255–71), we find a discussion of the 'fact' that men are marrying late or never; that fewer than fifty years before (thus bringing the turning point back into the 1630s) marriage was not primarily for money; and that the nobility are increasingly 'marrying into the City . . .'. 'I know no Remedy for this Evil under our Sun', he writes, 'but a Law providing that no Woman of what Quality soever shall have the Value of above Two Thousand Pounds for her Portion in Marriage, unless she be an Heiress; and that no such, above the Value of Two Hundred Pounds a Year, shall marry to any but younger Brothers' (Temple, p. 268). And it is easy enough to find quotations about heiresses and 'marrying estates' in Restoration comedies.[33] They are dubious evidence of anything except the existence of contemporary stereotypes.

Clarissa itself, however, supports these contemporary accounts, and Christopher Hill used the novel in his article as evidence for the existence of such marriage patterns. The reason that Solmes is such an attractive candidate in the eyes of the Harlowe family is purely economic. The estate that Clarissa inherited from her grandfather lies between two of Solmes's, and Solmes is prepared to offer generous settlements upon marriage which will eventually aggrandize the

Harlowe family fortunes at the expense of his own relatives. As Clarissa tells Anna when her persecutions begin, the younger Harlowes consider it necessary that she marry someone who is willing to make this concession, because her uncles intend to settle their estates on her, as her grandfather already has. Such testaments would of course violate the prevailing patterns of inheritance, which would have concentrated all of a family's wealth on the eldest son. The only way in which estates settled upon Clarissa, the youngest child, would not pass out of the family hands upon her marriage would be through the rare willingness of a husband to agree to their reversion back to the Harlowe family after his death. Clearly this is what Solmes has proposed.

Lawrence Stone, on the other hand, sees a steady progression in the development of the marriage for love as against the marriage of convenience. He maintains that 1660–1800 is a period not of deterioration, but of consolidation. According to him, the wealthy bourgeois and professional classes were responsible for these changes: he cites Jeremy Taylor's exaltation of marriage in support of his argument. While he admits that an obsession with property continued among the upper classes, he thinks that it was on the decline. Indeed, he accuses Mary Astell, the early feminist, of archaism when she complains in *Reflections on Marriage* (1705) that women have little choice in the selection of marriage partners.[34] The very documents which Habakkuk uses to support his thesis are used by Stone as proof of a massive disapprobation of marriage for gain; else such a policy would not be the subject of so much controversy.

There is, of course, much in this argument. Surely it is never the case that only one stream is flowing only one way in any historical period. But Stone reads his evidence about sexual behaviour very peculiarly elsewhere in his book. In his case histories of eighteenth-century figures, we find the scientist Hooker described as moderate in his sexual appetites because of ill health, while Mrs Boswell, tubercular, forever pregnant and terrified of the syphilis carried by her philandering husband, is described as 'frigid' because she lacks enthusiasm for the marriage bed. If we must take contemporary documents with a grain of salt, then how much more must the same caution apply to these pronouncements!

There is little doubt, if we read memoirs, letters and finally if hesitantly the literature of the period, that most women suffered under tremendous strain on the subject of marriage, for whatever complex of reasons we may choose to cite. There is some possibly suspect nostalgia in this passage from the section entitled 'Employment' in *The Ladies Library*:

There was an Age when women of the best Condition prided themselves in performing Christian Duties, in visiting and assisting the Sick, comforting and relieving the Poor; but Shew and Vanity usurp now the Places of Reason and Duty . . . It is now a Piece of good Breeding to ramble three or four Days in a Week from House to House, not in doing good, but in doing nothing, and to sit at Home the rest of it, expecting as great Triflers as themselves. *Dress, Meals, Visit, Park, Opera* and *Play*, take up all the Hours that are not given by them to sleep; in which, if the Morning is not spent, *Dress* continues it all: the Noon is not long enough for Dinner, the Afternoon is loiter'd away in the *Park*, and the rest of the Day at the *Theatres*: What Part of it can they spare for the Church and the Closet: What Part of it do they dedicate to God, who will most surely demand his Share, at the last Judgment and eternally punish those who have defrauded him of it?[35]

This passage reflects not so much an actual historical circumstance – it is always wise to treat with caution comments which glorify the past at the expense of the present – as the confused social position of women at the time of writing. It is doubtful if many aristocratic women ' of the best Condition' lived the virtuous life which the author describes. For one thing, unlike their accuser, they were not usually Nonconformist Anglicans. But if the author is referring to the well-to-do women of the middling stations, who began adopting the habits of their superiors in birth, then there may be grounds for the comparison. The combined and contradictory effects of secularization and an undoubtedly increasing mobility between classes, with narrowing moral and sexual pressures on women, were gently satirized by Pope in a famous portrait of a young woman from 'Epistle to a Lady' (1735):

> Why pique all mortals, yet affect a name?
> A fool to Pleasure, and a slave to Fame:
> Now deep in Taylor and the Book of Martyrs,
> Now drinking citron with His Grace and Chartres.
> Now Conscience chills her, and now Passion burns;
> And Atheism and Religion take their turns;
> A very Heathen in the carnal part,
> Yet still a sad, good Christian at her heart.[36]

In *Clarissa* itself, considerable attention is paid to the blurring of class as well as sexual lines. Anna Howe's admiring attention to Clarissa's dress is an example of the filtering down of aristocratic standards. Richness and charm, befitting Clarissa's rank, have a distinct advantage over mere quickness in dressing, modesty and seemliness, which were the cardinal virtues for the Puritan writers on the subject; yet Clarissa is seen as exemplary in this as in all else. It is a cliché of periodical and pamphlet writing of the time that female mores are decadent, that young women should not gad about to balls and masquerades. Richardson himself was fond of this topic: discussions of it appear in all his novels. It is at a masquerade that Pamela's Mr B. meets the countess with whom he has an affair.[37] In *Clarissa* the problem of disguise, and the false language that goes with it, is central to the novel, although the larger social world of London does not obtrude enough on private conflict to make masquerades in the ordinary sense a topic of discussion. Masquerades are often discussed at the beginning of *Sir Charles Grandison*. 'Masquerades,' says Sir Charles, 'are not creditable places for young ladies to be known to be *insulted* at them. They are diversions that fall not within the genius of the English commonality.'[38] And much more is said on the subject, on this page and elsewhere; see Richardson's letter to Edwards, 20 February 1753 (Carroll, p. 221), on Harriet Byron and masquerades.

The increasing fluidity between classes may be observed in other aspects of eighteenth-century life as well. The prosperous members of the London-centred middle class, for example, began, with varying degrees of ostentation, to divide their time between the city and their country houses, in modest imitation of the aristocracy. It has been noted by his biographers that Richardson, by mid-century, has already been affected by the urban urge to move into the country. His two successive retreats at North End and Parsons Green become the centres of a polite and (after the publication of *Clarissa*) increasingly female-centred way of life.[39] His favourite correspondent in later years is Lady Bradshaigh, a sturdy country gentlewoman from Lancashire, who, though she comes often to London, is fundamentally a provincial; and a good number of his friends, both male and female, live well away from London. We can read Lady Bradshaigh's own description of her country life (Eaves and Kimpel, p. 231). Among Richardson's other friends, Edward Young lived in Welwyn, Edwards in Turrick, Cheyne and Leake in Bath, Philip Skelton in a country parish in Ireland, Mrs Carter and Miss Talbot in Deal.

All three of his novels are at least partly country-centred, and so are their heroines. Pamela is a country girl of the lower classes whose contact with the 'high life' of the cities occurs well after her marriage; Clarissa is abducted into the city from a country estate, and there meets her end; Harriet Byron's misadventures (but also her future happiness) depend on her visit from her home in Northamptonshire to the gay whirl of London. Sir Charles Grandison's home is full of country virtues, but conveniently placed only a few miles beyond the city limits. It is located in Colnebrooke, which Harriet's cousin Reeves is able to reach from London by nine in the morning; and the Grandisons and Reeveses travel easily between their home and town in the course of a day.[40] Middle-class moderation has begun to make itself influential geographically as well as socially. England had, of course, been London-centred for generations by the time the admonisher in the *Ladies Library* was writing. It is still curious that Richardson, who was one of the few in his circle who had spent his youth as well as his adult life in London, and who hardly ever left it, should express more suspicion of the city in his writing than any other major novelist at the time.

Richardson's *Familiar Letters on Important Occasions* (1741), which contains the germ of *Pamela*, includes several letters from country people seeing the sights of London. They are usually disappointed or duped; their reactions in the first case are contrasted with the cynical looseness of the fashionable crowd. See, for example, Letter LXII, from 'A young Woman in Town to her Sister in the Country, recounting her narrow Escape from a Snare laid for her on her first Arrival, by a wicked Procuress' (p. 79); or 'From a young Lady in Town to her Aunt in the Country', describing Greenwich Park, Bethlehem Hospital, Vauxhall, Ranelagh and the theatres (Letters CLII–CCIX, pp. 218–38). Richardson's biographers, Eaves and Kimpel, point out that Richardson 'was primarily a city man . . . Few men have been more thoroughgoing Londoners . . .' (Eaves and Kimpel, p. 527). In his work, however, his view of city delights is unquestionably more ambiguous, though never decidedly hostile.

He does indeed make fun of 'arcadian scenery' in a letter to Susannah Highmore, 22 June 1750 (Carroll, p. 162), but he is concerned in this case with the elaborate artificiality of the bucolic world of romances. His own view of the countryside reflects a preoccupation with the possibility of living a simple and humane life; and he never seems concerned about aesthetic questions. He shows, in fact, almost no interest in landscape at all, except as it reflects the human predicament. Like Johnson and Fielding, on the other hand, he recognizes that the city offers knowledge along with its perils; Richardson's London is just as much the locus for revelations about self and society as Fielding's, or even as Johnson's Cairo in *Rasselas*.

It would be a mistake to assume that Richardson and his contemporaries thought of country and city as entities sharply opposed to one another: they still lived in a pre-industrial and at any rate pre-Rousseauvian world. Country and city did represent different life-styles, however, especially for women. When the upper middle class began splitting its year, like the aristocracy, between country estate and town house, the values of each style were illuminated even as class boundaries at the upper end of the social scale were cast into shadow.

The critic Mark Kinkead-Weekes has clearly seen something of this tendency when he remarks that Richardson and Defoe are city men because they show us the new and widening gap between individualism and morality, but he does not choose to explore the problem that arises when alternative worlds are created in these authors to contrast with the hypocrisy of city life.[41] Even Richardson seems to be seduced by the pastoral ideal, because morality for him does seem to be located outside the very London of which, in personal life, he was so vigorously a citizen.

Dorothy Marshall describes the mobility of the mercantile class; the elegant life which it developed in London, and the relative ease with which classes mixed at Ranelagh and Vauxhall.[42] We have a sense of this relaxation of class barriers in Richardson's own life. Richardson might write to one of his aristocratic female correspondents that 'There is a bar that separates us – Temple Bar',[43] and Lady Mary Wortley Montagu, for whom Richardson had much contempt, might boast after his death that 'The doors of the great were never opened to him',[44] but the fact remained that, after his first literary successes, Richardson's circle of acquaintance ranged from nobly born gentry and bishops through several degrees of respectability to distinctly less savoury characters like Laetitia Pilkington. For a man who began life in the working class, and who spent most of his life in St Paul's Churchyard, this fluidity of social possibility was considerable. Before a dinner in 1752 at Prior Park, the home of the great Bath philanthropist, Ralph Allen, Richardson remarked, 'Twenty years ago I was the most obscure man in Great Britain, and now I am admitted to the company of the first characters of the Kingdom' (Carroll, p. 14).

Laetitia Pilkington, at the other end of the scale, was an engaging if morally dubious lady for whom Richardson performed considerable charities (Eaves and Kimpel, pp. 175–9). She is an extraordinary example of the ease with which such a woman, the friend of Swift, Cibber and Richardson himself (though she seems to have been of decidedly easy virtue), could fall into destitution. Her letters are most touching. She and her illegitimate pregnant daughter are turned out, for example, 'because I would not let her lye in the street, my saint-like methodist landlady had padlocked the door, and turned us both there. My own writings she has secured, as well as a few small matters, she, my child, had provided for her child' (Eaves and Kimpel, p. 178).

The example of Laetitia Pilkington allows us to reflect again on the special pressures on women at a time of considerable general mobility. If we remember H. J. Habakkuk's assessment of the period, with its rise in the price of husbands and emphasis on the consolidation of wealth, the patterns of oppression in *Clarissa* are illuminated from the beginning. For middle-class women, of course, the possibilities for advancement were much less varied than for men. They could rise by accident of birth or by marriage, but not through efforts of their own. Social mobility and social success were not for them the result of the realization of ambition, the relatively orderly progress towards a goal, but a matter of chance. They benefited if the position of the father were favourable or the husband were kind; they were victimized if, like Clarissa, they were treated as objects of barter in the marriage market.

Early in the novel, Clarissa reports a conversation between herself and her brother, in which he maintains 'that a man who has sons brings up chickens for his own table . . . whereas daughters are chickens brought up for the tables of other men' (I, 54). James's remark is unpleasant but true. A rich mercantile family could actually go into bankruptcy in financing its daughters' marriages. Although such a family might gain the dubious privilege of connection to a great name, on the whole it stood to lose. Marriage patterns tended to favour the generation of the husband, whose wealth could be so enormously increased through an advantageous match, rather than, as in the old days, the generation of the father, whose wishes had once had the power to reverberate through several decades of offspring.

These pressures were reflected in the distortion of the ideal of the suitable marriage. Heiresses without family connections were desirable; they often came from mercantile backgrounds, where custom would make inheritance through the female more common than in landowning or aristocratic families. Merchants' daughters with families were often not desirable, even though their parents could offer high terms at great financial cost to themselves. These economic stresses were felt in all classes (see *Moll Flanders*), but for the working and lower middle classes the interest of necessity was already in mercantile accumulation, while in the upper and newly arrived leisured mercantile classes it was in land. Lawrence Stone may well be correct when he suggests that this sort of marriage, with its obsessional goal of acquiring land, was already on the way out when the seventeenth century turned into the eighteenth; but it certainly does not seem to have been *perceived* as such at the time. If our main concern were sociological realism, then we should have to note that *Clarissa* itself is in many ways a deliberately archaic novel. It is set in the early part of the century and plays upon a rhetoric already well past its days of glory; but the element of *Verfremdung* perhaps points up the conflicts even more sharply than contemporary accounts of such cases might.

In any case, new pressures on daughters of rich families were observed. It is possible that in response to these perceptions, the obedience to authority and the passivity recommended in the early conduct books became, like purity – and like religion itself – exclusively female matters. The contradictions in so strongly an individualistic morality as that embodied in the various forms of Protestantism became painfully clear. Richard Allestree's *Ladies Calling* is as good an example as any of the way in which manuals of practical religion put forward confused notions about the connections between sexual purity and all the other aspects of women's lives. The opposition between culture (male) and nature (female) is obvious: men's minds are like an enclosed common, cultivated and improved, while women's minds are like land left wild and rough. The comparison is made extremely frequently in the interminable discussions of women's education in the seventeenth and eighteenth centuries. In general, Allestree's argument is worth a close look, because its underlying assumptions are both widespread and subtle.

In his Preface, Allestree urges women to think more highly of themselves than they do, and not 'from a supposed Incapacity of Nobler Things, to neglect the Pursuit of them; from which God and Nature have no more precluded the Feminine, than the Masculine part of Mankind'. He emphasizes women's importance as educators and mothers, citing as 'proofs' examples from the Bible and classical antiquity; and comes close to admitting that their supposed intellectual inferiority is entirely the result of education:

Men have their parts cultivated and improved by Education, refined and stabilized by Learning and Arts, are like an inclosed piece of a Common, which by Industry and Husbandry becomes a different thing from the rest, tho' the natural Turf own'd no such inequality. And truly had Women the same Advantage, I dare not say but they would make as good returns of it; some of those few who have bin tried, have bin eminent in several parts of Learning . . . And were we sure they would have ballast to their sails, have humility enough to poize them against the vanity of Learning, I see not why they might not more frequently be intrusted with it; for if they could be secured against this weed, doubtless the soil is rich enough to bear a good crop. But not to oppose a received opinion, let it be admitted, than in respect of their intellects they are below men; yet sure in the sublimest part of humanity, they are their equals: they have souls of as divine an Original, as endless a Duration, and as capable of infinite Beatitude.

It becomes clear on closer scrutiny, however, that the divine essence in women has quite a different character than one would suppose it to have in men: it is intimately linked with virginity. If women realized their worth, 'they would be jealously vigilant against every thing, that might eclipse the radiancy, or contaminate the purity of their souls . . . Why should they not turn over all sensual inordinances to meer Animals, and creatures that have no higher principle than that of sense, whilst themselves soar up to those more sublimated *plesures*, which are at Gods Right Hand for evermore, Psalm 16.12'. When Allestree writes: 'We may therefore conclude, that what ever vicious impotence Women are under, it is acquired, not natural; nor derived from any illiberality of the Gods, but from the ill managery of his bounty', we can easily see that he is not referring to social conditions which might harm the innate virtue of women, but to their own self-discipline.

There is not much sense in any of these writers, despite their appeals to custom, of a dynamic social world which influences the individuals within it. The community, like the semifictional examples drawn from classical and biblical history to support such arguments, is perceived as static. Thus, women may be seen both as naturally inferior to men and naturally equal; but if they are equal they have become unequal through their own faulty behaviour. Though their powers of perception are meant to be less developed than those of men, they ought nonetheless to be able to recognize their own vices. This rather paradoxical point of view is particularly interestingly expressed in Allestree's assessment of woman's ability to receive God's grace. It is rather a touching argument because (not unlike Anna Howe) Allestree falls into contradictions even as he attempts to be unusually generous to the cause of women:

Nay give me leave to say farther, that as to an Eternal well-being, he seems to have placed them in more advantagious circumstances than he has don men. He has implanted in them som native propensions which (as I shall hereafter have occasion to observe) do much facilitate the operations of Grace upon them. Besides, there are many temtations to which men are exposed that are out of their road. How hard is it for a man to converse in the World, but he shall be importun'd to debauchery and excess, must forfeit his sobriety to maintain the reputation of a sociable Person? Again, how liable are they by a promiscuous conversation among a variety of humors, to meet with affronts, which the Maxims of Honor will tell them, must (in spight of all Christs interdicts) be reveng'd? And this engages them in Quarrels, sometimes in Murders. Now none of these are incident to women: they must in these and som other instances attaque temtation, violently ravish guilt, and abandon their Sex, the whole Oeconomy of their estate, ere they can divest themselves of their innocency.

Men can, in other words, abandon virtue because they are social beings: temptation can bring them down. No mention is made of will, the ability to resist temptation, as the highest form of virtue. Women, on the other hand, have a deeper identity. Their innate goodness is bound up so closely with their sexuality that they cannot be both vicious and female. This extraordinary conclusion is followed by one even more surprising:

So that God seems in many particulars to have closelier fenced them in, and not left them to those wilder excursions for which the customary liberties of the other Sex afford a more open way. In short, they have so many advantages towards Vertue, that tho the Philosopher made it one of his solemn acknowledgements to God, that he had made him a man, not a woman: yet I think Christian women have now reason enough to invert that form, and to thank God that he made them women, and not men.[45]

God seems to be demanding less than He did in the days of the Gouges: women are seen here as more likely to be virtuous simply because they are less distracted than men. They are asked to see their very restrictions as hidden blessings. We have in these paragraphs an early example of the simultaneous 'spiritualization' of womanhood and the lowering of the status of religion in the social life.

The early feminist, Mary Astell, has a considerably livelier sense of the power relationship between the sexes than Allestree when she discusses the religious discernment of women in a book printed in 1705. The half-apologetic waffling at the beginning of her assertion is some evidence that she thinks herself on controversial ground, though there is considerable sarcasm in her pose of feminine caution:[46]

Perhaps I may be thought singular in what I am about to say, but I think I have reason to warrant me, and till I am convinc'd of the contrary, since it is a Truth of great importance, I shall not scruple to declare it, without regarding the singularity. I therefore beg leave to say, that most of, if not all, the Follies and Vices that Women are subject to, (for I meddle not with the Men) are owing to their paying too great a deference to other Peoples judgments, and too little to our own; in suffering others to judge for us, when GOD has not only allow'd, but requir'd us to judge for ourselves.[47]

She shows little gratitude for the conditions which, according to Allestree, should make her more susceptible to grace than a man. But, though she draws quite different conclusions from his about the source of woman's lapse into vice, she seems to agree with him, though indirectly, on the question of male moral inferiority. It is men who lead women into folly, although they are supposedly given authority over them. Astell carefully avoids discussing the relationship between the male sex and evil, but one suspects from her repetition of the phrases 'Just' and 'Lawful Authority' that she finds much authority unjust and unlawful. It is their very power which makes men corrupt and hence corrupters:

How those who have *made themselves* our Governors, may like our withdrawing from their yoke I know not; but I am certain that this principle of judging for our selves, in all cases wherein GOD has left us this liberty, will introduce no disorder into the World, or disobedience to our *Lawful* Governors. Rather, it will teach us to be as tractable and submissive to Just Authority, as we are careful to judge rightly for our selves, in such matters wherein GOD has not appointed any to judge for us. The insinuations of those who have no right to be our Directors, but who have only usurp'd an empire over our Understandings, being one of the principal Causes of our disobedience to Lawful Authority. Both by rendering us disaffected to our proper Governors, as is their usual practice, that so they themselves may intirely command us: And also because sooner or later we shall be convinc'd of the dishonour and damage of being any ones Property, and thence grow suspicious of, and uneasy at the just commands of those who have a right to prescribe in some cases.

What is it that chains us down to the slavery of all the silly customs of the Age, to the waste of our Time, the expence of our Fortunes, nay even to the depraving of our very Reason, but because we must do as others do, and are afraid of the singularity of being Wiser and Better than our Neighbours? So that we force our selves to practice those Follies, which whilst we practise we condemn! What is it that engages Women in Crimes contrary to their Reason, and their very natural Temper, but the being over-perswaded and over-rul'd by those to whose conduct they commit themselves? And how do they excuse these Crimes, but by alledging the examples of other People?

And she concludes with a triumphantly epigrammatic sentence which could serve as a motto for *Clarissa*: ' I do not deny that singularity in trifles and indifferent things is a Folly and a Vice; but to be singularly wise and good in the midst of a crooked and perverse Generation, and in spite of all the persecutions we suffer for being so, is the most exalted pitch of heroick Vertue.'[48]

By 1705 middle-class women are leading the sort of life described in *The Ladies Library*, and Astell, like so many writers of her generation, condemns it. She is not so much concerned about women's being ' closelier fenced in ' than men, as about their being misled by public opinion. She still shares with Allestree, however, the conviction that women's powers of judgment (moral only, in Allestree's argument; both moral and intellectual, in Astell's) are being subverted and misused. Where Allestree is circular, telling his readers basically to pull themselves up by their own religious bootstraps, Astell is defiantly assertive: if women were not trained to suppress any individuality of thought or conduct, there would be many more exemplary women in society. Her insistence on 'Just Authority' suggests a narrow and demanding definition behind the term: she is well aware that encouraging women's individualism is encouraging rebellion against those ' authorities ' whose judgment may not be just; and she makes a distinction between civil and religious authority, though she will not say this directly. Even Astell, however, shares with Allestree the belief that sexuality and a woman's moral worth are intertwined:

one may lay it down as a rule, That no Man attempts to speak disrespectfully of GOD, or of the Holy Scriptures, but he is at the bottom a vain and wicked Man: And whoever he be who endeavours to corrupt a Woman's Faith, he has a design to ruin her in this World as well as in the next. If she has too much Vertue to be assaulted directly, the way is to undermine her Religious Principles, these being the only firm foundation of real Honour and moral Honesty; nor can any Vertue stand firm against all attacks, but that which is founded upon a Christian Principle.[49]

It is from works such as these, in short, that some of the substance and most of the rhetoric of the arguments in *Clarissa* are drawn. The words 'honour', 'honesty' and 'virtue', used by Astell in quick succession, are a key to the complexity of the moral dilemma for women. Each of them has one meaning which applies specifically to chastity in women; and examples of this meaning in all three, according to the *OED*, seem to be most abundant in the period from the seventeenth century to the late nineteenth. The first example of the word 'virtue' when used to mean 'chastity, sexual purity, especially on the part of women', comes from Shakespeare in 1599. The three subsequent examples are all from the eighteenth century, and two come from Richardson and Fielding. They are terms, in short, which are associated with that age when Puritanism in its various forms dominated English religious thought and especially practical morality; and they link goodness or badness in women with their sexuality.

In the eighteenth century, however, when women began inheriting the domain of religion as their political and economic power contracted, these words, contextually at least, took on broader meanings, while the original sexual construction of the terms was retained. In Astell's 'Rule', a woman has Christian principles in addition to her chastity: she can be raped spiritually as well as physically. Allestree tells us that passivity and understimulation make women more susceptible to grace than men; Astell goes further and sees male lust as an absolute evil. Both writers share the view that women are better than men, more responsible for their own deeds, and, through their greater moral worth, more vulnerable to failure than their male counterparts. They are given an awesome responsibility, and it depends completely on sex. Ian Watt seems to agree: ' It is, in all events, very evident that the eighteenth century witnessed a tremendous narrowing of the ethical scale, a redefinition of virtue in primarily sexual terms' (Watt, p. 157).

When Anna Howe outlines Clarissa's daily routine for John Belford, she is giving a picture of practical and moral excellence that, for the majority of the upper middle class, has already become archaic. The Clarissa of the testimonial letter is leading a life that is, as we have seen, lamented as a thing of the past even in the earlier part of the eighteenth century. It has become abstractly exemplary, just as religion has become abstractly 'spiritual'. All novels raise questions about realism, because the conventions of the form, however relaxed they may be, force some confrontation with the problems of imitation. The implications of the atavism in *Clarissa* have been far-reaching.

2

THE MORAL STRUGGLE AT HARLOWE PLACE

Anna Howe's first letter

The first letter from Anna Howe, which opens the novel, prepares us for the testimonial at the end in two ways. It serves first, of course, as an introduction to Clarissa's character. It also mediates between the heroine and a public which at this point also includes the reader, since the privileged intimacy which comes through reading this voluminous correspondence has not yet been established. The rather stiff and heavily qualified phrasing in which Anna offers her admiration (it is, in fact, a style she resumes only once, in the testimonial letter) suggests even at this earliest moment that unexamined praise is another version of Clarissa's persecution. It becomes clear that Clarissa has always been a public figure in her own circle; and from the beginning the reader is made ready for the trials that she will undergo. Clarissa's very desire to dodge the limelight, or at least the appearance of such a desire, contributes to her exemplariness: ' I know', writes Anna, ' how it must hurt you to become the subject of the public talk; and yet, upon an occasion so generally known, it is impossible but that whatever relates to a young lady, whose distinguished merits have made her the public care, should engage everybody's attention' (I, 1). There follows a description of all the comments Anna Howe has heard upon the duel between James Harlowe and Lovelace from ' Mr Diggs, the surgeon', Mr Wyerley and Mr Symmes (both former suitors of Clarissa's), and Anna's mother, Mrs Howe. ' Everybody pities you', Anna continues,

so steady, so uniform in your conduct: so desirous, as you always said, of sliding through life to the end of it unnoted; and, as I may add, not wishing to be observed even for your silent benevolence; sufficiently happy in the noble consciousness which attends it: *Rather useful than glaring*, your deserved motto; though now, to your regret, pushed into the blaze as I may say: and yet blamed at home for the faults of others – how must such a virtue suffer on every hand! – yet it must be allowed that your present trial is but proportioned to your prudence. –

As all your friends without doors are apprehensive that some other unhappy event may result from so violent a contention, in which it seems the families on both sides are now engaged, I must desire you to enable me, on the authority of your own information, to do you occasional justice . . .

You see what you draw upon yourself by excelling all your sex. Every individual of it who knows you, or has heard of you; seems to think you answerable to *her* for your conduct in points so very delicate and concerning.

Every eye, in short, is upon you with the expectation of an example. I wish to Heaven you were at liberty to pursue your own methods: all would then, I daresay, be easy, and honourably ended. But I dread your directors and directresses; for your mother, admirably qualified as she is to lead, must submit to be led. Your sister and brother will certainly put you out of your course . . .

(I, 2–3)

This passage is extraordinary for several reasons. First, the emphasis shifts twice in the first paragraph, which is one string of adjectival clauses, from Clarissa's intense privacy to her importance as an exemplum. The passage also suggests implicitly that Clarissa's persecutions are *merited*: ' and yet blamed at home for the faults of others – how must such a virtue suffer on every hand! – *yet it must be allowed that your present trial is but proportioned to your prudence . . .*' (my italics). Anna then asks for Clarissa's own account in order ' to do you occasional justice' and goes on to warn Clarissa that people who live so virtuously have a responsibility to their public. Later in the same letter, Anna makes the same point: ' If anything unhappy should fall out from the violence of such spirits as you have to deal with, your account of all things *previous* to it will be your best justification.' Like nearly any passage from Richardson, this one seems to reveal a darker side, upon scrutiny, than is at first apparent. Even Anna Howe, Clarissa's devoted friend, cannot escape the view (presumably the public view as well, since she is established at once as a reporter to Clarissa, and as a spokeswoman to the outside world) that Clarissa is in some way guilty; that were she not quite so excellent in all her virtues, she would not be made to suffer.

We can recognize the Miltonic and of course biblical origins of this notion; and it is not difficult to see that the assumption of precipitating guilt has religious roots.[1] The letter offers glimmerings of the comparisons drawn between Clarissa and Job in the third part of the novel. From the beginning we are aware of the direction of Clarissa's moral progress. Didactic references to Job abound, of course, in Puritan writing. We can take an example from Allestree's discussion of patience in *The Whole Duty of Man*:

it is but a counterfeit patience, that pretends to submit to God, and yet can bear nothing from men: We see holy *Job*, who is set forth to us as a pattern of true patience, made no such difference in his afflictions . . . when therefore we suffer any thing from men, be it never so unjustly in respect of them, we are yet to confess it is most just in respect of God; and therefore instead of looking upon them with rage and revenge, as the common custom of the world is, we are to look up to God, acknowledge his justice in the affliction, begging his pardon most earnestly for those sins which have provoked him to send it, and patiently and thankfully bear it till he shall see fit to remove it, still saying with *Job, Blessed be the name of the Lord*. (Allestree, p. 25)

Anna's letter, then, is solidly in the Puritan tradition, which demands that the saints of the church, in imitation of Christ, must bear their burdens in the most strictly theological sense – gracefully. But the religious connotations alone cannot give us a satisfactory explanation for the contradictions that Anna is presenting in such apparently generous words. It seems to be Clarissa's prudence that is being praised: not her faith, not her will, but rather the practical virtues of caution and perspicacity. There is a genuine blurriness about the ideal of moral behaviour in Anna's letter: Clarissa's stature quickly trivializes the rather narrow standards by which she is at first judged. Paul E. Parnell has discovered other vaguely suspect parallels between virtue and what he calls 'superiority of tactics' in the sentimental drama of the period; his study helps to give some understanding of the confusion of the ethical scale at the beginning of *Clarissa*.[2]

In any case, one might ask what her public is requiring of her when she has, until now, shown nothing but indifference, both to Lovelace and, apparently, to that public itself. It is true that she has been the cause of the duel, but she has had no share in events except through the sheer fact of her presence at Harlowe Place. The reader is drawn to ask why the passive centre of a violent struggle should need to have 'occasional justice done to her'; and why she can be thought exemplary and guilty at the same time, even by her closest friend.

This seems to be a view of moral responsibility of such profundity that it has been taken whole and unchallenged into the language even of a verbally skilled and self-aware character (Cynthia Griffin Wolff, for example, has even given Anna the office of conscience to Clarissa, which would suggest that Anna's moral susceptibilities have been regarded as fine rather than coarse).[3] Virtue, as we have seen in the development of the concept in the conduct books, tended towards a more exclusively sexual definition as the original Puritan impulse faded or, rather, changed; thus, the guardians of the moral code have become women. Clarissa's 'conduct in points so very delicate and concerning' must somehow prevent further violence. This suggestion is reinforced in the very construction of the sentence in which Anna asks, lawyerlike, for more information. She seems to accept, like Clarissa's 'friends without doors', that her correspondent is first of all guilty until proved innocent and, secondly, increasingly guilty with each consequence of the present action. While Lovelace and James Harlowe are certainly condemned for 'the contentions of these fierce, these masculine spirits' (I, 22), they are not as responsible for the consequences as is the woman who is the cause of their struggle. While she is on the one hand looked upon as primarily sexual (one can point to the eighteenth-century habit of referring to women as 'the sex'), she is also expected to exert self-control and to deny that sexuality, because women are meant to provide moral stability for society at large. It is almost as if the exertion of the will against an immovable identity in each individual woman provides the moral energy for a whole social world. This attitude recalls Allestree's attitude towards women as creatures whose low place in male esteem is entirely self-induced. Clarissa, as a lady of exemplary virtue, is expected to behave accordingly: she must deny herself in order to deny the possibility of the stain of involvement. One thinks of Fanny Burney's *Camilla*, which appeared much later in the century (1796), in which the heroine's father advises his daughter to 'struggle then against yourself as you would struggle against an enemy'.[4] Indeed, Richardson tells his readers as much in his 'Preface':

The principal of these two young ladies [the other being Anna Howe] is proposed as an exemplar to her sex. Nor is it any objection to her being so, that she is not in all respects a perfect character. It was not only natural, but it was necessary that she should have some faults, were it only to show the reader how laudably she could mistrust and blame herself, and carry to her own heart, divested of self-partiality, the censure which arose from her own convictions . . . As far as is consistent with human frailty, and as far as she could be perfect, considering the people she had to deal with, and those with whom she was inseparably connected, she *is* perfect. To have been impeccable, must have left nothing for the Divine Grace and a purified state to do, and carried our idea of her from woman to angel.   (I, xiv)

Anna Howe's letter, then, despite its evident kindness and concern, is written in treacherous language. Clarissa is informed that she is subject to the world's censure if she cannot 'clear' herself, but the message comes across in the very structure of Anna's sentences rather than in direct statements. From the beginning, Clarissa is being challenged. In the Harlowe Place section of the novel we can see this same language used in good faith by Clarissa and travestied by her gaolers, particularly by her brother and sister. Anna's mediating position between Clarissa and the attentive but anonymous public who waits to hear news of her allows her to use this language in what might be called an average way, in the novel's own terms: she neither lives according to Clarissa's standards, nor would she dream of subverting them. Unlike Clarissa, on the one hand, whose words are carefully chosen and closely integrated with the meaning she gives them, and unlike the younger members of the Harlowe family, on the other, who are consciously playing on the treachery of conduct-book language, Anna uses the words carelessly. They are like a skin of apparently solid ice: it is easy to fall through them into dangerous waters. We are at once alerted to the social and moral code which Clarissa must acknowledge. It is as ambiguous as it is stern.

While Anna Howe has given us an exposition of the terms of the trial, the Harlowes sit in judgment over Clarissa in this first section of the novel; and they are a family torn by discord. At first this disharmony is not expressed. The change occurs between Letters VI and VII. In Letter VI we learn that Clarissa is going to spend three weeks with Anna Howe. Though a family council gathers to give her permission to go, she has not yet fallen from favour; all the Harlowes ask of her is that she not receive visits from Lovelace during her stay. But she discovers upon her return that they have decided to take Solmes's offer of marriage (until then only mentioned in passing) very seriously indeed. She is met by another council, this time a solemn one: the Harlowes have learned that Anna has received visits from Lovelace (though Clarissa points out that she could hardly instruct another family to close its doors to him) and they blame Clarissa for permitting them. From this point onward, the persecutions begin in earnest. Clarissa and Anna recognize early that the Harlowes are driven by their own greed. Clarissa, having already incurred the family's displeasure when she inherited her grandfather's estate, has long before agreed to its administration by her father. It is not difficult for her to see that personal and economic jealousy, particularly in her brother and sister, are intertwined:

To obviate everyone's jealousy, I gave up to my father's management, as you know, not only the estate, but the money bequeathed me; contenting myself to take as from his bounty what he was pleased to allow me, without desiring the least addition to my annual stipend. And then I hoped I had laid all envy asleep; but still my brother and sister (jealous, as is now evident, of my two uncles' favour for me, and of the pleasure I had given my father and them by this act of duty) were every now and then occasionally doing me covert ill offices . . .

When James and Arabella (who had refused Lovelace out of pride when he courted her briefly, mistaking her for Clarissa) learn that their

uncles would be willing to settle estates on Clarissa even if she married
Lovelace – which would probably give Lovelace a baronetcy at
James's expense – they 'did behave to me as to one who stood in their
way; and to each other as having but one interest . . . Between them,
the family union was broken, and every one was made uneasy' (I, 55).

Here it becomes clear that Richardson can no longer depend upon
those social structures which are assumed in the conduct books.
Clarissa's conflict is not primarily a generational one, between parents
and children, though that it is how it appears to the elder Harlowes. It
is between those members of the family who stand to have potential
power. But Clarissa also understands how James and Arabella use the
language of the conduct books to persuade the older generation of the
rightness of their aims, on the one hand, and to break Clarissa's spirit,
on the other. In one of her very rare moments of irony, Clarissa repeats
the official line for Anna:

These desirable views answered, [if Clarissa marries Solmes] how rich, how
splendid, shall we all three be! And I – what obligations shall I lay upon them
all! – And that only by doing an act of duty so suitable to my character and
manner of thinking; if indeed I am the generous as well as dutiful creature I
have hitherto made them believe I am.

This is the bright side that is turned to my father and uncles, to captivate
them: but I am afraid that my brother's and sister's design is to ruin me with
them at any rate. Were it otherwise, would they not on my return from you
have rather sought to *court* than *frighten* me into measures which their hearts are
so much bent to carry?
(I, 59)

Clarissa, with some scepticism, analyses the reactions of the senior
members of the family and recognizes the speciousness of her siblings'
arguments: 'Hatred to Lovelace, family aggrandisement, and this
great motive *paternal authority*! – What a force *united* must they be
supposed to have, when *singly* each consideration is sufficient to carry
all before it!' (I, 61). The senior Harlowes are characterized not so
much by conscious hypocrisy, or even by greed, though both of these
sins are certainly evident, as by blindness (in the case of her father and
uncles) and passivity (a quality in Mrs Harlowe and Clarissa's Aunt
Hervey which is often remarked upon, and often lamented, by Clarissa
and Anna). It is the language which has tricked them, and because it is
being consciously manipulated by the younger Harlowes, the falsity of
the values behind it has been revealed for the first time.

'This great motive *paternal authority*', as Clarissa puts it, is a
secondary subject of family debate. The real source of conflict arises
out of the controversies about sexual identity and its moral power.
When Clarissa is left alone with her father early in the course of her

persecutions, for example, her obedience is clearly linked in his mind to her sexuality:

> He turned from me, and in a strong voice, Clarissa Harlowe, said he, know that I will be obeyed.
> – God forbid, sir, that you should not! – I have never yet opposed your will –
> Nor I your whimsies, Clarissa Harlowe, interrupted he. – Don't let me run the fate of all who show indulgence to your sex; to be the more contradicted for mine to you.
> My father, you know, my dear, has not (any more than my brother) a kind opinion of our sex; although there is not a more condescending wife in the world than my mother. (I, 36)

Clarissa's mother, during her series of visits to her daughter's room, uses the argument of parental authority in an attempt to persuade: 'If you mean to show your duty, and your obedience, Clary, you must show it in *our* way, not in *your own*' (I, 78). Clarissa tries to show her mother in some very lively exchanges that it is not parental authority that is at issue; but she is unable to make her see the contradictions in the family's attitudes.

James and Arabella, the architects of the family plan, use conduct-book language as a kind of torture of their younger sister. Arabella, in particular, whose jealousy is more personal than James's – after all, Clarissa excels her in everything and has been her rival for Lovelace – is particularly skilful in this method. She even refers to Clarissa's ordering of her daily life:

> She ridiculed me for my supposed esteem for Mr Lovelace – was surprised that the *witty*, the *prudent*, nay the *dutiful* and *pi-ous* (so she sneeringly pronounced the word) Clarissa Harlowe, should be so strangely fond of a profligate man, that her parents were forced to lock her up in order to hinder her from running into his arms. 'Let me ask you, my dear, said she, how you now keep your account of the disposition of your time? *How many hours in the twenty-four* do you devote to your needle? How many to your prayers? How many to letter-writing? And how many to love? – I doubt, I doubt, my little dear, was her arch expression, the latter article is like Aaron's rod, and swallows up the rest! – Tell me; is it not so?' (I, 213)

Perhaps it is a tribute to Arabella's nastiness and Clarissa's 'credibility' (an unpleasant journalist's word for the integrity of character in an old novel) that we interpret this attack as if we already knew about Clarissa's methodical and saint-like day; but we are only informed of the details of this moral account-keeping by Anna Howe, in her testimonial letter. We have not yet been given the information upon which this sneering is based, but we already know enough about Arabella and don't consider her a reliable critic.

A few pages later, Bella is accompanied by Aunt Hervey in another of the innumerable visits to Clarissa's room. This time Arabella links the question of Clarissa's estate to her disobedience: it is a brilliant piece of strategy, because the same motives that govern the rest of the Harlowes are attributed to Clarissa. Thus she can be accused of a double hypocrisy: she can pretend to condemn her family for practices in which she herself engages, and she can delude the world into thinking her a paragon. Yet, like Bella's first attack, this one is pure fantasy. It depends on a series of assumptions which, like Lovelace's later, serve only to deepen the gulf between attacker and attacked:

Yes, said my sister, I do not doubt but it is Miss Clary's aim, if she does not fly to her Lovelace, to get her estate into her own hands, and go to live at *The Grove* [the name of the estate], in that independence upon which she builds all her perverseness. And, dear heart! my little love, how will you then blaze away! Your mamma Norton, your oracle, with your poor at your gates, mingling so *proudly* and so *meanly* with the ragged herd! Reflecting, by your ostentation, upon all the ladies in the county, who do not as you do. This is known to be your scheme! and the poor *without* doors, and Lovelace *within*, with one hand building up a name, pulling it down with the other! Oh, what a charming scheme is this! But let me tell you, my pretty little flighty one, that your father's *living* will shall control your grandfather's *dead* one; and that estate will be disposed of as your fond grandfather would have disposed of it had he lived to see such a change in his favourite. In a word, miss, it will be kept out of your hands, till my father sees you discreet enough to have the management of it, or till you can *dutifully*, by law, tear it from him. (I, 229–30)

Those of us who have or are sisters can only be thankful that ordinary sibling rivalry does not usually take such vitriolic forms. Arabella, like all of Clarissa's persecutors throughout the novel, is after violation. These attacks are incursions, attempts to topple the boundaries of self which Clarissa has worked so hard to create. Her self, indeed, whatever that construction may turn out to be, at this stage resembles her estate. Both are squeezed hard between the lust of Solmes and the ambitions of the Harlowe family. In the first attack, Clarissa is accused of secret love for Lovelace, on the ground that she would not else refuse Solmes; in the second, she is accused of Harlowe-like greed in her supposed desire for financial independence. Clarissa's repeated declarations that she will never go to court for possession of the estate count for little, although she continues firm in this negative resolve until her death.

In both of these attacks by Arabella, Clarissa's moral behaviour is discredited, since she is accused of hypocrisy. Because Clarissa cannot marry Solmes, she is not allowed the neutrality of her former existence.

The assumptions of the past have crumbled, and she cannot accept the future which the Harlowes have prepared. Arabella's jibes constantly remind her of the fragility and terrible flexibility of a once benign language (there is no doubt that the endearments sharpen the cruelty of Arabella's remarks). The vocabulary of morality can become a weapon when it is detached from its original meaning. Clarissa, in her extreme isolation, is for the first time aware that she is surrounded by a world of words, and perhaps by little else.

It is only her correspondence with Anna Howe – at this point, at least – which saves her, because it gives her an opportunity to reassert her own values in her own language. One recalls, indeed, Anna Howe's hint in her first letter that all would 'be easy, and honourably ended', if Clarissa were 'at liberty to pursue [her] own methods'. Since Anna's letter has been written after a duel, the traditional chivalric recourse of high-born gentlemen, the reader is reminded that 'honour' for Clarissa is quite a different concept to that held by her brother and Lovelace. The situation can end 'honourably' for Clarissa only if she remains as she was, a virgin, or if she marries suitably. Honour in a woman, viewed conventionally, would have an exclusively sexual definition in the eighteenth century.[5] For Clarissa, however, sexuality and integrity are identified. Her use of the word does not exclude chastity, but generalizes the concept, so that it satisfies (or seems to, for the early Clarissa) both the social meaning of the term and her own individual one. Honour, for her, is personal integrity, which is symbolized, but not contained, in the notion of sexual integrity; honesty, and even faith in the power of communication, of common speech and common covenants. She uses 'honour' in this way, simply in passing, in one of her letters to Anna, when she disclaims any affection for Lovelace. The thoughtful reader might also recognize that the opening sentences of this passage recall Anna Howe's first letter and Richardson's prefatory remarks on self-distrust:

Indeed, my dear, THIS man is not THE man. I have great objections to him. My heart *throbs* not after him. I *glow* not, but with indignation against myself for having given room for such an imputation. – But you must not, my dearest friend, construe common gratitude into love. I cannot bear that you should. But if ever I should have the misfortune to think it love, I promise you *upon my word*, which is the same as *upon my honour*, that I will acquaint you with it.

(I, 47–8)

It becomes, in fact, Clarissa's perhaps central misery that she is no longer taken at her word. It is at that point that she begins the reassessment of a world which has split into irreconcilable internal and external fragments, and also of the language which used adequately to join them. One recalls Locke's equation of women and rhetoric: '*Eloquence*, like the fair Sex, has too Prevailing Beauties in it, to suffer it self ever to be spoken against: And 'tis in vain to find fault with those Arts of Deceiving, wherein Men find pleasure to be Deceived.'[6]

Of all her persecutors at Harlowe Place, however, it is of course her brother James who wields the real power; and he shows the same malicious skill with Puritan rhetoric as his sister Arabella. In an acrimonious exchange of letters with Clarissa, he informs her of a 'unanimous resolution' in a family council to force her to receive Solmes at her uncle Antony's (I, 255–6ff). Clarissa tries to direct a letter to her parents, who have refused communication with her, through the hopelessly implacable James. 'Let me not be cruelly given up', she writes, 'to a man my very soul is averse to. Permit me to repeat that I cannot *honestly* be his. Had I a slighter notion of the matrimonial duty than I have, perhaps I might. But when I am to bear all the misery, and that for *life*; when my *heart* is less concerned in this matter than my *soul*; my *temporary*, perhaps, than my *future* good; why should I be denied the liberty of *refusing*? That liberty is all I ask' (I, 260).

This is writing in Puritan style: the candid examination of conscience, earthly weighed against heavenly prospects. Clarissa invokes the most serious authority, the demands of religion, to support her disobedience. Marrying Solmes would put even her chance of heavenly grace in jeopardy, for she would be prostituting herself, and therefore sinning, if she gave her consent. Like 'honour' and 'virtue', the word 'honesty' carries both sexual and more general meanings.[7] Marriage with Solmes would (contrary to the popular phrase) make a dishonest woman out of one who has been, until now, both honest and honourable. The implicit hint that marrying Solmes would be a kind of prostitution shows that Clarissa has recognized that she is being sold into matrimony: and for her the act of selling, when it is carried into human relationships, is as sinful as it is personally repugnant. This attitude puts Clarissa radically at odds with the expectations of her family and the ambitions of her class. When the passage is compared to the response it receives in her brother's letter, it becomes apparent that James is all too ready to turn the language against Clarissa, making a parody of all her supplications:

You seem, child, to have a high notion of the matrimonial duty; and I'll warrant, like the rest of your sex (one or two, whom I have the honour to know, excepted), that you will go to church to promise what you will never think of afterwards. But, *sweet* child; as your *worthy* Mamma Norton [Clarissa's old nurse, who has been pleading her cause unsuccessfully] calls you, think a little less of the *matrimonial* (at least until you come into that state), and a little more of the *filial* duty.

How can you say you are to bear *all the misery*, when you give so large a share of it to your parents, to your uncles, to your aunt, to myself, and to your sister; who all, for eighteen years of your life, loved you so well?

If of late I have not given you room to hope for my favour or compassion, it is because of late you have not deserved either. I know what you mean, little reflecting fool, by saying it is much in my power, although *but* your brother (a very slight degree of relationship with you), to give you that peace which you can give yourself whenever you please.

The liberty of *refusing*, pretty Miss, is denied you because we are all sensible that the liberty of *choosing*, to everyone's dislike, must follow. The vile wretch [Lovelace] you have set your heart upon speaks this plainly to everybody, though you won't. He says you are *his*, and shall be *his*, and he will be the death of any man who robs him of his PROPERTY. So, Miss, we have a mind to try this point with him. My father, supposing he has the right of a father in his child, is absolutely determined not to be bullied out of that right. And what must that child be, who prefers the rake to the father?

This is the light in which this whole debate ought to be taken. Blush, then, Delicacy, that cannot bear the poet's *amor omnibus idem*: ['Love is the same for everyone', probably from Virgil, who has been referred to in their previous exchange] – Blush, then, Purity! Be ashamed, Virgin Modesty! And if capable of conviction, surrender your whole will to the will of the honoured pair to whom you owe your being: and beg of all your friends to forgive and forget the part you have of late acted.   (I, 262–3)

James has once again blocked her attempt at contact with her parents, whose sole authority, of all the Harlowes, Clarissa recognizes. His answer weaves Clarissa's own words in scattered phrases through-out the passage (a trick Richardson used rather more benignly in his own correspondence, particularly with his young lady friends).[8] Not only are Clarissa's pleas made to rebound upon herself (much as her own language does in the despairing lines that follow these from James), but the thrust of her argument is deflected.

James has caught the implications in Clarissa's letter. Her anger at 'being cruelly give up' comes of the awareness that marrying Solmes would, for her, bring moral disaster, whether or not her will were engaged; and James sees this. His response is to cut away the remaining ground from beneath her feet, much as Arabella has done. He implies, like Arabella, that Clarissa is a hypocrite, that she will take a lover (presumably Lovelace, if she marries Solmes) as soon as she marries anyway. He argues with maliciously specious logic that if the future is impossible to contemplate, then Clarissa should think about obeying her parents in the present; and he ends with another stab at the sincerity of her moral code. His warning about Lovelace is, like Arabella's imputation of her own motives to Clarissa, pure projection, if such wording is appropriate to a literary context: the reader, at least, has seen only three letters from Lovelace at this point in the novel, and none of them shows any obsession with Clarissa as property.

The effect on Clarissa of this manipulation of a once-trustworthy language slowly becomes apparent. She begins to get inklings of the chasm before her late in her captivity at Harlowe Place: 'Is it not a sad thing', she writes in a poignant letter to Anna Howe,

beloved as I thought myself so lately by every one, that now I have not one person in the world to plead for me, to stand by me, or who would afford me refuge, were I to be under the necessity of seeking for it! – I who had the vanity to think I had as many friends as I saw faces, and flattered myself too that it was not altogether unmerited, because I saw not my Maker's image, either in man, woman, or child, high or low, rich or poor, whom, comparatively, I could not love as myself. – I don't know what to do, not I! – God forgive me, but I am very impatient: I wish – but I don't know what to wish, without a sin: – Yet I wish it would please God to take me to his mercy: – I can meet with none here. – What a world is this! What is there in it desirable? The good we hope for, so strangely mixed that one knows not what to wish for! And one half of mankind tormenting the other, and being tormented themselves in tormenting! – For here in this my particular case, my relations cannot be happy, though they make me unhappy! – Except my brother and sister, indeed – and they seem to take delight in and enjoy the mischief they make.   (I, 264–5)

For Clarissa, spiritual awakening comes not from the dubious praise she once enjoyed, but rather from the agonizing realization that there is no space for a self in the world as she has conceived of it. Until this crisis, she had thought of herself as one who lived disinterestedly by the Golden Rule; now she learns that even this obedience was only the occasion for a display of spiritual pride ('I who had the vanity to think I had as many friends as I saw faces, and flattered myself too that it was not altogether unmerited . . .'). Her prose is full of first persons and reflexives, as if the Golden Rule had rebounded grammatically upon her with the discovery that the apparent kindness of those around her was a mask that remained in place only as long as its presence had been consistent with the self-interest of its wearers. Her piety, the practical and tolerant piety of the mid-eighteenth-century Anglican church, has been quite rejected by the very family who would have introduced her to its principles in her childhood.

Not for the first time in the course of her persecutions (see I, 4, for example), Clarissa wishes for death. Existence, squeezed between a deluded past, a hypocritical present and an unacceptable future, has become unbearable. The famous Richardsonian use of exclamations and hesitant half-phrases – of which we will see many more examples in the second part of the novel, when the gaoler is Lovelace rather than the Harlowes – intensifies the emotional turmoil. It also demonstrates how difficult the simple act of desiring has become, since her family persists, in its verbal torture, to divide Clarissa's decisions from their consequences. Clarissa almost articulates a wish for death, then withdraws from her impulse, then expresses it finally in a burst of feeling. She can no longer imagine a way in which she can exert her will against the newly exposed hypocrisies of her family.

Yet, as we have seen in the few examples that have been selected, this conscious manipulation on the part of Clarissa's persecutors creates its own hazards. It is as if the language, freed from its former denotations, has taken its users with it into a realm of uncontrolled imagery in which words create fantasies without the full knowledge of their manipulators. When Clarissa writes that mankind is tormented itself in tormenting, one hears the Miltonic echoes from the rhetoric-filled halls of Pandemonium. There, too, Beelzebub holds sway; there, too, the result of the conscious distortion of the purpose of language is the mutual estrangement of the sexes, and their expulsion from an orderly world. Richardson, needless to say, owes much to Milton,[9] as he does to the Puritan tradition in general. The effect of this debt is sometimes plain, but more often so diffuse and subtle that even the most casual examples leave the reader darkly aware that great moral forces run beneath the text.

'The devil's in her sex!'

I have tried to show how the language of an already ambiguous morality can be manipulated into expressing its own speciousness. This language is used naïvely (if a character's actions may be so described) by Anna Howe, carefully by the heroine, blindly by her parents, and with deliberate malice by her brother and sister. There is another example of suggestive language in *Clarissa* which is significant enough to merit some treatment on its own.

The variations on the notion that the devil inhabits women were extremely common in this period. In Restoration comedy, it is a lightheartedly blasphemous cliché, well suited to the explosive speech of the rakes who invoke it so often. Both heroes and buffoons partake freely of the imagery. In Wycherley's *Country-Wife* (1675), for example, Horner, the successful rake, describes the agent of his 'castration' as an

'*English–French* Chirurgeon, who has given me at once, not only a Cure, but an Antidote for the future, against that damn's malady, and that worse distemper, love, and all other womens evils'. In Horner's description the notion of the diabolical element in women is implicit; but it is made quite clear when Pinchwife, the aging cuckold of the piece, offers his views: 'Why should Woman have more invention in love than men? It can only be, because they have more desires, more solliciting passion, more lust, and more of the Devil.'[10] Etherege's *Man of Mode* (1676) is full of diabolical references to both sexes. But the devil in the rake Dorimant is rather an appealing fellow to the ladies. 'I know he is a Devil,' says Mrs Loveit, 'but he has something of the Angel yet undefac'd in him, which makes him so charming and agreeable, that I must love him be he never so wicked.'[11] Dorimant's activities make him devilish, but not completely so: his evil genius retains something of its heavenly origins, and he has a choice. He is *a* devil, not *the* devil.

The description of women in diabolical terms, on the other hand, is always an argument from essence. Women are taken over, possessed; and their demon has long since fallen from Heaven. The male version of diabolical identification derives from the poetically powerful image of Satan shortly after his plunge from divine favour. The female version has the tawdry prurience of seventeenth-century accounts of witchcraft. Even the slightest remarks, such as this one, made by Old Bellair in *The Man of Mode*, point up the difference: 'a wife is no Curse when she brings the Blessing of a good Estate with Her, but an idle Town Flurt, with a painted Face, a Rotten Reputation, and a crasie Fortune, a-dod, is the Devil and all; and such a one I hear you are in League with'.[12]

This imagery reflects the ancient but sturdy view of woman as the source of evil, Lilith as opposed to Eve. Genesis itself, especially as treated by Milton, is ambiguous on the subject: the step is not great from contempt for woman's weakness in submitting to temptation to fear of her power as a seductive ally of Satan. A gloss on such an ordinary turn of phrase would hardly be necessary, were it not that Richardson, perhaps because of his familiarity with colloquial rather than highly cultivated speech, often has a trick of transforming such clichés by use and placement.

In this case it is used first in a letter from Clarissa's uncle Antony. Clarissa has written two supplicating and carefully reasoned letters to each of her uncles, John and Antony, in the hope of winning them to her side. She makes the mistake of pointing out the illogicality of asking her to marry a man (Solmes) on the basis of her 'preposession' for another (Lovelace), and then compares them: 'But the one, it seems, has many faults: – Is the other *faultless*? – The principal thing objected to Mr Lovelace (and a very inexcusable one) is that he is immoral in his loves – is not the other in his hatreds? – Nay, as I may say, in his loves too (the object only differing) *if the love of money be the root of all evil.*' She goes on carefully to explain why she cannot accept Solmes, mentioning again the possibility of losing the chance of salvation in the next world (I, 156, 157). But she does not deny a 'prepossession' for Lovelace, though she has written earlier to Anna Howe that this is an intentional strategy, in the hope that her family will be more merciful (I, 191). The closest she comes is in her often-repeated promise not to marry without her family's consent, as long as she may be spared a union with Solmes.

Her uncle Antony, like Lovelace's uncle, Lord M., is no intellectual. One would expect catch-phrases from him, because his prose is full of proverbs, usually more than slightly misunderstood. It is nonetheless significant that his use of the phrase arises out of Clarissa's disobedience, however respectful, towards parental authority: she is plunged from her former place as an exemplum into the coarsest indignity of generalization about women. Antony Harlowe's crassness in financial matters, like Solmes's, is linked to his lack of sensitivity to people, to rational argument, and to moral worth. But he is seen as forthright, if stupid, and his sudden change of mind about a woman he has known and loved for eighteen years is one indication of the precariousness of her place in his and everyone's esteem: 'The devil's in your sex!', he writes. 'God forgive me for saying so. The nicest of them will prefer a vile rake and who – I suppose I must not repeat the word: – the *word* will offend, when the *vicious* denominated by that word will be chosen! I had not been a bachelor to this time, if I had not seen such a mass of contradictions in you all – Such *gnat-strainers* and *camel-swallowers*, as venerable Holy Writ has it' (I, 160). The comedy of this passage is surprisingly black, on scrutiny: it is another example of the sinister distortions of meaning in even the most common exchanges.

Antony has amusingly paraphrased a passage in the New Testament (Matthew 23:24) in which Jesus attacks the scribes and Pharisees for their hypocrisy. They are charged with neglecting mercy, justice and religion in the interest of material gain. Were he a better reader of Scripture, Antony would realize that this is exactly the accusation which could be brought against himself; Jesus in fact chastises the scribes and Pharisees in the same chapter for just the sort of blindness of which the older Harlowes are guilty. But Antony, like the 'gnat-strainers', cannot recognize the implications of his biblical quotation, while Clarissa, who is both pious and well read, will understand the reference and receive the full brunt of this hazily aimed blow. For her, the citation carries much the same meaning as Arabella's sharply worded attacks. Clarissa is once more accused of the very sins which have been practised by her family, and which are the source of the conflict. When Antony writes that women are a 'mass of contradictions', one is drawn to reflect that he at least partially defines 'contradiction' socially, rather than logically. Clarissa literally contradicts her parents. It is the fact of her opposition, and certainly not any inconsistency in her arguments, which is at issue.

Once more, we watch the crumbling of Clarissa's old sense of herself. Her reasons for her decision to resist her filial duties are ignored by her family, and the meaning of her opposition is effectively cancelled. The Harlowes try to swallow her up into their wickedly corporate identity: they try to make her one of themselves. She is seen as a hypocrite for disobeying her parents, and of course she would be sacrificing herself to their hypocrisy if she complied. At the same time, the devil is not merely her ally, in Antony's phrase: he inhabits her as he supposedly inhabits all women. A very few women, in Antony's eyes, are totally free from evil, as Clarissa was once; the rest are totally tainted. In this passage we have a complex example of how Antony has linked his view of women to his view of the world as a whole, and of his own place in it. After all, her hypocrisy would inevitably reflect upon his own, since he and the other Harlowes do not allow Clarissa to assert a separate individuality. There are no compromises in this morality; but Richardson's treatment of it shows a highly developed sense of irony.

The use of this particular invocation of the devil as the possessor of women is also interesting because of its placement. The letters to and from the uncles follow immediately upon the first letter from Lovelace in the novel. Here the debt to *Paradise Lost* is clear. Lovelace has been the hidden source of contention and has been constantly discussed by all the other characters. Clarissa has been corresponding secretly with him, but until now the reader has had nothing of him but her paraphrases to Anna of his letters. His letter bursts upon the novel with characteristic energy: he is full of witticisms, exalted visions of himself and quotations from Restoration poets. He is also, as so often in the novel, placed in implied comparison with Milton's Satan. Like Satan, he has been advancing steadily towards the scene of his project, even while the focus of the reader's attention is elsewhere: Richardson gives us the secret letters, rumours spread by spies, news of him from Anna and the conjectures of the jealous Harlowes as signs of his progress. Like Satan, too, he spends some time skulking around the periphery of the Harlowes' troubled garden – and it is from the garden that Clarissa is eventually abducted.

It would be a mistake to press comparisons too far. These are echoes, not duplications. One does learn quickly, on the other hand, that Lovelace, a literate and brilliant user of language, moves from the literary example to the personal (and especially sexual) predicament with dazzling speed. There is always an implied identification between Lovelace's sexual personality, which is shaped somewhere at the intersection of language and desire, and the satanism which is so often attributed to him by other characters, by Richardson's own literary habit of implication (as we have seen above) and, of course, by Lovelace himself.

Despite his own unquestionably diabolical qualities, however, even Lovelace uses the phrase which we have already encountered in Antony Harlowe's rebuke to Clarissa. It occurs in his second letter, in which he tells the story of Rosebud, the innocent young daughter of his landlord at the local inn, and her lover Johnny. He charges Jack Belford not to harm the girl when he comes to join Lovelace in the assault on Harlowe Place. Her grandmother has asked Lovelace to leave Rosebud alone, and he writes: 'This is the right way with me. Many and many a pretty rogue had I spared, whom I did *not* spare, had my power been acknowledged, and my mercy in time implored' (I, 170). He intends to double the couple's dowry so that they may marry comfortably. This act of charity is inspired by reflections which recall Satan's envious first look at Adam and Eve: 'What would I give [by my soul, my angel will indeed reform me, if her friends' implacable folly ruin us not both! – What would I give] to have so innocent and so good a heart as either my Rosebud's or Johnny's!' For the moment, then, Lovelace sees Clarissa as a heavenly angel, and himself as the fallen one: ' I have a confounded mischievous [heart] – by *nature* too, I think! A good motion now and then rises from it: but it dies away presently. A love of intrigue. An invention for mischief. A triumph in subduing. Fortune encouraging and supporting. And a constitution – what signifies palliating? But I believe I had been a rogue had I been a plough boy' (I, 172).

This constant setting-up and toppling of angels has interesting echoes for an alert reader, because between uncle Antony's letter and this second one from Lovelace there is a long transcription by Clarissa of her latest plea for mercy and its response. A direct appeal to Solmes has left the toadlike suitor unmoved but (in a house without secrets) has enraged her brother instead: 'No! you fallen angel, you shall not give your father and mother such a *son*, nor me such a *brother*, in giving yourself that profligate wretch for a *husband*' (I, 169).

It is not quite the same to refer to Clarissa as a 'fallen angel' as it is to use the rather coarser generalization that 'the devil's in her sex'.

Indeed, the fact that Clarissa is compared to Satan, as no woman is in Restoration comedy, gives us a hint about the shifting and ambiguous view of sexual morality in this eighteenth-century context. But the image, like Antony's, implies recognition of Clarissa's power as a source of moral energy. Her disobedience is compared to Satan's disobedience in heaven: in this way she is indirectly made responsible, in the smaller universe that is Harlowe Place, for the spirit of discord that prevails. The response of the Harlowes, when the image arises, seems always to involve silencing Clarissa. Both her sexuality and the possession of some greater knowledge ill-understood by the Harlowes themselves seem to frighten them: the image resonates with possibilities.

It is confusing, then, to return to Lovelace's letter about Rosebud. After all, he has taken the satanic mantle upon his own shoulders. But even he, when faced with parallel examples of virtuous women – the innocent country lover and the lady of great moral dignity – uses the same sort of language as Antony Harlowe: 'But the devil's in this sex! Eternal misguiders! Who, that has once trespassed with them ever recovered his virtue? And yet where there is not virtue, which nevertheless we freelivers are continually plotting to destroy, what is there even in the ultimate of our wishes with them? *Preparation* and *expectation* are in a manner everything: *reflection* indeed may be something, if the mind be hardened above feeling the guilt of a past *trespass*: but the *fruition*, what is there in that?' (I, 172).

Lovelace is never reticent about explaining his own character to his friend; and indeed, the reader is given a substantial and accurate portrait in these paragraphs. As countless critics have observed, Lovelace's interest is in the chase, not in the prize.[13] Like all the Don Juan figures of legend, he wants power. He is not fundamentally sensual, but rather a highly imaginative intellectual. He shares with Clarissa the ability to use language precisely and forcefully. While he is witty, and lies as a matter of course, he never uses words as James and Arabella do, as a kind of moral doubletalk. In his correspondence with Belford, we see him candid: his lies are reserved for those who do not belong to the brotherhood of rakes, and in particular for women.

Despite the trappings that Richardson has given him – an aristocratic background and a prominent place in London rakedom – Lovelace is an anomaly, a *Puritan* rake: he is part of a moral universe already familiar from the conduct books. Women are 'eternal misguiders': the more virtuous they are, the more they tempt men to destroy their virtue. This is not the misogyny of an Antony Harlowe, nor even of the rakes of Restoration comedy, but rather an acknowledgment of women's power as moral guardians. Sexual virtue here has become a fully general category, essential to every other sort of virtue, for he who 'trespasses' never reforms.

In this context, in fact, Lovelace's choice of the word 'trespass' has a certain resonance. It is, of course, biblical; but its more specific meaning for the Harlowes' England, in which public lands are being enclosed at a rapidly increasing rate, is also suggested. It is impossible not to make the obvious connection between the violation of person and the violation of property. In Clarissa's case, after all, Lovelace would not be trespassing *with*, but rather *on*, since there are several contenders, including Clarissa herself, for the rights of possession.

In tracing this single powerful thread of imagery like Ariadne's strand of silk through the labyrinth, we have stumbled on one of the many paths to an understanding of Richardson's crucial place in the history of culture. At this very early stage in the novel, Lovelace has already given us a new myth, an alternative to the biblical and medieval versions, to explain how guilt entered the world along with women. A cosmos is evoked in which there are evil male principles and good female principles. Once a woman is tainted with evil, the man who has violated her is polluted too. The violated (that is, sexual) woman is a reproach to mankind, and the road to repentance is closed anew by every victim. For Lovelace, as for Clarissa, an intolerable dilemma has arisen. When he addresses Clarissa, he writes frequently of the desire for reformation, since he maintains that salvation can come only through her. Occasionally, as in this letter to Belford, he even believes in this desire himself.

But the very pursuit is a sign of the impossibility of reform, since his goal is violation. The only way in which Lovelace could now reform would be to abandon his courtship of Clarissa; but that too would mean abandoning the hope of reformation. In Lovelace's view, and indeed in Clarissa's, a woman becomes active only by accident (perhaps Clarissa's belief helps to explain her enigmatic refusal to litigate for financial independence); but this does not mean that she lacks volition. Her virtue, passive when unassailed, becomes at most defensive under attack. Clarissa and Lovelace cling to the same myth, and therefore an understanding between them is forever out of reach.

These powerful undercurrents make *Clarissa* a religious novel, although, and partly because, the battleground is sex. We have two definitions of women's virtue before us: one which sees disobedience, any exercise of individuality or will, as a loss of grace, even as a return to type of an inferior, though potent, sort. Sexuality is here seen as the primitive seductiveness of a Lilith or a Salome (this is Antony's view).

That image is not uncomplicated, but neither is it one which developed specifically in the society which produced *Clarissa*. Lovelace's definition, on the other hand, encompasses the first one in a breadth of meaning that has the strength and vividness of magic. Virtue is destructive because it is constructive: sex is regarded, not only as a weapon against an individual, but against the values of a society. Clarissa, as a person and as a moral ideal, must find space to develop between these annihilating views of womanhood: it is hardly a surprise that the landscapes of the novel become increasingly claustrophobic. In the Harlowe Place section of the novel, at least, one suspects that the very structure reflects the testing of the proposition that the devil is in Clarissa's sex. She is often referred to as a witch and is sometimes treated like one; and the waves of interrogation and relenting which assail her are like the stratagems of an inquisition.

Clarissa's 'witchcrafts' and a delayed marriage

It is difficult to account for the eight delays which the Harlowes grant when they are trying to force Clarissa to marry Solmes unless one recognizes that Richardson's fictional world is no more 'natural' than that found in any other modern narrative (despite Ian Watt's categorization of the novelist as a 'formal realist'). Instead, a grand moral structure forms and underlies the specific conflicts of personalities. The issue, as indeed it appears to have been in the witchcraft trials, mostly of the previous century, is Clarissa's independence of will and her related power to express and adhere to her own decisions.[14] The Harlowes are not after forced marriage. If their motives were entirely material, it would not be difficult for them physically to compel Clarissa to the altar, as James indeed tells her in one of his many harsh answers to her pleas during her imprisonment at Harlowe Place. She has been threatened with a removal to her uncle Antony's moated castle of a house, where she will be forced to receive Solmes's visits. At the end of a trial period at her uncle's, the family will decide (if she has not accepted Solmes) whether she should be allowed to marry Lovelace, or be banished for ever from Harlowe Place. Not unnaturally under the circumstances, Clarissa thinks that she will be spirited away to a secret marriage; but James points out that her fear of the chapel at Antony's house is 'the more foolish as, if we intended to use force, we could have had the ceremony pass in your chamber as well as anywhere else' (I, 263–4).

Instead, they attribute to her a predilection for another man – a man who is best known for his sexual exploits, and who is surrounded with satanic imagery – and they demand her renunciation of him. Her trials are reminiscent of ecclesiastical trials in the length and intensity of their interrogations, the limited number of permissible correct answers, the imprisonment and mental torture which follow each refusal; but also in the sudden apparent turns of mercy when each of her requests for a postponement of the wedding date is granted. That she recognizes the notion of a wedding date at all is itself a victory for the Harlowes: the next step, they hope, will be consent. In this sense the trial is more like an inquisition, because, like Joan of Arc and the ministers whose trials are described in Foxe's *Book of Martyrs*, Clarissa is allowed to have the dignity of a point of view which must be changed if her power as a figure in society is to be broken. The constant sexual bombardment, however, is the other side of this struggle of conscience: from this perspective Lovelace becomes a kind of demon, or incubus, who must be exorcized before Clarissa can regain her purity. It is as a pure – that is, utterly unattached – figure that she must be sacrificed to Solmes (who, indeed, has more than a little of both Mammon and Moloch about him). Perhaps it is this underlying notion which makes Clarissa refer so often to the danger to her soul if she allies herself with Solmes. He is a pagan 'monster', as she calls him, a devouring money-machine who feeds on the children of the rich at the expense of his own family.

It must be said that this structure is not clearly defined, nor are the parallels with the witchcraft trials or the trials of Puritans under Bloody Mary anywhere stated. But there is no doubt that *Clarissa*, as Leslie Fiedler has seen, is as much a mythic work as it is an early 'realistic' novel.[15] Because it is at a transitional stage between the Bunyanesque allegory and the straight didacticism of religious manuals, on the one hand, and the novel of feeling, on the other, we arrive in *Clarissa* at a particularly rich moment in literary history, where a new perspective on the individualism and autonomy of a literary character meets an established code both of literary and moral value that is itself in the process of change, though it still offers a structure for belief and practice. What makes analysis difficult (and rewarding) is that Clarissa's trials have a sexual as well as a religious or moral content: were only the second in question, one could see a model for the *form* of her persecutions in the *Book of Martyrs*.

As it is, one would be hard-pressed to look for exact parallels in a popular demonology like Joseph Glanvill's *Saducismus Triumphatus* (1689), whose most famous ghost, the Drummer of Tedworth, inspired a play by Addison unstartlingly entitled *The Drummer* (1716). This apology for the supernatural had been written to refute a sceptical work by John Webster, *The Display of Witchcraft* (published 1677) and it was widely read in the eighteenth century.[16] It is even mentioned by Lovelace in *Clarissa*.[17] There are very many tiresomely similar accounts of supposed crimes of supernatural origin and descriptions of trials in Glanvill; but since the author is trying to expose a pattern of witchcraft, with its own pathology and symptoms, the enumeration of cases is not surprising. Glanvill was a good friend of the Mathers of Boston: one forgets how late the Salem trials actually occurred in the history of the western world until one sees that a comparable phenomenon was to be found in the England of Newton and Locke. These accounts, with their emphasis on the repulsive physical habits, violent crimes like murder and cattle-killing, suckling of 'familiars' and even flying about on broomsticks of suspected witches, have superficially little to do with a mid-eighteenth-century sensibility like Richardson's. They are, of course, the dying spasms of a stern Puritanism which no longer answered the spiritual needs of a new generation. Nevertheless, Glanvill had an enormous readership in the following century, as has already been noted, and the debate over a world of evil spirits continued. We observe a transformation of the original impulse in Richardson. Witchcraft has always been defined as an antisocial activity engaged in mainly by women, and it has always been associated with special knowledge unavailable to the common run of mortals. Glanvill tells his audience as much in his opening definition of terms: 'As for the words *Witch* and *Wizzard*, from the Notation of them, they signifie no more than a Wise Man, or a Wise Woman. – So that a Witch, thus far, is no more than a knowing Woman . . . But use questionless had appropriated the word to such a kind of skill and knowledge, as was out of the common road or extraordinary . . .' and nowadays the words are used, he adds, for 'one that has the Knowledge or skill of doing or telling things in an extraordinary way, and that in vertue of either an express or implicate association with some Evil Spirit'.[18]

The aspect of witchcraft dependent on the supernatural no longer troubles the secularized, if still pious, world of Richardsonian Anglicanism, though the Wesleys revive this aspect, as so many others, of the old faith. But the notions about women's special powers remain, even if those powers are now defined almost exclusively by a social rather than by a theological standard. Clarissa is a 'wise woman' through her very superiority; at least there is no more precise category available for her powers. Her individuality and integrity are frightening to the Harlowes, who are forced to see her serious embracing of a morality which they have essentially forsaken as a challenge and a reproach.

They attack her power over language as if they were not proof against her charms, and they treat her possible marriage to Solmes, correctly, as if the act itself, however involuntary, would be a recantation of a former position.

One of the most violent and emotional scenes in the first part of the novel illustrates the Harlowes' attitude. After the sixth postponement of marriage or forced marriage (represented in an unclear but sinister way by the threatened trip to uncle Antony's house), Clarissa is made to endure a visit from Solmes. She first refuses to see him, and the interview, when it occurs, is dramatic. An exchange between Clarissa and her uncle in the presence of Solmes reveals the profound relationship that exists in the Harlowes' minds between sexual desire and the unacceptable exertion of the will. Clarissa assumes too much when she tries to satisfy merely their greed; and even though she offers never to see Lovelace, much less to marry him, this is not convincing enough proof for them of her neutrality. It is her will itself which must be broken, and that can never occur, for volition is the source of Clarissa's integrity:

Miss Clary, replied my uncle, you have had your will in everything till now; and this makes your parents' wills sit so heavy upon you.

My will, sir! be pleased to allow me to ask what was my will till now, but my father's will, and yours and my uncle Harlowe's will? Has it not been my pride to obey and oblige? I never asked a favour, that I did not first sit down and consider if it were *fit* to be granted. And now, to show my obedience, have I not offered to live single? Have I not offered to divest myself of my grandfather's bounty, and to cast myself upon my father's; and that to be withdrawn, whenever I disoblige him? Why, dear good sir, am I to be made unhappy in a point so concerning to my happiness?

Your grandfather's estate is not wished from you. You are not desired to live a single life. You know *our* motives, and we guess at *yours*. And let me tell you, well as we love you, we would much sooner choose to follow you to the grave, than that *yours* should take place.

. . . Then, sir, you shall sooner follow me to the grave *indeed*. . . . And, Mr Solmes, turning to him, take notice of what I say: *this* or *any* death, I will sooner undergo (that will soon be over) than be yours, and for *ever* unhappy!

(I, 379–80)

Clarissa's uncle, enraged, assures her that she will be married within the week, and her brother adds: 'O thou fallen angel . . . O, thou true woman – though so young! But you shall not have your rake: remember that; . . . You shall be redeemed, and this worthy gentleman . . . will be so good as to redeem you from ruin – and hereafter you will bless him, or have reason to bless him, for his *condescension* . . .' (I, 381). James physically mistreats Clarissa for the first time, and she is left sprawling on the floor when the door she has thrown herself against (because her father is on the other side) suddenly opens. Even this act of physical torture recalls an ancient tradition of interrogation. And despite the threats, her request for a delay is granted.

The eight postponements of the marriage to Solmes occur in a verbal tempest, as this example suggests. The language is argumentative: we are faced with accusations, denials, epithets and attempts at persuasion. But we are never allowed to forget the nature of the arguments. Arabella, for example, cuts off her sister's pleas in revealing language: 'I tell you I see through your *witchcrafts* (that was her strange word). And away she flung, adding as she went, and so will everybody else very quickly, I dare say' (I, 35). Later, Clarissa describes another quarrel with her sister. This time, Arabella maintains 'That I half-bewitched people by my insinuating address: that nobody could be valued or respected, but must stand like cyphers wherever I came. How often, said she, have I and my brother been talking upon a subject, and had everybody's attention till *you* came in with your bewitching *meek* pride, and *humble* significance . . .' (I, 215–16).

Clarissa describes the tactics of persecution to Anna. Her brother and sister profess amazement at her stubbornness:

Such a strange perseverance in a measure so unreasonable! But my brother and sister are continually misrepresenting all I say and do; and I am deprived of the opportunity of defending myself! My sister says that had they thought me such a championess, they would not have engaged with me: and now, not knowing how to reconcile my supposed obstinacy with my general character, and natural temper, they seem to hope to tire me out, and resolve to vary their measures accordingly. (I, 238–9)

On the other hand, Lovelace, who has been manipulating events behind the scenes through his agent, Joseph Leman, tells Clarissa when he surprises her in the garden that he desires to repent, and that 'he so much valued my *free* choice . . . and my *unbiassed* favour (scorning to set himself upon a foot with Solmes in the compulsory methods used in that man's behalf) that he should hate himself were he capable of a view of intimidating me by so very poor a method' (I, 182).

The most obvious rhythm of compulsion, then, arises from the menacing threats of the Harlowes and the comparative release offered by Lovelace, even though he is actively engaged in intensifying the pressure. But there is another rhythm (one is inevitably reminded of the systole–diastole of a heartbeat, so passionate and so *closed* is life at Harlowe Place) which the Harlowes have developed for themselves; and that is the one of deadline and postponement. One example is enough, because things become so tortured and Chinese-box-like as the pages roll on.

After Clarissa has for the first time weighed her feelings about Lovelace, whose letters have become more frequent as the conditions of Clarissa's imprisonment become more severe, a deadline for a marriage date comes from her mother, along with the supposed enticement of promised clothes and jewels. The wedding is to be in a fortnight's time; 'but if you determine as we would have you, and signify it to us, we shall not stand with you for a week or so' (I, 208). Not only has an extension been offered on this date, but the Harlowes seem to have forgotten about their first threat, when Clarissa was asked to sign the already completed marriage contracts.

By the time several more bouts of threats and relenting have occurred, Clarissa asks Anna for advice. Her friend comes to the crux of the matter: 'What *can* I advise you to do, my noble creature? Your merit is your crime. You can no more change *your* nature, than your persecutors can *theirs*. Your distress is owing to the vast disparity between you and them. What would you have of them? Do they not act in character? And to whom? To an alien. You are not one of them' (I, 282). And indeed, this view soon seems to be confirmed by the family itself. When Clarissa again refuses to see Solmes, her family will neither see her nor write to her: they return her letters unopened. Her uncle John Harlowe's is the only reply she gets. It is tenderly worded, but expresses the deep fear her family has of her:

since you have displayed your talents, and spared nobody, and moved everybody, without being moved, you have but made us stand the closer and firmer together. This is what I likened to an *embattled phalanx*, once before. Your Aunt Hervey forbids your writing for the same reason that I must not countenance it. We are all afraid to see you, because we know we shall be made as so many fools. Nay, your mother is so afraid of you that once or twice . . . she shut the door, and locked herself in, because she knew she must not see you upon *your* terms, and you are resolved you will not see her upon *hers*.
(I, 305)

Much later, when the wedding plans have been changed seven times, the Harlowes confiscate Clarissa's pens and ink. With true Richardsonian foresight, however, she has kept some writing materials hidden away. Reflecting on her 'strange situation', Clarissa writes to Anna: '*Strange* I may well call it; for don't you see, my dear, that we seem all to be *impelled*, as it were, by a perverse fate which none of us is able to resist? – and yet all arising (with a strong appearance of self-punishment) from ourselves?' And she continues:

> Your partial love will be ready to acquit me of *capital* and *intentional* faults: but oh, my dear! my calamities have humbled me enough to make me turn my gaudy eye inward; to make me look into myself! And what have I discovered there? Why, my dear friend, more *secret* pride and vanity than I could have thought had lain in my unexamined heart.
>
> If *I* am to be singled out to be the *punisher* of myself and family, who so lately was the *pride* of it, pray for me, my dear, that I may not be left wholly to myself; and that I may be enabled to support my character, so as to be *justly* acquitted of wilful and premeditated faults. The will of Providence be resigned to in the rest: as *that* leads, let me patiently and unrepiningly follow! I shall not live always. May but my *closing* scene be happy! (I, 419–20)

The next letter, written on a Thursday, informs Anna of the eighth postponement – this time because the Harlowes have heard that Lovelace plans an ambush if they set out for Antony's moated house – but this does not alter their resolve. Instead, her parents will go to Antony's the following Tuesday, and Clarissa will be married to Solmes in her own chamber on Wednesday morning. Lovelace has already informed her of this plan, but Clarissa still asks for another week's respite. Her aunt tells her that on the morning of her wedding she is to be led before the assembled family: 'When this awful court is assembled, the poor prisoner is to be brought in, supported by Mrs Norton; who is to be first tutored to instruct me in the duty of a child; which it seems I have forgotten' (I, 439). On Monday night she flees with Lovelace, although, hoping for more delays, she has since changed her mind about escaping with him.

Taken together, these complex passages form a pattern which owes little to a conventional idea of realism. We are given each character's perceptions of Clarissa in terms of an involved symbolic order – or, rather, disorder; and Clarissa, uncomprehending, is thrown back upon her own perception of herself. Sets of oppositions are evolved which are important to the Harlowes (even though the family's hypocrisy complicates interpretation still further): eloquence versus the performance of duty; disobedience versus sexual purity; language versus action; passion versus honesty. Once teased out, the oppositions themselves reveal the nature of this tortured and original world. They are not obvious dichotomies unless one engages in a necessary act of literary and moral empathy. Even the terms thus opposed are hardly basic. Clarissa is not so much a person to those around her, as a symbolic object. Her existence centres and absorbs all the obsessions of her society: the Harlowes stand or fall with her success or failure in a moral sphere to which they no longer have access and which they do not understand.

Her letter to Anna, in which she reflects on the 'perverse fate' that impels her family, and which arises from within each individual, is a recognition of her special function. Joblike, she accepts the role of punisher of herself and her family; but unlike Job she locates divine vengeance within the human spirit. The inner light of Puritanism burns at Harlowe Place with a hot and uncertain flame: it is not difficult to see why Antony and James so easily confuse it with the ancient diabolical heat of female lust. Clarissa can accept a symbolic attitude towards herself, if she understands it: she found the public view easy enough to bear in the days of her exemplariness. Even in these times of suffering, she has biblical models and a faith to support her. She can identify her own confused despair, that of punished righteousness, with Job's. But she adds, significantly, 'pray for me, my dear, that I may not be left wholly to myself; and that I may be enabled to support my character, so as to be *justly* acquitted of wilful and premeditated faults'.

The process of Clarissa's being left to herself is the subject of this novel, and of many which follow it in the Richardsonian tradition. She will learn to become a person, even without the support of conventional morality, and without being 'taken at her word'. She will, of course, retain and develop a deep and increasingly mystical faith; but she will have done so only by testing every received assumption. In this again, she is profoundly important to an impatient and secularized world that has not examined its own foundations; but she is also profoundly dangerous.

One is drawn once more, in an attempt to understand this extraordinarily rich text, to Glanvill's accounts of seventeenth-century witch trials. He records the confession of Alice Duke, in 1664, who describes her pact with the devil: 'He promised her when she made her Contract with him, that she should want nothing, but ever since she hath wanted all things.'[19] Like Faust, the witch who desires as a mere mortal only finds herself tormented by an entirely different magnitude of desire once she has yielded to her tempter. Both the Harlowes and Lovelace believe that something similar occurs in the realm of female sexuality. It is for this reason that the Harlowes try to suppress any sort of desiring or volition in Clarissa, while Lovelace tries to encourage it. The Harlowes, whose greed is a kind of culmination of earthly desire, fear the increasing individualism of Clarissa because she has become their protection against a consciousness of their own sins. Once they abuse her, she is forced to develop in her own way; and they must recognize that they can no longer stand behind her exemplariness. Her development away from them must inevitably be construed as a challenge (as we have seen in Antony's letter and uncle John's rebuke in the interview before she escapes). The sexuality which made her exemplary is also, according to the Harlowes, her weak point and the cause of her rebellion. They are too blind to search for the more immediate causes for her behaviour; and it is not surprising that they turn to Lovelace as the source of their daughter's disobedience. It is important to remember, however, that all these views of Clarissa's sexuality are spiritual: the morality of a society depends upon the fate of one persecuted virgin.

When James cries: ' O thou fallen angel . . . O, thou true woman – though so young . . . You shall be redeemed, and this worthy gentleman . . . will be so good as to redeem you from ruin . . .', one can observe the distortion of a moral idea. James yet again inverts Clarissa's religious scruples against marrying Solmes, and turns her repulsive suitor into a kind of saviour. He has the resources to mock his sister in this way because any of the views of womanhood which have been discussed in these pages may be used against her. She is a 'fallen angel' because her sexuality can always be invoked as the root of her disobedience. His view is, of course, not far from Lovelace's; but Lovelace, like Clarissa, has a defined code within which to place his attitudes (even if his is a distorted and cynical one), while James, like the other Harlowes, is trapped by his own relentless temporality.

Like James, Antony and Clarissa's father, on the other hand, Lovelace also believes the generality of women to be creatures of extreme carnality. Once they are violated, he expects them to focus their existence on sexual pleasure, and give up the pretence of virtue. That is the assumption (as Mark Kinkead-Weekes has observed)[20] which serves as the basis for his seductions. But, unlike the Harlowes, Lovelace has a compelling moral reason for wishing for his own failure, and that is his belief in the possibility of an extraordinary woman's redeeming or damning power.

3
'CLARISSA LIVES: *LET THIS EXPIATE!*'

Sex and the epistolary novel: preliminaries

Clarissa, then, has delivered herself into the hands of her complex and dangerous suitor, Lovelace. Once she leaves Harlowe Place, the interplay of plots, the confusion between authentic and manufactured identities, the counterpoint of voices, create such a dense fabric that any analysis leaves as much behind as it accounts for. If we were to make comparisons between *Clarissa* and other art forms, indeed, we could choose the opera, a genre which was of great interest to Diderot and Rousseau. What is lacking, however, is that staple of operatic menus, the lovers' duet. There are quarrels in abundance between Clarissa and Lovelace, but only one occasion (the day before the rakes come to supper) when tenderness prevails on both sides (II, 224–5). Even then, Clarissa only admits some affection for Lovelace, and that grudgingly, in a letter to Anna Howe. There are no direct confessions of true feeling between these troubled lovers. The area of actual contact between them is always a battlefield. Only after the skirmishes are over do they retreat and reflect on the reality and depth of their love (or hatred).

The few letters which *are* exchanged between the two protagonists are invariably misinterpreted. 'Never was there such a pair of scribbling lovers as we', remarks Lovelace in a letter to his confidant, John Belford, 'yet perhaps whom it so much concerns to keep from each other what each other writes' (II, 19). The most famous example of such a failure of communication is Lovelace's misunderstanding of a letter which Clarissa sends him near the end of the novel. 'Sir', she writes,

I have good news to tell you. I am setting out with all diligence for my father's house. I am bid to hope that he will receive his poor penitent with a goodness peculiar to himself; for I am overjoyed with the assurance of a thorough reconciliation, through the interposition of a dear, blessed friend whom I always loved and honoured.

94

Lovelace believes that the Harlowes have taken her back. Overjoyed, he exults in a letter to Belford about the happiness he will now enjoy with Clarissa (IV, 156–7). Belford, engaged in other matters, cannot enlighten him about the true state of things until very much later. Clarissa, of course, is referring to her imminent death: by 'my father' she means God. She is thinking allegorically, as if she were only half present in the literal world.

We can compare this spiritual *double entendre* to the many examples of sexual *double entendre* which are so common in French novels of the same period. It is curious, after all, that a work which is so deeply concerned with sexuality has so little to do with romantic love. It has been commonly said that the gap between love and sex, and indeed between marriage and love, was far greater in the social life of upper-class Paris than it ever was in London, and there seems little reason to doubt the assertion. But if we turn to the novels of Diderot and, later, Laclos for confirmation of these social facts, we must also remember that they reveal as much about their literary origins as about their social environment. Diderot and Laclos had perhaps the deepest insights of any of their contemporaries except Rousseau into the Richardsonian world-view. While Rousseau chose to amend the original vision by giving love an ascendancy over sex, Diderot and Laclos recognized that Richardson was exploring the assault on individuality through sex, and they took this notion to extremes that would probably have shocked the English novelist.

Clarissa, then, would most likely make a bad opera because there are no love-scenes, no opportunities for harmonious reconciliation, in this merciless world of letters. This seems quite surprising when we think about letter-writing. Correspondence has been a favoured means of expressing and even enlarging romantic love; but it does not function in such a way in *Clarissa*. The epistolary technique, however, is enormously subtle, because it reflects the tensions in and the development of character under stress. One can take the changing attitude of John Belford as an example: he grows from a rather passive defender of Clarissa into her executor, and becomes the main source for an account of her death. It allows us to learn of subplots which parallel and illuminate the main action: the lively Anna Howe's courtship by the dull but virtuous Hickman, for instance. Through it, we may be treated to several versions of the same events, so that we can know the true depth of Lovelace's duplicity and of Clarissa's innocence. Much has been made of the intimacy of the epistolary structure. We see the characters at their most 'relaxed', as it were, because they are writing to their closest friends, who are sometimes critical but never dismissive.

But in another way, the epistolary structure also distances us. We learn of events at second hand; they are always being retold.

Clarissa's raving after the rape, for example, is recounted entirely by Lovelace. Here the epistolary style is used most advantageously. We can observe the counterpoint between Lovelace's account of her behaviour and his own commentary upon it. The breakdown is a time of self-revelation for Clarissa. All the while we are aware of the irony in learning of these truths from the man who has brought Clarissa to them through his duplicity. The effect of the lengthy ellipsis is stunning: we are slowly led to realize the enormity of the rape through its repercussions. It is the great unmentionable, like a religious epiphany, and we are told what happened only after Clarissa has had the presence of mind to escape from the brothel for good. This long first 'absence' prefigures Clarissa's death: it is followed by a great deal of writing from her. When she grows too weak to continue, detailed accounts from Belford to Lovelace take over. After her death there is a flood of posthumous letters from her, while the novel ends with Lovelace's death. In this way, her consciousness dominates the book.

But throughout the novel it has been a strangely disembodied consciousness, just as Lovelace's has been. When we consider Richardson's emphasis on the integrity of the person, it is odd that the active expression of the self through deeds carries relatively little weight. We are given direct access to thoughts and emotions, but not to events: it is as if plot were an outer shell, an encumbrance like Clarissa's richly dressed suits, to be got rid of as soon as possible. This attention to the inner life seems extremely modern today, and helps, again, to explain the novel's ineligibility for opera. There is very little spectacle, very little dialogue between the main figures. As Johnson said in a celebrated remark: 'Why, Sir, if you were to read Richardson for the story, your impatience would be so much fretted that you would hang yourself. But you must read him for the sentiment, and consider the story as only giving occasion for the sentiment.'[1]

On the other hand, the contortions of the plot certainly make for liveliness when they occur, but they depend largely on a misreading of one character by another. Lovelace can trick Clarissa into thinking that Tomlinson is a deliverer, and that the prostitutes are ladies, by playing on her ignorance of the world. But *we* are not allowed to be ignorant. We are co-conspirators, and the moving principle is dramatic irony. The plot doesn't function the way a thriller's would, for example, and there are few surprises. Even Lovelace's stratagems are literary or dramatic: we have impersonation, forged letters, tampering with correspondence, and *coups de théâtre* such as the escape from Harlowe Place or Lovelace's appearance at Hampstead dressed as an old man, after Clarissa's flight from Mother Sinclair's and before the subsequent rape. They are not developed for or from the novel as such, the way they might be in Balzac, Dickens or Tolstoy. The social context and events in themselves have little meaning and no independent momentum. Even when the prostitutes have Clarissa arrested, the situation and language suggest that we are confronting something which is not so much a narrative event as a linguistic and moral one. In this case, it centres around one of the preoccupations in the novel: the proper sphere and content of Law.

From Clarissa's point of view, criminality has little to do with conventional ideas about law. This ambiguity of definition is one of the great ironic currents in the novel. 'The Law shall be all my resource: The Law, . . . The Law only shall be my refuge!' she cries, on the verge of suicide after the rape (III, 289). It is quite clear that she is not referring to the law of the land, nor even to conventional religious notions of legality, since she is about to plunge a penknife into her heart. After all, she has refused to litigate with her father for the control of her estate (which would have granted her freedom from her family and from both her suitors); and she never consents to bringing charges against Lovelace. Shortly after her escape from him, she is arrested on false charges. The description of the scene of the arrest, as related by Belford to Lovelace, who has had nothing to do with this particular trick, is illuminating:

as she came out of the church, at the door fronting Bedford Street, the officers, stepping to her, whispered that they had an action against her.

She was terrified, trembled, and turned pale.

Action! said she. What is that? I have committed *no bad action*! Lord bless me! men, what mean you?

That you are our prisoner, madam.

Prisoner, sirs! – What – How – Why – What have I done?

You must go with us. Be pleased, madam, to step into this chair.

With *you*! With *men*! I am not used to go with *strange men*! Indeed you must excuse me!

We can't excuse you: we are sheriff's officers. We have a writ against you. You *must* go with us, and you shall know at whose suit.   (III, 426–7)

This little scene, like so many others in the book, is full of precise detail. The officers meet Clarissa on the Bedford Street side of the church; she trembles and goes pale; every turn of dialogue is recorded. But it is also fraught with the quality of nightmare. For Clarissa, the encounter is an effect without a cause. She is being arrested without having committed a crime, without even a clue as to what she might be accused of. As in a dream, she misunderstands what the men are saying. Her *malentendu*, however, reveals another awareness: it serves to reinforce the strong sense of her own identity, made deeper by suffering. She is terrified, because she *does* have a secret, the rape, and she has no idea how much the sheriff's men know about her. We may look at part of the passage again: '. . . the officers, stepping to her, whispered that they had an action against her . . . *Action!* said she. What is that? I have committed *no bad action!*'

Indeed she has not. Clarissa's story is of a passion, in the Christian sense, which must be strongly distinguished from mere passivity. Like all moral passions of this kind, her suffering is purposeful, and offers a direct challenge to society. While we think of the Christian martyr as one who rejects the flesh in favour of the spirit, we have in Clarissa a heroine for whom the flesh is essential. It is true that she transcends earthly rewards in her death, but it is important to remember that the source of her spiritual triumph has all along been her insistence on the integrity of the person, body and spirit. It is this consciousness that gives her the courage to refuse Solmes, and that destroys any hopes for worldly happiness after the rape. In the passage under discussion, the men 'have an action against her'. It is not difficult to see that by now Clarissa identifies men with action and action with evil. Hence her disbelieving reply: 'Action? . . . I have committed *no bad action!*'

Here, the legal word 'action' functions in several ways. It brings home to Clarissa the constant necessity of defining her own limits, of being clear in her mind that *she* is not guilty of the rape. But the men, by bringing an 'action' against her, force her into the polar thinking which we have described. Men are active, but do not feel; women are feeling, but cannot act; therefore she cannot have committed a *bad action*. Action has become a sexual distinction, because all Clarissa's experience of men shows that they cannot both feel and do. The brilliantly changeable Lovelace, champion of freethinking, is but the most extreme example.

If we continue further in our analysis we notice, of course, that the passage identifies 'action', which is both male and negative, with the law, which comes apparently out of nowhere to punish Clarissa. The charge has actually been brought by the prostitutes, who are women in complicity with men. This blurring of sexual roles has some importance in other contexts, particularly in connection with Diderot. But the significant point in this bit of dialogue is that the undertones tell us about Clarissa's consciousness and the impressions that events (which are always secondary in importance to their human impact) make on it. Even her misinterpretations of the world are characteristic.

One can contrast this view of action (which takes its sexual form in the rape) with Ian Watt's. 'In the realm of action', writes Watt, 'the rape itself, when Clarissa is unconscious from opiates, may be regarded as the ultimate development of the idea of the feminine sexual role as one of passive suffering: it suggests that the animality of the male can only achieve its purpose when the woman's spirit is absent.'[2] This view, while a common one, is mistaken. Many critics and novelists have seen Clarissa in this way, and the trivializations that followed her *have* portrayed 'the lass with the delicate air' (to borrow loosely a chapter heading from *Pamela's Daughters*, that amusing book by Robert Utter and Gwendolyn Needham), for whom sex itself is the ultimate evil. But it is nonetheless curious that even so perceptive a critic as Watt has not seen that this novel centres on a rape, not on conventional expressions of sexuality. Faced with this particular violation, many readers seem to lose their literary alertness. Instead of seeing the rape as a kind of murder of the identity for which the sexual aspect is only a metaphor, they are reduced to conventional phrases about female masochism and sexual passivity, as Watt is later in the same passage.

But Watt has touched on the deep mythological structure in *Clarissa* (indeed, it is difficult not to do so, since it informs the text at every point). The male world in *Clarissa* is seen as potentially criminal, though individual men are not necessarily evil. We can reflect, however, that even the wise and decent cousin Morden becomes a duellist and a murderer, though he deliberately breaks his promise to the dying Clarissa to do so. At the least, one may conclude from a reading of *Clarissa* that the institutions which men have created are powerful, and therefore not to be trusted by their victims, who are usually women. Indeed, the very scantiness of the plot may be a result of a sexual mysticism which is suspicious of energetic action and its consequences.

We can again consider Clarissa's reluctance to litigate with her father for her estate, which would give her independence, or to bring Lovelace to court for rape. Lovelace plays upon this ambivalence in Clarissa and knows that she will never bring suit against him. Indeed, even before Clarissa's rape (which has already been planned and is included in his exalted reverie) he fantasizes about raping Anna Howe, whose letters he has been intercepting, and even Anna's mother. He includes his band of four rakish friends in the enterprise, describes in detail what the rapes would be like, and goes on to consider the consequences:

Well, but shall we not be in danger of being hanged for three such enormous rapes . . .?

Yes, to be sure, when caught. But is there any likelihood of that? Besides, have we not been in danger before now for worse facts? and what is there in being in *danger*? If we actually were to appear in open day in England before matters are made up, there will be greater likelihood that these women will *not* prosecute than that they *will*. – For my own part, I should wish they *may*. Would not a brave fellow choose to appear in court to such an arraignment, confronting women who would do credit to his attempt? The country is more merciful in *these* cases than in *any others*: I should therefore like to put myself upon my country.

If caught, he continues, he would turn the trial into a triumphant occasion. He compares himself to a public figure, a general mayor, or ambassador, and ends the elaborate description complacently:

Then we shall be praised – even the judges, and the whole crowded bench, will acquit us in their hearts; and every single man wish he had been me! – the women, all the time, disclaiming prosecution, were the case to be their own. To be sure, Belford, the sufferers cannot put half so good a face upon the matter as we . . .

Well, but suppose, after all, we are convicted; what have we to do, but in time make over our estates, that the sheriffs may not revel in our spoils? There is no fear of being hanged for such a crime as this, while we have *money* or *friends*. And suppose even the worst, that two or three were to die, have we not a chance, each man of us, to escape? The devil's in 'em, if they'll hang five for ravishing three!

I know I shall get off for one – were it but for family sake: and being a handsome fellow, I shall have a dozen or two of young maidens, all dressed in white, go to court to beg my life. And what a pretty show they will make, with their white hoods, white gowns, white petticoats, white scarves, white gloves, kneeling for me, with their white handkerchiefs at their eyes, in two pretty rows, as his majesty walks through them and nods my pardon for their sakes! – And, if once pardoned, all is over: for, Jack, in a crime of this nature there lies no appeal, as in a murder.   (II, 421, 422, 424)

Lovelace is, of course, justified in his confidence that the law – the law of the land, that is – would be on his side if Clarissa or Anna were ever to bring suit. In the eighteenth century as in the twentieth, it is the victim who is on trial when an accusation of rape is brought before a court of law. As we shall see, Richardson amplifies this insight in a variety of ways throughout the novel. But this passage is also typically Richardsonian in its use of a real social situation as a reflection, or perhaps even refraction, of a character's imagination. The description expands from a hard-headed perception of Lovelace's legal position into an inflation of the external world in which the rake becomes a public figure, almost a god, accompanied by his vestal virgins, over whom only a king has authority.

Political comparisons abound in Lovelace's letters. Tyrants, kings and generals from ancient history are often invoked. The real helplessness, in legal and social terms, of the women Lovelace encounters contributes greatly to his sense of his own power. But his power is exercised almost entirely in fantasy. The impulse to remake the world in the image of that fantasy breaks into actual deeds only now and then: the discarded plans, the almost hallucinatory exaltations, are evidence enough that an internal life only slightly enlarged by contact with real women is quite enough for Lovelace. He is no Robespierre: he is on the side of authority, and knows it to be his friend. It is quite striking that he has no political or military aspirations at all, unlike real-life eighteenth-century rakes such as John Wilkes. His dominion is internal. He is really a sportsman, like his aristocratic ancestors, but he stalks ideas and identities rather than the game-birds with which he so often compares his female prey. The imperial parallels which he frequently draws remind us of the society and tradition which support and affirm him.

Clarissa may therefore be looked upon, with reason, as the perpetual victim, the unjustly accused political prisoner in a male world where rapists and the rapacious alike go free. Clarissa's crime, if it could be called such, is her unwillingness to go against an inner principle of wholeness. Anna Howe points this out early in the novel (and Clarissa's awareness of her own integrity remains a constant topic in the correspondence). The famous passage in which Anna points out that virtue itself marks Clarissa off from her persecutors is a constant point of reference throughout the novel (see my discussion of it on p. 90). Clarissa's insistence upon chastity as a vehicle of integrity has perhaps led to her lack of popularity in our own century. Readers have tended to see her as a representative of the most unpleasant side of the Puritan ethic, that which treats women as property, and unwed deflowered girls as damaged goods (even though Clarissa herself makes numerous comments on the interaction of love and property relations). It is confusing that Clarissa was seen, even in her own time, as an apotheosis of womanhood: for us this blurs the clarity of her moral struggle. But in the novel she is singleminded, a person absolutely unable to compromise, whose will cannot be broken or even bent by anyone. Such behaviour hardly conforms to an ideal of female passivity.

Death and exegesis in *Clarissa*

There is another way in which the letters contribute to the reader's initial impression that *Clarissa* is fundamentally a religious novel. They are, on the whole, familiar letters, detailed, conversational, often domestic. But there are moments (as in Anna Howe's two 'framework' letters, and in her response to Clarissa's father's curse) when they take on the elevated style which we have come to associate with Puritan saints' lives. The tradition from which the saints' lives themselves spring, however, is as ancient as the Bible itself. We can go backwards from the seventeenth century through innumerable writers – Petrarch, Dante and St Augustine among them – to the Old and New Testaments.

The interpretation of the Bible has always, of course, been an inexhaustible source for secular literature. With the Gospel according to St John, language, which had always served as a figure for man's relationship with God, took on new dimensions. The 'word made flesh' could become a metaphor for time and history, and the space at the end of a sentence gave full meaning to what came before. Biblical typology, the study of symbolic patterns or types, has been a particularly rich method for saints and sinners alike. Originally, typology was a technique of exegesis which helped Christian theologians to prove that the Old Testament was nothing but a preparation for the coming of the Christ in the New; they were particularly concerned to show the connection in the books of Job and Isaiah, which abound in Christlike figures. More generally, however, this way of looking at the Bible gave a new perspective to reading. The rhythm of anticipation and fulfilment which was discerned, not only in the content of the prophetic books but in their very structure, thrust the emphasis of the writing onto the endpoint of narrative. That is, the *true* meaning (as opposed to the apparent or benighted meaning which the unrepentant Jews might find in the Old Testament) of events and of language was clarified only at the point of its own extinction. The significance of Christ's life is not fully understood without the Resurrection; and similarly, the significance of the prophecies in the Old Testament is opaque to a mind not enlightened by the story of Christian passion.

Milton exploited such a moment in *Paradise Lost*, when he allowed Adam to review and understand the future in the light of his own past at the precise moment when the idyll of spiritual bliss had drawn to a close. Moses, dying on a mountain-top on the wrong side of the Jordan, while his people pass through into Israel, is another example of a biography whose meaning is illuminated through death. The particular typology of life, suffering, vision and death is a structure which allows an individual, in this case the prophet or the Christ, at once to experience mortality and to transcend it. But the point at which mortality is most excruciatingly clear is also the moment of education: to understand mortal time in the shadow of immortal time is to give meaning to the brevity of a human life, which is analogous to the history of the world. A human word has the same importance within history as God's word has in eternity. In this sense, Revelation may be seen as God's autobiography. Certainly the forms which theological criticism discovered in it have become archetypes for secular auto-biographies. And the principle, of course, extends much further: any study or poetic rendering of life in which symbolic importance is given to recurring images or figures, whether these are classical, biblical, or original with the author, draws some power from this pattern in the arrangement of its own ending. Joyce's *Ulysses* and Eliot's *Four Quartets* may be seen in this tradition, along with St Augustine's *Confessions*, Dante's *Vita Nuova* or Milton's *Paradise Lost*.[3]

We can apply this notion of typology to *Clarissa* in a number of ways. Indeed, it may be easier to forgive Richardson for the length of his heroine's death-scene if this apparently unseemly weightiness is given a context. As in tragedy, an inexorable logic of misunderstanding seems to push the story to its unhappy conclusion. But this logic does not arise, as far as we are able to see, out of a kind of divine chess-game in which human beings are unwitting pawns (as in some Greek tragedies), nor even out of the blindness of passions such as sexual jealousy or the lust for power (as in Shakespeare). The struggle for Richardson's characters takes place entirely within the limits of human relationships. Self-education arises out of the collision of one individual with another: the subsequent damage contributes to what we call the shaping of personality. Not surprisingly, then, we find ourselves dealing with special sorts of internal conflicts, particularly in Lovelace's case.

His lack of integration comes partially from his inability to distinguish between knowledge and belief. He is one of those rationalists who doesn't even believe in belief, despite the exhortations of his friend Belford to the contrary. Clarissa, on the other hand, must learn to temper her spiritual pride. But she undergoes a sexual humiliation where Job or Augustine, or even Jesus, would experience a spiritual humiliation. There are many points of contiguity between biblical and religious precedents and Clarissa's own sufferings. Job's humiliation, though divinely arranged, is horribly physical; Christ, like Clarissa, suffers physical violation at human hands, and nearly succumbs to despair. But Clarissa is a young woman, and for much of the novel she has only one tormentor. He is not entirely an enemy, despite the fact that he is, of course, constantly described in satanic terms. Although Clarissa's violation has a larger social meaning, it depends *primarily* on a definition of bodily integrity. Unlike Christ, she is not the human embodiment of a spiritual entity; unlike Job, she is not singled out in a one-to-one relationship with her Creator. If there is to be a link to God at all in this conflict, then it is she who must forge it, she who, as it were, must begin her correspondence with the deity at a point when communication with other people is no longer possible.

Clarissa's death, therefore, is in one way not really 'impelled by perverse fate', as she writes to Anna Howe while still at Harlowe Place. No matter how hard we try to make the struggle of wills in the novel fit the tragic pattern, after all, we cannot really consider volition and conviction in quite the same category as fate, in tragedy. Clarissa herself is not hopelessly driven and consumed by her obsessions. Rather, it is Lovelace who conforms to some of the conventional ideas about tragic characters. He writes in a famous passage, for example, that 'I have three passions that sway me by turns; all imperial ones, Love, revenge, ambition or a desire of conquest' (II, 495). But even he is not to be taken entirely at his word. His language is as seductive and deceptive as are his disguises; and it is not always clear that his feelings are as powerful as he likes to suggest. He is also an intellectual and an aesthete. He delights in forms and sounds; he is a cavalier who (unlike some of his unfortunate predecessors under Cromwell) never loses his head.

Even so, the general structure of his character has literary antecedents, not only in the obvious lineage of Restoration rakes but in the literature of love on a grander scale. We are reminded, for instance, of Paolo and Francesca, the lovers in Canto V of Dante's *Inferno*. They are whirled on a ceaseless wind in the second circle of Hell. It is their punishment, as Dante tells us: 'I learned that to such torment are condemned the carnal sinners who subject reason to desire.'[4] Certainly, the second circle would be a fitting place for Lovelace. But he would be partnerless; even in Hell, his desire would be unlimited. And unlike Paolo and Francesca, who have been tempted into their single sin of adultery through the reading of the romance of Lancelot and Guinevere, Lovelace distances himself from the object of his desire even as he strives towards it, committing many crimes along the way. It is curious, however, to find a thirteenth-century poet warning against the reading of romances in a fashion which would not have seemed at all strange to the eighteenth century. Literature gives a name to the ineffable, a structure for formless yearning, a pattern to be followed in the commission of sin.

For Lovelace, literature is both stimulus and justification. Even 'high' literature acts upon his imagination as pornography might upon lesser men. In this way, he is one of the first truly modern characters in literature. His relationship with reading is eroticized: Roland Barthes would be proud of him. He ravishes classic texts, quotes and misquotes them so that they serve his purposes. But more often he sets up models from literature, however loosely conceived, as rivals. In his first letter to Belford we are treated to a flood of references. He cites Otway, Dryden, Cowley and Shakespeare, and reflects: 'But was ever hero in romance (fighting with giants and dragons excepted) called upon to harder trials?' (I, 149). The trials to which Lovelace so cheerfully refers are, of course, tests of manhood: they are about admission into a worldly order, the society of knights-errant, rakes, knaves and lovers. The comparison is strangely archaic; but then Clarissa, as we have amply seen, belongs to another age as well.

Letters, for Lovelace, serve as a kind of proving-ground. We sense the presence of his brother-rakes, particularly Belford, in the background, as if there were an audience in a shadowy gallery. Even though Belford roundly condemns his friend, there is a stylized quality to the self-consciousness with which Lovelace flings off his lines. Indeed, his confidant's dire warnings seem to have no effect on our cavalier. Belford is regarded by Lovelace, it seems, rather as Hickman is regarded by Anna Howe. He is, in his way, as ineffectual as Hickman as well: he tut-tuts at every opportunity, but appears at Lovelace's supper party for Clarissa. It is only when he becomes a relayer of messages and information between the lovers (at the point, of course, when they are fatally and impossibly estranged) that he comes into his own as a character. Lovelace's eclipse is Belford's shining-time, to borrow a phrase from Anna Howe (who writes several times to Clarissa that 'adversity is your shining-time, my dear'); and the element of rivalry – one could profitably say homosexual rivalry – which exists in all such hunting brotherhoods is clarified.

Solmes and James Harlowe, who are Lovelace's ugliest and most obvious rivals, function differently altogether. Their claim is purely economic and political. They are unable to recognize the real quality of the struggle while Clarissa is still at Harlowe Place; and they are almost incidental to it by the time Lovelace and Clarissa begin the long journey into mutual destruction and partial renewal. They contribute, however, to the universal definition of Clarissa as an object – to be won, lost, bought or sold – with which we are confronted in the first two books of the novel.

The question of Clarissa's identity is a very complicated one, even more complex than it appears at first. It is easy enough to talk of her integrity. The flattest reading of the novel (which is of course the version taken up by Clarissa's Victorian admirers) would invite us to appreciate our heroine's unflinching devotion to the cause of her own chastity, with which spiritual perfection is so intimately bound up. But if we are seriously to regard *Clarissa* as a mythic work, as well as a work of fiction in all the conventional senses, then we cannot help noticing that Clarissa's *meaning* changes as the novel unfolds. She is always viewed by others, as well as by herself: though it would be unjust to compare her perfectly composed soliloquies to Lovelace's thespian rants, she too stands on a stage, or perhaps better a rostrum; for her gifts are rhetorical, rather than histrionic. We could almost imagine *Clarissa*, especially in its middle sections, as one of those eighteenth-century fairs, with their jumble of attractions: the actor stands next to the soap-box orator, the prostitute next to the clergyman. But Clarissa holds the cards: she plays all the heavenly roles in this updated and topsy-turvy morality play.

Clarissa's *meaning*, to others as well as to herself, is therefore the central question in the book: that is why it may be seen as one of the first *Bildungsromane*. The problem is that she is carrying out an independent inquiry, as it were, while her kinfolk, friends and lover are engaged upon quite another. She is searching for individuality, but the people around her are trying to redefine her symbolically: she moves away from exemplariness as they never do. Clarissa is forced into fleeing Harlowe Place when she realizes for the first time that she is, in fact, regarded as an object by her family. We could amplify to some extent by borrowing a term from René Girard's *Deceit, Desire and the Novel*,[5] if we call her a 'mediator'. It is through her, and only through her, that material gain and social rank are attainable for the Harlowes: in this obvious sense, she is an economic mediator, a kind of currency.

But in addition, there is a less visible 'triangle of desire' – to borrow again from Girard (Chapter 1) – in operation at Harlowe Place; it is the one which I have discussed in the opening chapters of this study. Clarissa's constancy could be called external as well as internal: she is forced into a complicated spiritual position by her family. She is seen as a guide, fixed and predictable as the North Star, a spiritual mirror in which the members of her family – and, indeed, of her immediate society – can confront their own images. Again, it is through her, and only through her, that the Harlowes are able to draw on an illusory moral insurance, the certainty of grace. As long as her desiring and their desiring of and through her are one, there is peace at Harlowe Place. But when Solmes arrives at the mansion, they look into their spiritual mirror and are found wanting. Clarissa's disobedience is a condemnation of their values and motives, and they know it. Thus, one sort of crisis is created for them, and another for Clarissa, who has discovered the meaninglessness of volition when the self is prised loose from its old place in a society and a moral code. All this sounds like a rather pretentious mixed metaphor; but in fact Clarissa is both icon and person, and therefore impossibly complicated. Once she is torn loose from this particular role of mediator she is thrust into a new one, equally excruciating, in which she is seen (by Lovelace) as a means to knowledge and salvation; and a different cycle begins.

She learns throughout, however, about the limits of social understanding, and must begin again internally whenever she comes to the recognition that the meanings others give her do not correspond with the results of her own explorations. Clarissa, after all, desires too: the misreadings of her character have consistently failed to take into account the truth that 'mediators' and 'objects of desire' usually come equipped with psyches of their own. Clarissa desires the freedom to be; and she at first mistakes Lovelace for her mediator, the means by which she can achieve it. She is quickly relieved of her illusions. It is not surprising, that *Clarissa* has a fairy-tale like quality. If one recalls the story of Snow White (a nineteenth-century tale, indeed, but with earlier antecedents), in which a truth-telling mirror brings a curse upon the innocent daughter of a witchlike stepmother, one can see how impossible the expectations in this novel are, for Clarissa is the mirror, the daughter and, in some sense, the witch. The second part of the fable, in which the sleeping Snow White, like Sleeping Beauty, is awakened by a handsome prince, also has some meaning for us; but alas, when our Beauty awakens, it is with the horrified realization that she has been kissed by the Beast.

Lovelace is beastlike or monstrous exactly because, like Dante's rather more lovable Paolo and Francesca, he has 'subjected reason to desire'. Clearly, desire is, as Lovelace says himself, an imperial passion. By nature, it must seek an object, and that object must stand automatically as victim or vassal: if union or equality were sought, then desire would be satisfied in its object, and that could not happen in a personality in which desire held sway. In this sense, again, we are not dealing with the fatal logic of tragedy, but with the rhythm of a drive which eternally seeks an end or satisfaction which it cannot find.[6] The distinction is important because a notion of character as educable and responsive develops from this sense of emotional limitation: it is one of the generic differences between tragedy and fiction. I hope I do not diminish the characters in plays by making such a point. They, of course, learn supremely through suffering. Novels are merely able to record the slower development of characters, who must learn to recognize themselves as their own fatality. Lovelace never comes to this realization, and pays the price of his humanity for his blindness.

The 'triangle of desire' which operates in the central scenes of the novel until Clarissa's final escape, then, is a rather more heavily decorated figure than its Euclidean original. Lovelace, of course, desires Clarissa, but he also desires salvation, and Clarissa is the only means to obtain it. He regards Clarissa both as object and mediator: this is an essentially modernist stance, for such a situation could be seen as a species of 'internal mediation'. In René Girard's model for this sort of mediation Stendhal is used as an example, and the distance between subject and mediator, rather than between mediator and object, is the one which is reduced or even collapsed into identification. Still, we need only make the figure lopsided on the far side of the apex (that is, by bringing the mediator and the object close together), and we are left with a Richardsonian geometry of passion. The vision which sustains both Clarissa and Lovelace is, at first, essentially nostalgic. Both try to find ways back into the Garden of Eden, that long afternoon of untroubled unity, where desire and fulfilment, self and world are one. Clarissa soon learns to set her face to the future, not merely in imagination, but in fact: Lovelace remains uneducated. We sense that Richardson disapproves of rationalistic optimism on the ground that it is backward-looking: Lovelace tries to undo history. But Clarissa is a religious object, as well as a persecuted girl. She is more like a female Christ than like a Madonna. Can she indeed bear the weight of her cross, or does she succumb under the intolerable weight of this mythic identity?

Lovelace's proposals of marriage and the impossibility of union

We are never allowed to forget this mythic content: the very structure of the novel reminds us of it. In the period between Clarissa's flight from Harlowe Place and her escape to Hampstead, Lovelace's marriage proposals come thick and fast. There are something like a dozen situations in which marriage is the subject of conversation or of private reflection. These repetitions serve, of course, as a parallel to the endless baiting about marriage to which Clarissa was subjected at Harlowe Place. But while she remained in the malevolent bosom of her family the alternatives at least were clear. Like an accused witch, Clarissa was seen as guilty, whatever her plea. For a witch, immolation would have followed, whether the victim chose to keep still or to make her confession. All that would have changed would have been the social meaning of the burning. If a witch kept silent, she had to be destroyed so that society could be rescued from her evil presence; if she confessed, the fire was a penance, a way of purifying her soul for the Hereafter. Strangely enough, a possible marriage to Solmes has taken on a similar mythic significance at Harlowe Place. Clarissa would have had to marry Solmes, whatever her scruples on the subject, because her family were seeking to fulfil their economic and social ambitions through the alliance. Even so, as we have had many opportunities to observe, the battle has been for Clarissa's soul, for her meaning within the family. Clarissa would have had to enter Solmes's odious bed wholeheartedly. Otherwise the sacrifice – and it would have been a sacrifice, to an English Baal – would have been deprived of meaning and made useless.

When Lovelace, on the other hand, begins to play on Clarissa's expectations, as a cat plays with a mouse, the social situation has changed. Anna Howe no longer wrings her hands on the sidelines, urging Clarissa to stick to her principles. Now she urges marriage at every possible moment. In a way, she has replaced the Harlowes: her voice has become nearly as insistent as their obsessive clamour. Clarissa, at this point, is inclined to agree with her friend, because she is still more concerned with the *que-dira-t-on* than with the larger view of her own future. She is looking back over her shoulder, still longing to return to the Harlowes' garden and her former centrality in a predictable and supportive moral world.

The epistolary air is thick with suspense. Will Lovelace ask Clarissa for her hand? Will she be able to accept him? The unhappy lovers try hard to 'read' each other throughout the central part of the novel. Each looks for a gap, a 'way in', as some of the more aggressive critics of poetry are fond of phrasing it: Lovelace, of course, looks for the moment when Clarissa might be willing to surrender her chastity. But Clarissa watches for authenticity, for an offer honourable on her terms, which include an assumption of equality. She stops looking for such a gap in Lovelace's defences very much earlier than he does; and the dwindling of the suspense surrounding the possibility of a marriage between them is a signal that she has done so.

In the meantime, however, the tension on the matter is so palpable that Lovelace's veering off when a proposal is expected is as much of an event as his asking for Clarissa's hand at inappropriate moments. Both of these strategies (that is, *not* making a proposal when one is anticipated, and making an offer when the mood is clearly wrong) consistently deflate action, making a non-event out of what is in fact the most serious matter in the novel. Clarissa tells Anna Howe about the first discussion of marriage after the escape from Harlowe Place. Characteristically, it comes up during a quarrel. First we hear Lovelace, then Clarissa's aside to Anna Howe:

'Forgive me, madam – I have just done. Have I not, in your own opinion, hazarded my life to redeem you from oppression? Yet is not my reward, after all, precarious? For, madam, *have you not conditioned with me* (and, hard as the condition is, *most sacredly will I observe it*) *that all my hope must be remote?* That you are determined to have it in your power *to favour or reject me totally*, as you please?'

See, my dear! In every respect my condition changed for the worse! Is it in *my power* to take your advice, if I should think it ever so right to take it?
(I, 501)

In this letter, and in some of Clarissa's later comments on Lovelace's proposals or non-proposals of marriage, we can see Clarissa's own attention to the social world, and a certain residual lack of candour. Even after her father's curse has been brought down on her head, she refuses Lovelace on grounds of 'punctilio' (II, 197). During one of her conversations with Lovelace before they decide to continue to London, she says:

To go to town upon an *uncertainty*, I own, is not agreeable; but to be obliged to any persons of your acquaintance, when I want to be thought independent of you; and to a person especially to whom my friends are to direct to me, if they vouchsafe to take notice of me at all, is an absurd thing to mention.(II, 95)

It requires little discernment to see that Clarissa is more concerned with appearance than with fact in this passage: she wants 'to be thought independent', even if Lovelace actually holds her captive. But at this point, even Lovelace is not certain whether she is his prisoner or not; he changes his mind from paragraph to paragraph, as in this letter to Belford:

'Tis certain I can have no pretence for holding her, if she will go. No such thing as force to be used, or so much as hinted at; Lord send us safe to London! . . .
But why will this admirable creature urge her destiny? Why will she defy the power she is absolutely dependent upon? Why will she still wish to my face that she had never left her father's house? (II, 31)

In lesser mortals, of course, such mild dissembling in the interest of self-preservation would be understandable, and even admirable; but Clarissa is on trial. She must move into an entirely different realm of moral experience on the saint's characteristic path of spiritual and physical humiliation. When we reflect for a moment, in fact, it becomes clear that Lovelace and Clarissa are in fact more equal in their power over one another during this period of their relationship than at any other time, even though Lovelace gloats and Clarissa mourns over the apparent loss of her freedom.

Nonetheless, proposal follows proposal, and Lovelace's reflections follow Clarissa's. Slowly, Lovelace discovers that he sometimes almost believes in his offers himself. The trial of her womanhood informs his language at every point. When he describes a scene in which his acting has almost become sincere, he writes: 'Was the devil in me! I no more intended all this ecstatic nonsense than I thought the same moment of flying in the air! All the power is with this charming creature. It is I, not she, at this rate, that must fail in the arduous trial' (II, 142).

'Men–women' and the boundaries of sexuality

The debate about the nature of the sexes continues, however, even when marriage is not in question. Both Lovelace and Anna Howe make full use of diabolical comparisons when they reflect on his rakery, and everyone, except Clarissa herself, continues to refer to Clarissa as 'angelic'. But there are more subtle explorations of the differences as well. The two debates (between Anna and Clarissa, and between Belford and Lovelace) parallel each other, just as Lovelace's pre-liminary string of marriage proposals parallels the form of the emotional torture at Harlowe Place. The culmination of this par-ticular debate occurs when Clarissa learns of her father's curse; shortly afterwards Lovelace takes her to London. From this point on, the trials increase in severity, while the marriage proposals almost disappear. There are attempts at suicide; the ruses become more complex; and Clarissa's very thoughts are interfered with, because Lovelace begins to intercept the correspondence between the two women. Clarissa seems to sense that the Harlowes' garden gate has finally closed for ever when she writes to Anna immediately before Arabella's terrible letter (containing the curse) arrives:

But far, far be banished from me fruitless recrimination! Far banished *because* fruitless! Let me wrap myself about in the mantle of my own integrity, and take comfort in my unfaulty intention! Since it is now too late to look back, let me collect all my fortitude and endeavour to stand those shafts of angry Providence which it will not permit me to shun! That whatever the trials may be which I am destined to undergo, I may not behave unworthily in them, but may come out amended by them.   (II, 168)

But the discussion leading up to and surrounding the curse and the flight to London is illuminating. Both Anna Howe and Belford see women as different in kind from men (and Clarissa as the most different of all, of course) while Lovelace and Clarissa, for varying reasons, suggest that the difference is merely one of degree. In a very important letter, Anna compares Clarissa to the soul and the Harlowe family to the body: 'What an unequal union, the mind and body! All the senses, like the family at Harlowe Place, in a confederacy against that which would animate, and give honour to the whole, were it allowed its proper precedence' (II, 117). Belford, much later, writes similarly, when he is in the thick of his struggle with Lovelace to abandon the pursuit of Clarissa:

She is to my eye all mind; and were she to meet with a man all mind likewise, why should the charming qualities she is mistress of be endangered? Why should such an angel be plunged so low as into the vulgar offices of domestic life? Were she mine, I should hardly wish to see her a mother, unless there were a kind of moral certainty that minds like hers could be propagated. For why, in short, should not the work of bodies be left to *mere* bodies? (II, 243–4)

Indeed, the Harlowes themselves seem to be determined to stamp out any proofs of Clarissa's existence with the vehemence we associate with lapsed believers when they turn against their church. They are iconoclasts in the most literal sense of the word. Arabella writes in her most vicious style when she tells Clarissa about her father's curse, and doesn't neglect to tell her that:

Your drawings and your pieces are all taken down; as is also your own whole-length picture, in the Vandyke taste, from your late parlour; they are taken down, and thrown into your closet, which will be nailed up, as if it were not a part of the house, there to perish together: for who can bear to see them? (II, 170)

Lovelace, on the other hand, often lets remarks slip which suggest that the difference between virtuous and fallen women is not really the gap between the angelic and the merely mortal. Fallen women become, by definition, so much like him that femaleness is no longer their most conspicuous feature. It is the evil (male) principle which dominates. To be a chaste woman is enough; it is rather like being Eve before the Fall. But the fallen are all in the clutches of Satan, and are less different from each other than all of them, men and women, are different from the virtuous, even though women, like Satan himself, have had a deeper plunge from Grace than men. Lovelace's constant suggestions that Clarissa be proved either woman or angel refer to two kinds of mortality: the fallen and the pure. A virtuous woman is the closest fleshly equivalent to the angels, and thus a spiritual battle can be fought between 'mere bodies', as Belford would say. When

Lovelace compares himself to modest women, then, it is worth paying attention.

One argument let me plead in proof of my assertion: that even we rakes love modesty in a woman; while the modest women, as they are accounted (that is to say, the *slyest*), love, and generally prefer, an impudent man. Whence can this be but from a likeness in nature? And this made the poet say that every woman is a rake in her heart. It concerns them by their *actions* to prove the contrary, if they can. (II, 55)

Clarissa, for different reasons, also points to a common source of feeling in men and women when she begs Anna Howe not to disobey her mother:

Learn, my dear, I beseech you learn, to subdue your own passions. Be the motives what they will, excess is excess. Those possessions in our sex which we take no pains to subdue, may have one and the same source with those infinitely blacker passions which we used so often to condemn in the violent and headstrong of the other sex; and which may be only heightened in *them* by *custom*, and their *freer education*. Let us both, my dear, ponder well this thought; look into ourselves, and fear. (II, 236)

Clarissa shares Lovelace's view that men and women are alike in their passions, but this is a strange way of phrasing a warning. She seems to fear the possibility that passionate women may find themselves becoming like, or even (spiritually) turning into men. The debate altogether has the flavour of late medieval discussions on the nature of women. But unlike that famous Council of Trent in which a question was raised about whether women have souls at all, Richardson seems to be wondering whether women *are* souls, that is, the nobler essence of a society, or whether they are cut from the same stained cloth as their irredeemably fallen brothers.

If spiritual identity is sex-linked in this way, we would expect that much would be made of the maintenance of sexual distinctions. And indeed, there are constant running references to unseemly behaviour, especially in women. In both *Pamela* and *Clarissa*, of course, there are the ogre-like procuresses, gigantic in stature, lesbian in inclination, who betray virgins for profit. The very fact that they engage in commercial transactions, selling human flesh instead of buttons or books, seems to create a dubious sexuality. Ladies simply do not enter the marketplace: to be so conspicuously greedy, so vulgarly active, seems almost a greater evil than the actual nature of the business. It is significant, therefore, that Mrs Sinclair does not appear as manlike to Clarissa when they are first introduced (II, 193). While Clarissa never finds her sympathetic, her opinion of her as 'odious' and 'vile' is only slowly developed. It might be added that we learn about Mrs Sinclair's true nature mostly because characters other than Clarissa find her so as well. Lovelace, for instance, describes Clarissa and Mrs Sinclair in confrontation for the first time. Clarissa, who has been brought back from Hampstead by prostitutes disguised as Lovelace's aristocratic kinswomen, realizes that she has been trapped:

Having never before seen anything but obsequiousness in this woman [Mrs Sinclair], little as she liked her, she was frightened at her masculine air, and fierce look – God help me! cried she – what will become of me now! . . .
. . . The old dragon straddled up to her, with her arms kemboed again, her eye-brows erect, like the bristles upon a hog's back, and, scowling over her shortened nose, more than half hid her ferret eyes. Her mouth was distorted. She pouted out her blubber-lips, as if to bellow up wind and sputter into her horse-nostrils; and her chin was curdled, and more than usually prominent with passion. (III, 195–6)

The most complete physical description of the old woman (by Belford) occurs very late in the novel, when Mrs Sinclair is on her deathbed. The point at which Mrs Sinclair is finally perceived as Lovelace's accomplice, of course, is the rape itself: and Clarissa, at that moment, is hard put to distinguish vision from hallucination.

Throughout the novel, then, Mrs Sinclair is seen first as a creature of Clarissa's own perception and imagination. Since she is also seen to degenerate as Clarissa approaches spiritual perfection, she is literally diminished as she grows more horrific. In this sense, she is Clarissa's victim, an agent of disease which is effectively overcome. At the same time, her alliance with Lovelace reminds us that her 'nieces' were created by Lovelace, who first seduced them. The old woman is often called Mother Sinclair; and the violation of Clarissa is a kind of Black Mass, with Lovelace officiating and the procuress acting as assistant priestess. But perhaps an apter analogy could be made with childbirth. Mother Sinclair could be seen as a midwife, since she is partly responsible for the birth of a new identity in Clarissa. The relationships, in any case, are incestuous: it is as if the prostitutes were a mock family, the Harlowes painted in their true colours.

Clarissa will either have to join the other fallen women, becoming, like them, both wife and ritual daughter to Lovelace, or she will have to perish. Vampirized, like them, she would have to be a vampire to new prey. It is not a great step from this moment in *Clarissa* to the sexual rapacity of Dracula: in fact, this particular sort of cruelty reminds us more of Bram Stoker than of Sade. Really, of course, a notion of sexual disease (which includes sexual dishonour) lies behind this traditional view of the madam as the betrayer of her own sex.

Desire is infectious, destructive and immortal. The more it is indulged, the more monstrous and powerful becomes the personality that harbours it, until even the distinctive characteristics of each sex are eaten away as if by the pox which is itself a result of sexual greed. Eventually, the lustful person renounces humanity altogether, and becomes the personification of his or her vice, a gargoyle-like caricature perched on the very walls of a sanctuary. In this scene, too, then, we can see the roots of the late-eighteenth-century neo-Gothic style: sexual terror replaces the fear of God. Of the seven deadly sins, the eighteenth century finds lust the deadliest. It is curious that writers in mid-century France made the same connection, for we see an identical preoccupation with the distortion of sexual identity in Diderot and Laclos.

The first sign that sexual boundaries are in danger for women, however, lies in the effervescence of too much energy. When Anna Howe writes at length about her suitor, Mr Hickman, she has much to say on the subject of 'men–women':

I do assure you, my dear, were I a man, and a man who loved my quiet, I would not have one of these managing wives on any consideration. I would make it a matter of serious inquiry beforehand, whether my mistress's qualifications, if I heard she was notable [that is, a capable, bustling and energetic manager], were *masculine* or *feminine* ones . . .

Indeed, my dear, I do not think a *man–woman* a pretty character at all; and as I said, were I a *man*, I would sooner choose a dove, though it were fit for nothing, but, as the play says, to go tame about the house, and breed, than a wife that is setting at work (my insignificant self *present* perhaps) every busy hour my never-resting servants, those of the stud not excepted; and who, with a besom in her hand, as I may say, would be continually filling me with apprehensions that she wanted to sweep me out of my own house as useless lumber. (II, 118)

As is so often true in Richardson, most of this passage relies on a cliché about busy housewives that probably could be traced to the beginnings of cultural history. Certainly, there are other roughly contemporary examples of the same sort of harangue against over-energetic household management (Linda K. Kerber, for example, has collected some amusing American examples of male mistrust of spring-cleaning and whitewashing from the 1780s),[7] and we can go back at least to the Wife of Bath, and certainly to Shakespeare, for other instances. Implicit in this attack on wifely excess is the familiar charge of sexual voracity which we have already seen in other guises. A single man, a mere husband, dwindles into insignificance before such a wife, who seems to need many men. And how humiliating to be castrated with a broom! Even the reference to the servants of the stud carries a tinge of sexual innuendo. A woman who rides horses regularly (*astride*, doubtless – one can almost hear Richardson's disapproval, rendered visible in the italicized word on the page) is perilously close to doing the same with her grooms. One recalls the talk about *mésalliances* between duchesses and grooms during the controversy over *Pamela*. Anna's description, like the one of Mrs Sinclair, has ancient origins and comes from the primitive belief in female insatiability. But it is curiously juxtaposed against an accepted notion of *male* insatiability. This fear that the sexes have more in common than was previously imagined gives a peculiarly eighteenth-century twist to the cliché.

The rape

As Lovelace draws his net closer, there is a flurry of incidents in the plot: more actually *happens* between the arrival of the lovers at Mrs Sinclair's and Clarissa's rape than anywhere else in the novel. The possibility of marriage is pushed firmly into the background, though there is much talk about obtaining a marriage licence, and though it never disappears altogether. And Clarissa is tried and tried again. Lovelace makes himself temporarily sick to ascertain Clarissa's affection for him; he interprets her concern and tenderness as sure signs of love. He uses the occasion of a small accidental fire in the middle of the night to attempt her virtue, but instead brings on Clarissa's escape to Hampstead. By now Clarissa is clear in her mind that she will never marry Lovelace. The language on both sides becomes more and more spiritualized, as if all sides are beginning to recognize the larger dimensions of their struggle. When Lovelace writes of Clarissa's successful fight against him when he tries to persuade her to yield during the confusion over the fire, he is forced to admit defeat: 'What a triumph has her sex obtained in my thoughts by this trial and this resistance?' (II, 507). She refuses to see him for a week, and he tries to justify himself in terms of her virtue: 'She called me *villain*, Belford, within these few hours. And what is the sum of the present argument; but that had I *not* been a villain in her sense of the word, she had not been such an *angel*?' (II, 516).

Lovelace's ruminations before the final and successful attempt on Clarissa are particularly fascinating. Nowhere is one more strongly reminded of *Paradise Lost*: Lovelace is about to make an assault on Clarissa, just as the fallen angels in pandemonium finally agree that Satan should be sent to lure the newly created Adam and Eve out of the Garden of Eden. Lovelace's arguments, like Beelzebub's, are magnificently specious:

Do we not then see that an honest prowling fellow is a necessary evil on many accounts? Do we not see that it is highly requisite that a sweet girl should be now and then drawn aside by him? And the more eminent the girl, in the graces of person, mind, and fortune, is not the example likely to be the more efficacious?

If these *postulata* be granted me, who, I pray, can equal my charmer in all these? Who therefore so fit for an example to the rest of the sex? – At worst, I am entirely within my worthy friend Mandeville's assertion, *That private vices are public benefits*.

Well then, if this sweet creature must *fall*, as it is called, for the benefit of all the pretty fools of the sex, she *must*; and there's an end of the matter.

(III, 145)

But there is an important difference between the debate in Hell and this chain of arguments: all the voices in this internal discussion are Lovelace's own. Even his fellow rake, Belford, to whom his reasonings are addressed, is no sympathetic interlocutor but a strayed Christian on the point of returning to the flock. Lovelace finds, indeed, that his first smug conclusions are followed by others. His conscience has seized the pen, and written down the feelings unspoken before: the remorse, the fear, the sense of an ineluctable and tragic purpose impelling even his own plots. His dismay is by no means entirely facetious:

Yet already have I not gone too far? Like a repentent thief, afraid of his gang, and obliged to go on, in fear of hanging till he comes to be hanged, I am afraid of the gang of my cursed contrivances.

As I hope to live, I am sorry (at the present writing) that I have been such a foolish plotter, as to put it, as I fear I have done, out of my *own power* to be honest. I hate compulsion in all forms; and cannot bear, even to be *compelled* to be the wretch my choice has made me! So now, Belford, as thou hast said, I am a machine at last, and no free agent.

Most significant of all is the burst of despair when he exclaims: 'Why was such a woman as this thrown into my way, whose very fall will be her glory, and perhaps not only my shame, but my destruction?' (III, 146). This sentence carries the full mythological weight of Richardson's novel. One can take Lovelace's two cryptic utterances ('The affair is over. Clarissa lives', after the rape; and 'LET THIS EXPIATE!', his dying words after a duel with Clarissa's cousin Morden) as the two poles of an implicit Christian typology which the rake has fully perceived and expressed, though he is conscious of his own helplessness in the face of it. Like a good biblical scholar, he has seen that he is moving in another time-scale altogether from the historical one. He has recognized that destiny can act through sexuality, that most human and socially palpable of all qualities, as clearly as through any other medium.

Sex and Enlightenment

The recognition that passion and apotheosis can be experienced in what until now has been looked upon as the realm of human action most remote from God is, quite simply, terrifying for Lovelace. He puts the paradoxes into a sharp aphorism: Clarissa's fall will bring her eternal life and a coronet in heaven, while he will suffer not only shame (a purely social punishment to which Clarissa has already developed an immunity) but eternal destruction. Only at this point can Lovelace see that all his delight in Satanic imagery is the hubris of a mere fallen man. After the rape of Clarissa, he recognizes he will indeed fall utterly and permanently, like the dark angel with whom he so often compares himself. The scale of his volition is entirely different from Clarissa's: he is only willing himself into destruction, while Clarissa must wrench herself out of an old identity into a new and greater one. The phrasing of Lovelace's message, in fact, suggests this. The cadence of 'The affair is over. Clarissa lives' (III, 196) is reminiscent of the royal announcement: 'The King is dead. Long live the King'.

It is Clarissa, then, who escapes the relentless drive of sexuality. Desire forges a straight trail through history by its own energy. The search for fulfilment is never culminated, the need is never met. Clarissa, after all, does not answer Lovelace's need either: he despairs afterwards. But she has become an object, a 'mediator' for the last time. She is held only once in the tight coils of sexuality (I choose this imagery deliberately, since she undergoes a violation, not an embrace), and then she is released for ever, just as Christ's agony on the cross, or any death agony, is an exquisite excess of mortality, after which a certain kind of freedom (if we continue to follow Richardson's own pious Christianity) becomes possible at last. Clarissa is susceptible to 'fatality' only up to a point: after the rape she is free to create herself anew, and die. If we take this sexual mythology to heart, indeed, we cannot argue even that the direction and structure of the narrative itself, for purely literary reasons, call for Clarissa's death. Richardson has shown us the inexorable grip of spiritual necessity, so that the aesthetic aspect of the novel is only an effect, and not a cause, of the mythic or religious one.

I have taken rather great exegetical liberties with this single line of text, but I think them justified in the light of the sufferings which follow this internal argument of Lovelace's. If we return now to our text, we will see that the murder of Clarissa's identity is also foreseen metaphorically. For the letter ends with the rhetorical murder of Lovelace's conscience – and conscience, for him, is *feminine*:

Thus far had my *conscience* written with my pen; and see what a recreant she had made me! I seized her by the throat – *There*! – *There*, said I, thou vile impertinent! Take *that*, and *that*! How often have I given thee warning! And now, I hope, thou intruding varletess, have I done thy business!

Puling and low-voiced, rearing up thy detested head, in vain implorest thou *my* mercy, who, in *thy* day hast showed me so little! – Take *that*, for a rising blow! And now will *thy* pain, and *my* pain from *thee*, soon be over, Lie there! Welter on! Had I not given thee thy death's wound, thou wouldest have robbed me of all my joys. Thou couldst not have mended me, 'tis plain. Thou couldst only have thrown me into despair. Didst thou not see that I had gone too far to recede? Welter on, once more I bid thee! Gasp on! *That* thy last gasp, surely! How hard diest thou!

ADIEU! Unhappy man! ADIEU! (III, 147)

This killing of the conscience is a particularly horrifying moment in the book. She speaks, after all, with Clarissa's gentle voice, and she dies (critics of Richardson might be compelled to jeer a little) so very slowly. Lovelace's viciousness is directly expressed – we must constantly distance ourselves as a defence against the blood, reminding ourselves that after all this physical description refers to an abstract entity. But there is no doubt that Lovelace's omnivorousness (we could as aptly call it carnivorousness) has actually managed to swallow up something of Clarissa's spirituality, without, however, diminishing his victim, whose soul becomes large enough to provide consciences for any number of rakes.

This passage probably anticipates Sade more fully than any other in the novel. We see Lovelace's sexual fury against Clarissa in all its unbridled violence; but we must also recognize it as a kind of suicide. Lovelace is killing the better part of himself, of course. It would be interesting, and probably important, to know if Richardson has transformed or originated yet another cliché, the one in which men refer to their wives as their 'better halves'. Clarissa has become part of Lovelace; but no matter how many chances he is given to recognize what is at stake, he cannot help himself, and kills her. He has become 'a machine at last', as he writes to Belford, and has lost the battle before it has properly begun. The marriage between heaven and hell, such as it was, has already been celebrated and dissolved.

As I remarked earlier, Clarissa does not herself describe the rape until 150 pages after Lovelace's announcement that it has taken place. Her description, when it comes, is of the trauma suffered rather than of the event. She vaguely recalls that the rape was committed in the presence of the prostitutes:

I grew worse and worse in my head; now stupid, now raving, now senseless. The vilest of vile women [she means Mrs Sinclair] was brought to frighten me. Never was there so horrible a creature as she appeared to me at this time.

I remember I pleaded for mercy. I remember that I said *I would be his – indeed I would be his* – to obey his mercy. But no mercy found I! My strength, my intellects failed me – And then such scenes followed – O my dear, such dreadful scenes! – fits upon fits (faintly indeed and imperfectly remembered) procuring me no compassion – but death was withheld from me. That would have been too great a mercy!

. . . I was so senseless, that I dare not aver that the horrid creatures of the house were personally aiding and abetting: but some visionary remembrances I have of female figures, flitting, as I may say, before my sight; the wretched woman's particularly. But as these confused ideas might be owing to the terror I had conceived of the worse than masculine violence she had been permitted to assume to me, . . . and as what I suffered from his barbarity wants not that aggravation; I will say no more on a subject so shocking as this must ever be to my remembrance.   (III, 371–2)

Shortly after the rape, Lovelace reports to Belford on her ravings. Ostensibly, this breakdown, which lasts only a few days, is a result of her sedation by the prostitutes; but in fact it is clearly a reaction to the violation, though the opiates may have helped to contribute to the effect of shock alone. Clarissa writes fragmented, Ophelia-like utterances on scraps of paper. One of them is a parable:

A lady took a great fancy to a young lion, or a bear, I forget which – but a bear, or a tiger, I believe it was. It was made her a present of when a whelp. She fed it with her own hand: she nursed up the wicked cub with great tenderness; and would play with it without fear or apprehension of danger: and it was obedient to all her commands: and its tameness, as she used to boast, increased with its growth; so that, like a lap-dog, it would follow her all over the house. But mind what followed: at last, somehow, neglecting to satisfy its hungry maw, or having otherwise disobliged it on some occasion, it resumed its nature; and on a sudden fell upon her, and tore her in pieces. And who was most to blame, I pray? The brute, or the lady? The lady, surely! For what *she* did was *out* of nature, *out* of character, at least: what it did was *in* its own nature.

(III, 206)

The sexual connotations in this passage are obvious. The beast is distinguished by its native voracity. The lady of the parable has tried to tame a wild animal so that it would become as docile as a lap-dog, just as Clarissa has deluded herself into thinking that her sexual feelings for Lovelace were really philanthropic impulses towards reforming him. It is not even clear, however, whether her own sexuality is meant to be the beast, or whether we are supposed to think of Lovelace in this comparison. The distinction is a little blurred, because mindless animality is not what has been associated with Lovelace in the novel. Since the beast was 'made . . . a present of when a whelp' and since 'its tameness . . . increased with its growth', it does not fit the picture of a Lovelace very closely.

Instead, we have a parabolic story of *development*. Just as Clarissa's perception of monstrosity – of unnaturalness – in Mother Sinclair is a function of her experience, so here the ability to see (if it comes at all) comes only with death. This young lady, to begin with, is blind. Her moral blindness allows her to engage in the unnatural act of taming a wild beast. A defect in one sort of nature, moral nature, leads to annihilation. But the young lady is blamed, like the Pharaoh in the Book of Exodus whose heart is supernaturally hardened by God, for a defect which by definition is irremediable: blindness cannot be overcome by an act of sight. It is a curious comparison for Clarissa to use when we remember that first letter of Anna Howe's, with its suggestion that merely being the subject of a quarrel is enough evidence to convict the troubled maiden of impropriety.

The important thing about this animal is its beastliness. Our raving narrator, after all, is not clear about whether it is a bear, a lion or a tiger. It was 'presented to her', possibly by parents, as a gift. We do not know whether she too was a 'whelp', or little girl, at the time. The suggestion is that she was already adult (with the implication that she should therefore have known better) while the 'wicked cub' grew before her very eyes. In the sentence which climaxes the parable, however, we are given a grammatical ambiguity which I think highly significant: suddenly our gifted stylist makes a grammatical error. 'Dangling participle!' a schoolteacher would say today, marking the sheet with a red pencil. But what is the effect of this apparent infelicity? We don't quite know whether *she* is the one who neglected 'to satisfy its hungry maw', or whether the beast itself finally loses its veneer of civilization through a slight offence or break in routine. Suddenly, virgin and monster become oddly one; and I hope I don't over-emphasize the grotesque aspects of the tale when I say that their unity is complete by the end of the passage. This little parable is a frightening inversion of the medieval pairing of the virgin and the unicorn. In iconography, the unicorn, monstrous and pure, lays its head on the virgin's lap and looks contentedly at itself in a mirror. The lady, in not seeing the beast straight, has not seen herself straight either. This lap-dog of a beast, however, must have been quite well disguised. Someone, after all, *gave* it to her when it was small and not only inoffensive but apparently attractive. Offstage, then, we can imagine the trusted hand of authority giving the girl the gift of her own destruction. In accepting it, she immediately moved '*out* of character, at least' – out of character if not out of nature. All her loving and motherly efforts, the nourishing, the nursing, the tenderness, have been wasted on the very creature who will eat her up. The beast, unlike the wolf in Little Red Riding Hood or even in The Three Little Pigs, is not to blame. The animal is at the very least the young lady's creation. The text tells us that much, even though I think that most modern readers would take this story as a parable about parts of the young lady's identity. She has, to all appearance, reared a monster, whose true identity and monstrousness remain ambiguous till the end. Yet it is she, and not the beast, who is finally condemned as monstrous, 'out of nature'. Even in this moment of extreme stress, however, she confirms the view of sexuality that she shares with Lovelace: men and women may differ in the degree of their passions (if, indeed, in that), but they do not differ in kind, in *essentials*, as Anna Howe would say. Nonetheless, it is impossible to escape the conclusion that Clarissa thinks of sexuality as deeply wrong. Desire itself creates the space for Satan. It may, in fact, be the sign of Satan's very presence in her spirit. When Clarissa discovers her own desire, whether sexual or spiritual, she discovers the man in herself. Perhaps that is the reason for the eighteenth-century preoccupation with *hommes–femmes*: sexual fear has taken on a male body.

All the while, however, she attempts to restore her identity and 'to bring herself back to herself', as she puts it, after the shock of the rape. She learns in the process that restoration is impossible; that reformation must occur, not in Lovelace, but in herself. But first she must put the original experience by, nullify it in the sense in which one nullifies a marriage, without denying the importance of what has happened. When she sees Lovelace again, a week after the rape, she is imperious, not humble. For the first time, she has dressed herself in the spotless white which becomes her badge for the duration of the novel. This is, of course, no longer the white of virginity. Clarissa has begun to attain knowledge through experience and suffering, and has learned to reject the notion that experience (any experience, but particularly the sexual one) sullies both the body and the spirit of the unfortunate woman who undergoes initiation, in whatever form. The radical mistrust of herself has not killed her, after all, but she is slowly becoming someone else altogether:

Hadst thou not sinned beyond the *possibility of forgiveness*, interrupted she; . . . the desperateness of my condition might have induced me to think of taking a wretched chance with a man so profligate. But *after what I have suffered by thee*, it would be *criminal* in me to wish to bind my soul in covenant to a man so nearly allied to perdition.

Marriage is now out of the question. It is only a matter of time before it becomes clear that the only alternative is death.

Clarissa's death

Although Clarissa has a small breakdown after the rape, her sufferings become most harrowing after she is arrested and brought to a sordid room in an officer's house. Belford quickly rescues her and brings her back to her lodgings at a glover's, but this final blow to her self-esteem seriously weakens her and smoothes the way, as it were, for death. We see her now perpetually arrayed in brilliant white (see III, 445, for example). She has lost her anxiety about 'punctilio', the *que-dira-t-on*, which played such a prominent role in the first days of her relationship with Lovelace. Belford, reporting her return to her lodgings, expresses his amazement at her lack of concern for her reputation:

O Mrs Smith, said she, as soon as she saw her, did you not think I was run away? You don't know what I have suffered since I saw you. I have been in a prison! – Arrested for debts I owe not! . . .

. . . But dost thou not observe what a strange, what an uncommon openness of heart reigns in this lady? *She had been in a prison*, she said, before a stranger in the shop, and before the maid-servant: and so, probably, she would have said had there been twenty people in the shop.

The disgrace she cannot hide from *herself*, as she says in her letter to Lady Betty, she is not solicitous to conceal from the *world*! (III, 455–6)

When she finally offers Anna Howe her reasons for preferring death over life, she shows quite convincingly that both marriage and a single life are now impossible for her. Since she cannot actually choose to die without a violation of her religious principles, she promises that she will not do physical harm to herself. Nonetheless, she senses the imminence of her death, and has begun to look at her life as if it were already past:

In short, I will do everything I can do to convince all my friends, who hereafter may think it worth their while to inquire after my last behaviour, that I possessed my soul with tolerable patience; and endeavoured to bear with a lot of my own drawing; for thus, in humble imitation of the sublimest Exemplar, I often say: Lord, it is Thy will; and it shall be mine. Thou art just in all Thy dealing with the children of men; and I know Thou wilt not afflict me beyond what I can bear: and if I *can* bear it, I *ought* to bear it; and (Thy grace assisting me) I *will* bear it. (III, 522)

Clarissa has renounced all claims to exemplariness herself, and has thereby humbled her pride at last. We should not confuse her concern about the manner of her death with an anxiety about decorum. The dignity of the deathbed scene is a sign, the seal of the deity on each individual life; and it gives meaning to everything which precedes it. The rake Belton and Mrs Sinclair die badly, but Lovelace and the prostitutes are unable to apprehend the significance of the message of their dissolution. Clarissa, on the other hand, is in a privileged position: she is given not only understanding of the event itself, but pre-knowledge that it is going to occur. The first step towards death is the stilling of desire, for, as we have said, desire always needs an object and thus demands the supremacy of an ego. But, as we know, it takes a great deal of volition to 'close the valves of our attention' (to paraphrase Emily Dickinson). What is at issue is not the suppression of the will, but a final redirection or sublimation of it. This occurs first in the matter of eating; for, however Clarissa may protest on the subject, it is quite clear that the *physical* cause of her death is starvation. Belford calls her a 'lovely skeleton' (IV, 154) when he sees her in her last days.

On the other hand, Clarissa produces an enormous amount of writing: it is as if the taking in of the phallus, however involuntarily, demands two penances: abstinence first, followed by catharsis, a creative but grimly asexual parody of childbirth. Here, again, the misunderstanding between the lovers is clear; for Lovelace, after the rape, spends much time dreaming about the possible birth of an heir. He cannot recognize the birth that is actually taking place in the person whom he watches with such obsessiveness. Clarissa, meanwhile, moves more and more deeply into a symbolic existence, and begins to take her place in a vividly realized Christian history. She has her coffin brought into her room, where it becomes the altar for her meditations; and Belford describes it for Lovelace:

The principal device, neatly etched on a plate of white metal, is a crowned serpent, with its tail in its mouth, forming a ring, the emblem of eternity: and in the circle made by it is this inscription:

CLARISSA HARLOWE

April x

[Then the year]

AETAT XIX.

For ornaments: at top, an hour-glass winged. At bottom, an urn. Under the hour-glass, on another plate, this inscription:

HERE the wicked cease from troubling; and HERE the weary be at rest. Job iii. 17.

Over the urn, near the bottom:

Turn again unto thy rest, O my soul! For the Lord hath rewarded thee. And why? Thou hast delivered my soul from death; mine eyes from tears; and my feet from falling. Ps. cxvi. 7,8.

Over this is the head of a white lily snapt short off, and just falling from the stalk; and this inscription over that, between the principal plate and the lily:

The days of man are but as grass. For he flourisheth as a flower of the field; for, as soon as the wind goeth over it, it is gone; and the place thereof shall know it no more. Ps. ciii. 15, 16.   (IV, 257)

These symbols are clear enough; but Clarissa's special plight has given unusual significance to some of these standard funerary devices. The urn and lily together are one of the most common emblems of the Virgin Mary; the urn on its own is a symbol of containment and hence femininity, while the white lily, of course, stands for purity. The winged hour-glass is primarily a literal rendering of the expression 'Time flies'; but an hour-glass without wings is also an emblem of the inversion of the relationship between the upper and lower worlds. The *ouroboros*, or serpent with its tail in its mouth, is the richest symbol of all. It was used by the Gnostics in Greek antiquity to represent the unity of all the cycles of life in the cosmos, and hence has become an emblem of eternity. But the snake itself has other deeply sexual connotations. Serpents have always been associated with goddesses, with the feminine, material and destructive principle, rather than with the masculine, spiritual and creative principle embodied in the Cross (or in the sword of St George). For Jung, the snake is a symbol of the anguish of recognizing the primeval and destructive forces in the human psyche.[8]

If we have had any doubt until this point that Richardson's narrative has been doing some extraordinary things with the psychology of everyday life, this funerary description should convince us that Clarissa is no ordinary young lady. She has taken the device of the Virgin Mary and has snapped off the lily's head to show how literally she has been deflowered. She moves with ease into the Christian pattern of prophecy and fulfilment, and seems to have no difficulty in making the implicit comparison between herself and the Virgin, since she sees herself as so antithetical in the matter of purity. (That the Madonna appears at all, even symbolically, in this Puritan context is remarkable: we are reminded yet again that female sexuality is being brought to the centre of a religious quest.)

Clarissa has also adopted two devices which are extremely ambivalent on the question of female sexuality (the 'lower world' of the hour-glass and the destructive energy of the snake are linked in this) and given them new power. The serpent is not only a promise of eternal life to come, but an effective iconographic containment of the evil of sexual feeling. Desire has been stilled: the serpent's destructiveness rebounds on its own body, and Clarissa's integrity, symbolized in the vagina-like centre around which the snake arranges itself, remains intact. The space for her new personality has been created at last, even if only symbolically, on the lid of a coffin. But the serpent has become masculine, self-enclosed and, fundamentally, impotent. The voracious Lovelace must finally cannibalize himself. Clarissa, indeed, describes Lovelace as a self-destructive snake in one of her last letters to Anna Howe: 'Yet I am glad that this violent spirit *can* thus creep; that, like a poisonous serpent, he *can* thus coil himself, and hide his head in his own narrow circlets; because this stooping, this abasement, gives me hope that no further mischief will ensue' (IV, 275–6).

Even the biblical quotations contribute to the pattern of anticipation and fulfilment: they are all from the Old Testament, as if Clarissa were herself the Christ, the missing last term of the prophecy. The humility of the last quotation is, of course, belied by the existence of the novel itself; while the apotheosis of victimhood, with its oblique reference to Lovelace, is clear enough in the quotation from Job. As Clarissa says to Belford just before she dies: ''Tis a choice comfort, Mr Belford, at the winding up of our short story, to be able to say, I have rather *suffered* injuries *myself* than *offered* them to *others*' (IV, 324).

Like Christ in medieval iconography, Clarissa is making her cross bear fruit. But her cross is a psychological one, internal and invisible, like her own sexual organs. She has proved the spiritual equality of the sexes by bypassing the material process of reproduction altogether. It is Lovelace, not she, who has become the baser principle in this epic struggle. Her progeny, unfortunately, are the insipid 'spiritual' heroines which Victorian ideology somehow managed to create out of the genetic material of this powerful novel. The fact that her sacrifice has so little *social* effect is part of the mythic structure: Christ, too, left a chaos of remorse and unbelief behind him. But Clarissa has shown that moral and religious battles can be fought in the person, body and spirit, of a woman, and has thus pointed the way, ironically enough, to a fundamental secularization of literary concerns. Readers today, who might understandably be repelled by the ultimate rejection of physical sexuality, will nonetheless recognize a profound respect for the integrity of the personality in Richardson; younger writers all over Europe helped to enlarge upon the ideal of 'organic unity', and it has become central to our views of the development of the individual. The eventual separation from religion occurs, not because Clarissa's femininity lessens the seriousness or importance of the struggle, but because human relationships and human generation have been made central, and not secondary, to an understanding of the place of mankind in the divine order. It soon became easy enough to forget the Christian context: but the mythology of the virtuous woman has not yet lost its power.

4

DIDEROT'S *ÉLOGE DE RICHARDSON* AND THE PROBLEM OF REALISM

Diderot and Richardson

In the opening chapters of this study, I have tried to clarify the connection between Richardson's originality and the Puritan tradition of conduct books in England. It is difficult, when we turn to the tangled question of his influence abroad, to understand exactly what in his work appealed to the sophisticated *philosophes* of Catholic France. Richardson's own ties to the Continent, as his biographers tells us, were personal and sporadic; and his contacts with France were particularly insubstantial.

To begin with, he was no francophile; and, unlike many of his contemporaries, he had no knowledge of French.[1] There is no evidence that he read either Marivaux or Prévost, the authors in whom critics have most often tried to see predecessors. He read Mme de La Fayette's *Princesse de Clèves* in English (though we do not know in whose translation), but disapproved of it on moral grounds.[2] Indeed, one of his characters inveighs against Mme de La Fayette and La Calprenède at rather great length in *Sir Charles Grandison*.[3] When Warburton sent him a preface for *Clarissa* in which he was linked with the French tradition, Richardson thanked him, but added: 'All that know me, know, that I am not acquainted in the least either with the French Language or writers: And that it was chance and not Skill or Learning, that made me fall into this way of Scribbling.'[4]

His one constant French correspondent, de Freval, had intended to translate *Clarissa*, but Prévost was quicker off the mark and published a bowdlerized translation which was supposedly more in keeping with French delicacy than the original (*Lettres angloises, ou Histoire de Miss Clarisse Harlove*, Dresden, 1751). Richardson was not consulted, and was disappointed with what he knew of the translation – a copy of Prévost's introduction, translated back to English, was found among Richardson's papers.[5] Through a young Swiss geologist, Richardson almost came into correspondence with Mme d'Épinay, the protectress of Rousseau, friend of Diderot and mistress of Grimm, but illness prevented the ageing novelist from taking up the contact.[6] These few biographical facts are all we know of his relations with the French literary world.

The cult of Richardsonianism rose, however, regardless of the novelist's personal connections with literary figures abroad. Richardson's admirers recognized that he had given new life to a much-maligned genre; but perhaps his greatest gift to his posterity, as readers at the time saw it, was his ability to moralize art, to arouse people to controversy over ethical issues. He was able to make such an impact by giving his characters immediacy and vitality in his use of dialogue: even the letters are really written conversation. When they turn into monologue, as in *Clarissa*, we become aware of the isolation of the writer through the misapplication of this essentially sociable form. And when silence or the description of a gesture replaces direct discourse, it carries all the more weight against the mass of words which we usually associate with Richardson's highly articulate characters.

These two innovations, the moralization of fiction and the rendering of psychological development through dialogue and gesture, were taken into drama by Diderot and Lessing, and to a lesser extent into painting.[7] If we are to judge by Diderot's own efforts at a moral drama, and by what we know of the engraver and painter Greuze, whom Diderot idolized in his *Salons*, the Richardsonian transplants were not very successful. We could happily overlook Diderot's two plays, *Le Fils naturel* of 1757 (accompanied by *Les Entretiens sur le Fils naturel*, a work of theory) and *Le Père de famille* of 1758 (accompanied by the treatise *De la poésie dramatique*) if we were discussing their literary merits alone. Only his friends, who hinted darkly at the corruption of a society which did not recognize his originality, could applaud them as great achieve- ments for the stage. The history of their performance, which is extremely short, is not, however, as insignificant as had once been thought.[8] There is no doubt that Diderot tried to use Richardson's techniques in these plays; and his dramatic works did have influence, particularly in Germany. One of Diderot's modern editors, Jacques Chouillet, goes so far as to suggest that the *philosophe*'s dream of total drama finally came true with Wagner and Verdi.[9]

What especially attracted Diderot to Richardson during these years was the novelist's talent for rendering conversation and gesture as if they were being performed on a stage. This ability to create non-verbal meaning through language, and to give language itself the vividness which we associate with the spoken rather than with the written word, in a form where a dramatic performance could take place only in the imagination of the reader, fascinated Diderot, who was never able to resist a paradox. Diderot, like many critics after him, may have erred in taking Richardson's obvious dramatic gifts too literally: a novelist with an eye for dialogue and 'staging' will still not necessarily make a good playwright. It is instructive to observe what happens to Diderot's attempt to transpose the Richardsonian rendering of strong feeling into the drama. We get scenes like this one, from *Le Fils naturel*:

Clairville – Excusez mon impatience. Eh bien, Dorval! . . .
Dorval (Dorval est troublé. Il tâche de se remettre; mais il y réussit mal. Clairville qui cherche à lire sur son visage, s'en aperçoit, se méprend, et dit:)
Clairville – Vous êtes troublé! Vous ne me parlez point! Vos yeux se remplissent de larmes! Je vous entends, je suis perdu!
(Clairville, en achevant ces mots, se jette dans le sein de son ami. Il y reste un moment en silence. Dorval verse quelques larmes sur lui, et Clairville dit, sans se déplacer, d'une voix basse et sanglotante:)
Clairville – Qu'a-t-elle dit? Quel est mon crime? Ami, de grâce, achevez-moi.
(DPV, X, 34)

This passage makes breathless reading. As if we do not have enough stage directions in the parentheses, we discover that most of the actual text is nothing but a continuation of them. We can almost hear Diderot puffing at the emotional bellows in the background, trying, through the series of dots and broken sentences, rhetorical questions and melodramatic gestures, to invest the play with Richardsonian depth and dignity of feeling. But too much is made of too little, and a reader today is more than once tempted to tears of laughter, rather than of distress.

Diderot boldly makes an illegitimate son the central character of his play, to show us that true sensibility, not noble birth, makes a hero. Dorval is a more liminal figure in society than Richardson's Grandison, but no more endearing. He is more interesting in the *Entretiens* which follow the play than he is in the drama itself, because in them we are allowed to see his closeness to nature as he becomes a vessel for that creative energy which surrounds him in the natural world. He rises and subsides with every influence, a perfect man of feeling. The 'Second entretien', indeed, opens with a famous passage, analysed by Leo Spitzer in his essay on Diderot in *Linguistics and Literary History*,[10] which is a disconcerting verbal orgasm. All of these innovations – the use of everyday language, ennobled only by feeling, not by neoclassical convention; the introduction of characters who are distinguished by intrinsic worth, rather than by their rank in society; the sympathy with external nature; the implicit eroticism in the portrayal of creative energy – were more important to the talented generation of playwrights who appeared in Germany in the 1770s than to Diderot's own compatriots. Indeed, one might see another side of the notion of closeness to nature in Goethe's *Natürliche Tochter*, one of the plays in which the maturing poet/playwright had to rethink his own youth, and his debt to a French literary heritage, in the wake of the Reign of Terror.

If in the writers of the *Sturm und Drang* we get genuinely antisocial, or at least seriously questioning, heroes such as Karl Moor or young Werther, we are pulled firmly back to society in the plays of Diderot, for he envisaged bourgeois drama as a cure for misanthropy. Constance, the wise and virtuous young widow with whom Dorval is eventually united, is responsible for some surprisingly undramatic lectures. Here again, Dorval's temporary gloom and desire to flee from society have nothing of the real darkness which Richardson shows us at the heart of the social structure. The terrors of both Harlowe Place and Mrs Sinclair's brothel, so at odds with their elegant appearance, and the cowardice and timid admiration of the guests at a ball to which Lovelace has actually been invited despite his by then widely known misdeeds, are some examples of Richardson's insights into social hypocrisy. Dorval, on the other hand, is not able to hold out against society for very long. He has no real objections to its structure and meaning, and is easily swayed by Constance, who has the only famous lines in the play: 'Vous, renoncer à la société!' says she. 'J'en appelle à votre coeur, interrogez-le, et il vous dira que l'homme de bien est dans la société, et qu'il n'y a que le méchant qui soit seul' (DPV, X, 62). (This is the line, of course, which was one of the causes of the rupture between Diderot and Rousseau. There is little doubt that Diderot had Rousseau in mind when he wrote these words: Rousseau had just moved to the Hermitage, on Mme d'Épinay's estate, La Chevrette, to the consternation of his Parisian friends.) After a rather long Shaftesburyan excursion, in which Constance assures Dorval that virtue, like beauty, must have good effects on us because ' [il] est dans le coeur de l'homme un goût de l'ordre, plus ancien qu'aucun sentiment réfléchi . . .' (DPV, X, 64), we come to a touching declaration of faith:

Il y a sans doute encore des barbares; et quand n'y en aura-t-il plus? Mais les temps de barbarie sont passés. Le siècle est éclairé. La raison s'est épurée. Ses préceptes remplissent les ouvrages de la nation. Ceux où l'on inspire aux hommes la bienveillance générale, sont presque les seuls qui soient lus. Voilà les leçons dont nos théâtres retentissent, et dont ils ne peuvent retentir trop souvent. Et le philosophe dont vous m'avez rappelé les vers [Voltaire], doit principalement ses succès aux sentiments d'humanité qu'il a répandus dans ses poèmes, et au pouvoir qu'ils ont sur nos âmes.   (DPV, X, 65)

Good taste, reason and virtue are all properties of the same feeling heart: Dorval, the possessor of these qualities, must act 'naturally', that is, sociably, if he is to remain true to himself. This is very thin stuff indeed for Diderot. Perhaps we detect a hint of the quarrel between Rousseau and him, which ended in rupture shortly after the publication of this play: Dorval is pulled back sharply, if not with much conviction, from the Rousseauvian brink of self-pity. Diderot's attitude towards Richardson in the late 1750s and early 1760s is to some extent influenced by his relationship with Rousseau. The extravagance of his praise in the *Éloge*, and the uncharacteristically old-fashioned didacticism in his plays, are two extremes to which he could well have been led by his pain and annoyance at his difficult friend.

Nonetheless, Richardson's novels were very much on his mind during this period, even if, in Diderot, we see the didacticism and the concern with virtuous sensibility skimmed off from the original, and poorly adapted for the stage. If proof is needed, the reader may turn to the spirited exchange between Diderot and the actress/novelist, Mme Riccoboni. Mme Riccoboni, piqued because Diderot has not asked her opinion on the staging of the *Père de famille*, very sensibly points out that the long silences written into the text, and the attempts to imitate domestic behaviour, are not well suited to the conditions of the French stage. She complains, amusingly, that she is afraid that some praise for the play might involuntarily escape her: 'Mais je ne veux pas parler de votre pièce, de peur qu'il ne m'échappe d'applaudir à la diction ou aux sentiments. Je ne veux vous dire que des injures pour vous apprendre à traiter votre amie comme une femme, comme une sotte femme.'[11]

Diderot's answer is remarkable. He tries to refute her charge that the silences destroy dramatic tension by drawing an example, not from other dramas, but from the novels of Richardson:

Un tems déplacé est une masse de glace jetée sur le spectateur [quotation from Mme Riccoboni's letter].

– Mais ce tems ne sera point déplacé s'il est vrai. C'est toujours là que j'en reviens. Vous observez par-ci par-là quelques-uns de ces tems; à moi, il m'en faut à tout moment. Voyez combien de repos, de points, d'interruptions, de discours brisés dans *Pamela*, dans *Clarisse*, dans *Grandisson*. Accusez cet homme-là, si vous l'osez.[12]

Clearly, the distinctions between the genres are not sharply drawn in his own mind. But Richardson is very much in his thoughts, since he even uses Richardsonian style in his response. He repeats each point of Mme Riccoboni's letter before launching into his defence, just as Richardson's characters do in *Clarissa*. Uncannily, he adopts a teasing tone (often addressing Mme Riccoboni as 'Fanny', for example, after the heroine of one of her novels, *L'Histoire de Miss Fanni Butlerd*, itself derived from Richardson). One is reminded more of Richardson's personal correspondence with his circle of female admirers, to which Diderot could not possibly have had access, than of the novels. Nonetheless, the archness is there, suggesting that Diderot, with his sensitive ear, had picked up Richardson's cadences in the English originals of the novels, even without a knowledge of Richardson's writing style in private life. The opening of the letter is characteristic:

J'ai tort, j'ai tort, mais je suis paresseux et j'ai redouté vos conseils. Faut-il se jeter à vos genoux et vous demander pardon? M'y voilà, et je vous demande pardon.

O homme, tu as de l'orgeuil! [quotation from Mme Riccoboni's letter]. – Oui, j'en ai, et qui est-ce qui en manque? Vous, femmes, vous n'en avez point?[13]

Diderot's dramas, and the treatises that accompanied them, had an importance out of all proportion to their stage success.[14] It was, however, as a theorist, and later as a novelist, that Diderot made the best use of his admiration for Richardson. Since the interrelationships – or rather the distinctions – between the arts fascinated him, however, it would be wrong to brush his dramatic efforts aside.

In addition, of course, he was a great publicist; and of all the *philosophes*, he was the most open to English ideas. Before he took up Richardson's banner, he had already read widely among English philosophers, novelists and scientific writers. From the time of his first published work, a free translation of Shaftesbury's *Essay Concerning Merit and Virtue* (published by Shaftesbury in 1699; translated and published by Diderot in 1745), he kept up a keen interest in English thinkers. He shared a passion for English science with the rest of his contemporaries: it could be said that Bacon was one of the guiding spirits of the *Encyclopédie*. His debt to Sterne, particularly in such fictions as *Le Neveu de Rameau* and *Jacques le fataliste*, has been thoroughly researched.[15] Diderot's conception of the form of a bourgeois drama came, in the main, from England, as it did for his contemporaries in France and Germany; and Diderot at first thought that Richardson's moral realism could be successfully grafted upon it. The work of George Lillo, the author of *The London Merchant* (1730: translated into French in 1748), was particularly influential.

When we look at the cluster of works and letters which represents the culmination of Diderot's passion for Richardson – the letters to Sophie

Volland from 1759 to 1762; *La Religieuse*, 1760; and the *Éloge de Richardson* of 1762 – it is useful to remember that these same years were pivotal ones for European literary history in general. The *Éloge*, for example, was only one of several works which helped to signal a change of literary and philosophical direction. But even by these standards, Diderot, with his often uncanny publicist's instinct for change, was at the centre of new literary developments. It is useless to try to categorize the thinkers and events of the time with any firmness: Dr Johnson, who in many ways seems of an older generation than Diderot and Rousseau, was nonetheless their contemporary; while Richardson and Young were of the same generation as Voltaire. And Lessing, whose writings in the dozen years from 1755 (*Miss Sara Sampson*) to 1767 (*Minna von Barnhelm*) were particularly influential, was fifteen years younger than Diderot, though in the internationally fertile year of 1759 he had already begun contributing daring essays on drama and taste to the periodical *Briefe, die neueste Literature betreffend*, edited by his friend Mendelssohn.

In any case, the *Éloge de Richardson* and its accompanying documents could not have been better timed historically. In 1759, Voltaire's *Candide* and Johnson's *Rasselas* were published within months of one another. They were both fictions of the old school, lying somewhere between fable and satire (two dominant forms at the end of the seventeenth century and beginning of the eighteenth), with no attempt at the domestic realism or psychological characterization which Johnson's friend Richardson had introduced into prose narrative. For Voltaire, *Candide* was a vehicle for attacking the philosophers of moral optimism, in particular Shaftesbury and Leibniz; though he was no sentimentalist himself, his work contributed to the downfall of neoclassical complacency. *Rasselas* was sometimes nothing more than an excuse for strings of aphorisms. For the English, the shadows of Shakespeare and Milton loomed large, making tragedy impossible (though the playwrights of the time in both countries had what now seems a pathetic inability to recognize this) and epic poetry unapproachable, at least with a straight face. For the French, of course, the golden age of Molière, Corneille and Racine, La Fontaine and La Rochefoucauld, was recent history.

The background of great dramatists in the two countries meant that tragedy had remained the noblest of genres for aspiring writers, at a point when it had become perhaps the most unattainable. In addition, there were the Greek classics, whose influence over the educated imagination was more powerful than ever in the eighteenth century. The fact that Voltaire, despite the impact of his *Lettres angloises*, was often no anglophile, and thought Shakespeare vulgar; or that the French tragedians had little success on the English stage (Diderot comments on this problem in his *Observations sur Garrick*),[16] perhaps only reflects the intensity with which the older – or more old-fashioned – writers of the eighteenth century had to grapple with their own traditions. It was not until well into mid-century that writers began to be able to look about them in search of new forms. Diderot, as always, was well aware of the exhaustion of the old genres. 'Eh bien, tout est perdu!' cries Dorval in the 'Second entretien', appended to *Le Fils naturel*:

Corneille, Racine, Voltaire, Crébillon, ont reçu les plus grands applaudissements auxquels des hommes de génie pouvaient prétendre; et la tragédie est arrivée parmi nous au plus haut degré de perfection.

. . . Il y a cependant une ressource: il faut espérer que quelque jour un homme de génie sentira l'impossibilité d'atteindre ceux qui l'ont précédé dans une route battue, et se jetera de dépit dans une autre; c'est le seul événement qui puisse nous affranchir de plusieurs préjugés que la philosophie a vainement attaqués.   (A–T, VII, 118–19)

Among the writers who recognized the need for innovation was Edward Young, the poet, whose *Night Thoughts* was published in the 1740s when Richardson's first two novels were appearing; he later became both Richardson's friend and, somewhat inadvertently, a fellow idol for sentimental writers in England. The habitual melancholy of his later years suited the mood of the times well. Like Johnson and Voltaire, he published an important work, the *Conjectures on Original Composition*, in 1759. He was already eighty: the *Conjectures* were addressed to Richardson, and reflected some of the new ideas about creativity and genre. Thus, another old writer had modern literary notions; but in 1722, when he was younger, more cheerful and less original, he composed an epigram upon meeting Voltaire which was a deliciously neat persiflage of some of the obsessions of the poets of his generation:

> Thou art so witty, profligate, and thin,
> At once we think thee Milton, Death, and Sin.[17]

While Diderot recognized the possibilities which the novel offered, the distinctions between fiction and drama, and between the kinds of realism each form demanded, were not easy ones for him to maintain. In Richardson, he recognized a writer who had successfully managed to combine some of the expressiveness of gesture and suggestiveness of symbol which Diderot himself valued so much in drama and poetry; while the quality of Richardson's realism, and the strength of moral impact, were new and exciting departures for him.

Neither Voltaire nor Rousseau shared Diderot's joy at these discoveries. Roger Kempf gives us several choice quotations which make it quite clear that Voltaire hated *Clarissa*: 'un fatras d'inutilités', he called it at one point. In a letter to Mme du Deffand, who was herself enthusiastic about Richardson, he added that he read 'neuf volumes entiers dans lesquels on ne trouve rien du tout'.[18] Rousseau, who owed so much to Richardson, was ungrateful to him in his *Confessions*. The *philosophe* from Geneva was already at his phobic height when his *Nouvelle Héloïse* appeared in 1761.

But it is hardly surprising that Rousseau would, as it were, burn his bridges behind him. Just as he later repudiated Diderot's contributions to his *Discours sur l'inégalité*,[19] so he here impugns Richardson's originality. He classifies Richardson, with some qualifications, among those novelists of earlier generations who introduced marvellous and exotic adventures into their books. 'Il est aisé de réveiller l'attention', he writes,

en présentant incessamment et des événements inouïs et de nouveaux visages qui passent comme les figures de la lanterne magique: mais de soutenir toujours cette attention sur les mêmes objets, et sans aventures merveilleuses, cela certainement est plus difficile, et si, toute chose égale, la simplicité du sujet ajoute à la beauté de l'ouvrage, les Romans de Richardson, supérieurs en tant d'autres choses, ne sauraient, sur cet article, entrer en parallèle avec le mien.[20]

The attack tells us more about Rousseau than about any of the novels in question. But the circumstances under which it was written suggest that Diderot's essay has a certain objectivity of which Voltaire, with his classicist's impatience at *longueurs* and inelegances of style, on the one hand, and Rousseau, with his paranoia and his hunger for absolute originality, on the other, were not capable. The *Éloge* and, to a lesser extent, *La Religieuse*, form a critical link between the *Candide* of 1759 and the *Nouvelle Héloïse* of 1761, even if the *Éloge* comes chronologically slightly after Rousseau's novel. The writings of this period proclaim the change of emphasis, with a disinterestedness that Diderot alone of his great contemporaries was able to muster, from fiction as a sideline of serious literary production to fiction as the new vehicle of moral and poetic power. In the *Éloge*, Diderot gives us a discerning critique of Richardson's originality and importance. Not least among his achievements in the *Éloge*, which appeared in the abbé Arnaud's *Journal étranger* in January 1762 (Richardson having died on 4 July 1761), was his criticism of the ubiquitous Prévost's 'adaptation' of *Clarissa* into French. Prévost had, for example, entirely omitted the last scenes of the novel, Clarissa's funeral and the reading of the will. After Diderot's attack, Prévost published a *Supplément aux lettres angloises de Miss Clarisse Harlowe* (1762), which appeared, along with the *Éloge*, in all subsequent editions from 1766 to 1777.[21]

Indeed, long before, the abbé Raynal had had to confess in his semi-clandestine periodical, *Nouvelles littéraires*, that he had experienced 'le plaisir le plus vif et l'ennui le plus assommant' when he read *Clarissa*, presumably in Prévost's translation, in January 1751. But by 1756 and 1758, Grimm, the new editor of the journal, which had since become the *Correspondance littéraire*, attacked Prévost's audacity in tampering with the original:

M. l'abbé Prévost, qui avait déjà fort tronqué les derniers volumes de *Clarisse* dont il n'y avait pas un mot à perdre, a absolument estropié le roman de *Grandison*; il a osé abréger et gâter jusqu'au morceau de Clémentine qui est un chef d'oeuvre de génie d'un bout à l'autre. (Garnier, *OE*, 23)

Since Grimm and Diderot were intimate friends, and Grimm was influenced by Diderot in many of his opinions, it is likely that Grimm and Diderot had by then had the occasion to read Richardson's works in English.[22]

A close look at the *Éloge*

What Diderot discovered in Richardson is that reality is fallible; and, with his preternatural eye for paradox, he made the most of his recognition that the best illusionists in art can expose a fraudulent, even if empirically palpable, world. Four years earlier, indeed, Diderot was unable to resist a playful example of his ability to distort even the shaky illusion of fiction. He lists himself, the interlocutor, among the characters in Dorval's play (where he does not appear) and raises questions in the reader's mind: who is the author? who the character? – 'je reconnus toujours le caractère que Dorval avait donné à chacun de ses personnages. Il avait le ton de la mélancolie; Constance, le ton de la raison; Rosalie, celui de l'ingénuité; Clairville, celui de la passion; moi, celui de la bonhomie' (DPV, X, 162).

Diderot's own mistrust of reality is apparent when he writes in the most famous passage in the *Éloge*:

C'est lui qui porte le flambeau au fond de la caverne; c'est lui qui apprend à discerner les motifs subtils et déshonnêtes qui se cachent et se dérobent sous d'autres motifs qui sont honnêtes et qui se hâtent de se montrer les premiers. Il souffle sur le fantôme sublime qui se présente à l'entrée de la caverne; et le More hideux qu'il masquait s'aperçoit. (Garnier, *OE*, 32)

One can see this metaphor as an early recognition of a darkness in humanity: that motivation comes from a frightening and hidden place; that a rational explanation of behaviour is not necessarily a true one. Diderot's Moor has been seen as one of the most striking personifications of the unconscious. Indeed, there are numerous examples in Diderot's work of a disconcertingly modern awareness of unconscious behaviour and sexual sublimation.

Richardson unmasks the Moor, however, by letting us see how language betrays him. Diderot, the discerning musical critic, has learned from Richardson to listen for clues to character in words and their pitch:

C'est lui qui fait tenir aux hommes de tous les états, de toutes les conditions, dans toute la variété des circonstances de la vie, des discours qu'on reconnaît. S'il est au fond de l'âme du personnage qu'il introduit un sentiment secret, écoutez bien, et vous entendrez un ton dissonant qui le décèlera. C'est que Richardson a reconnu que le mensonge ne pouvait jamais ressembler parfaitement à la vérité. (Garnier, *OE*, 32)

There seems ample justification for thinking that Diderot has taken careful note of Richardson's ability to manipulate the expectations in language. What appears to us as arrant hypocrisy, even cruelty, in the abuse of conduct-book phraseology which we encounter in, for example, Arabella and James Harlowe, can seem a piously appropriate application of good sense to the older Harlowes. Moral deafness makes these characters bad listeners: they cannot hear the dissonant tones in a language whose falsity strikes the reader (morally acute, thanks to Clarissa's mediation) like the gong of doom. But Diderot, being Diderot, is not specific in this passage. He has, intuitively, it appears, seen a rhetorical principle, a literary method, at work in Richardson; but its operation has not crystallized in his mind into concrete examples.

Superficially, he suggests that Richardson has greatly expanded the familiar eighteenth-century notion of typicality. We are used to thinking of the typical representative of a group or class of individuals in seventeenth- and eighteenth-century literature: the rake, the honest apprentice, the clever lady's maid, the miser, and so on. Though each of these figures may be a type within a class, the types are distinct from one another. Each has its unique, and instantly recognizable, mode of discourse. Diderot is undoubtedly making the point which we would expect from him: that Richardson is a master of this sort of typicality. He adds later, when he again admires the number and diversity of Richardson's characters, that it is impossible to confuse one voice with another. They are all distinct: ' Dans ce livre immortel, comme dans la nature au printemps, on ne trouve point deux feuilles qui soient d'un même vert' (Garnier, *OE*, 39).

But behind this admiration for Richardson's obvious ability to create individuals, there lies an interesting tendency to find a unifying principle in the very act of individuation. There is some ambiguity even in the phrasing of the paragraph: is there *one* discourse common to all individuals, or is *each* discourse recognizable according to the type of person who uses it? Another comparison reminds us more of *Le Neveu de Rameau* than of Richardson's novel: 'Il y en a jusqu'à quarante [personnages] dans *Grandisson*, mais ce qui confond d'étonnement, c'est que chacun a ses idées, ses expressions, son ton; et que ces idées, ces expressions, ce ton varient selon les circonstances, les intérêts, les passions, comme on voit sur un même visage les physiognomies diverses des passions se succéder' (Garnier, *OE*, 39).

This analogy may be seen simply as a testimony to the lifelikeness of the characters, or it can be seen as an analogy which makes the work of art itself anthropomorphic. The individuality of the characters seems to be less significant than the expressiveness of the novel as a whole; it is as if the novel were an actor, in fact, whose gestures were the characters. Perhaps it is the discourse we recognize, and the characters who are merely expressions of it, secondary qualities of an expressive essence.

If one is to judge on the basis of Roger Kempf's approach to Diderot, such a conclusion does not seem at all farfetched. Kempf suggests that for Diderot the book is so much an expression of the self that it, in a sense, chooses its reader. Total engagement is demanded: anything less is an insult to the author. Kempf adds that this contempt for the readers of his own time, most of whom would have been unable to commit themselves to his work in this way, had much to do with Diderot's obsession with posterity. Like Stendhal, he envisioned a chosen few in future generations who would give his ideas, give *himself*, as he was embodied in those ideas, the passionate appreciation which they deserved.[23] Richardson, because he engaged his readers so totally, became Diderot's standard for the ability to absorb the reader into the intensity of participation which reading should become: 'Les ouvrages de Richardson plairont plus ou moins à tout homme, dans tous les temps et dans tous les lieux; mais le nombre des lecteurs ne sera jamais grand: il faut un goût trop sévère. . .' (Garnier, *OE*, 32). When Diderot himself is the reader, observer, or critic, rather than the creator, he, too, experiences the extinction of personality that such an effort requires. It is the sign of a person of sensibility, 'd'un goût exquis' (Garnier, *OE*, 33).

As Kempf suggests, the work of art for Diderot operates upon the reader or observer in mysterious, enchanting ways.[24] It is unified by the consciousness of its creator, which is bodied forth in what appears to be pure energy (in the case of literature, this would be language, or linguistic energy). The characters and the situations of the Richardsonian novel, as we have seen, are only a way of clothing the creative force. There is nothing moral about this process: in fact, it is remarkably like that described in *Le Rêve de d'Alembert*, where energy is co-original with matter, and inseparable from it.[25]

If the applications of this notion of a single creative force seem at first wildly disparate, since they are drawn from the fine arts, from language, from cosmology or from the biological sciences, the notion itself is consistent – for Diderot, remarkably consistent. Kempf is probably right to link the obliteration of the reader in the sheer power of the work of art to Diderot's unceasing subjectivism. It is the self that talks, that writes, that creates characters on stage. If, morally, the self cannot act, or be anything but passive, it is all action when it can pour itself, as energy, into an object: a conversation, a role in a play, a book, a painting. Even the universe, if one can dehumanize the image enough, may be seen as an integrated self on a cosmic scale, subject to the same processes as the lesser selves of artists. Diderot's famous digressions are nothing more than an expression of his trust in himself: integration may be a mysterious process, but nothing is irrelevant to it.

By this criterion, Diderot's comparison of Richardson's novels to the Bible is less extravagant than it at first appears. Like the Bible, Richardson's work is the exuberant outpouring of natural energy into a multiplicity of creations. Yet we are immediately brought up short. For the Bible is first of all, of course, a collection of moral laws, and only secondly an extended poem full of 'hieroglyphs' that invite readers to wonder and to lose themselves in contemplation. Because we are readers, we must eventually give ourselves up to reality, and become moral beings again.

Richardson's novels, like the Bible, not only embody truths but help us better to perceive truth in all things: they force us to take sides on moral issues. Diderot tells us about the effects which *Clarissa* has on some of his acquaintances. It has kept a woman from engaging in a potentially adulterous relationship (we know from his correspondence that the woman in question was Sophie Volland's married sister, and her epistolary lover a man whom Diderot later considered as a possible husband for his daughter, Angélique), and it has caused a rupture between two friends (probably Mme d'Épinay and *her* daughter Angélique) because the latter had the baseness to laugh at some of the most touching scenes in *Clarissa* (Garnier, *OE*, 42–3). By the way those closest to us read Richardson, we learn about their real nature. Sometimes the lesson is painful:

J'ai vu, de la diversité des jugements, naître des haines secrètes, des mépris cachés . . . Alors, je comparais l'ouvrage de Richardson à un livre plus sacré encore, à un évangile apporté sur la terre pour séparer l'époux de l'épouse, le père du fils, la fille de la mère, le frère de la soeur; et son travail rentrait ainsi dans la condition des êtres les plus parfaits de la nature. Tous sortis d'une main toute-puissante et d'une intelligence infiniment sage, il n'y a aucun qui ne pèche par quelque endroit. Un bien présent peut être dans l'avenir la source d'un grand mal; un mal, la source d'un grand bien.   (Garnier, *OE*, 38)

For the priests of Diderot's century – with the possible exception of such worldly *abbés* as Raynal, Galiani, Arnaud and Prévost – this passage would have been yet another outrageous example of the *philosophe*'s almost continual blasphemies. We, on the other hand, might well be shocked by the damage which Richardson suffers in the comparison. If the Bible has caused so much unhappiness and bloodshed, and driven apart those who should be most intimately connected, it is difficult to see how it can be considered morally good. How can Diderot compare a work he so admires to the collection of prejudices which he believes the Bible to be? His retreat into a Shaftesbury-like optimism is not convincing, though we can as easily read the same lines as an example of Diderot's tolerance of disparity and injustice: the dispassionate scientist in him recognizes an organic, if mysterious, necessity in the order of things. We may agree that, as in life, there is no character in Richardson 'qui ne pèche par quelque endroit', though it is difficult to think of Richardson's hand, twitching with palsy and nervousness, as 'une main toute-puissante'.

But for Diderot, characteristically, the line between fiction and reality is shifting and blurred. We can see that the ways of God are enigmatic; that causality is hidden from us, that good and evil are 'so strangely mixed', as Clarissa would say, that we can never know if we do not carry the seeds for our own destruction in our present happiness, and so on. All of this is truism; and Diderot himself no longer believed in the benevolent intelligence who had all things in hand. But this speculation applies to human reality: even most Romantics would not claim as much unconditioned mystery for art. It is difficult to imagine that Diderot thought Richardson's novels capable of as rich a spread of possibility as life itself. Yet it is not clear that his implicit analogy is meant to be about the *effects* which reading Richardson might have on future generations. He himself seems to shrug his shoulders and move on to easier matters (that is, the effect that the novel has on him in the present) when he writes:

Mais, qu'importe, si, grâce à cet auteur, j'ai plus aimé mes semblables, plus aimé mes devoirs; si je n'ai eu pour les méchants que la pitié; si j'ai conçu plus de commisération pour les malheureux, plus de vénération pour les bons, plus de circonspection dans l'usage des choses présentes, plus d'indifférence sur les choses futures, plus de mépris pour la vie, et plus d'amour pour la vertu; le seul bien, que nous puissions demander au ciel, et le seul qu'il puisse nous accorder, sans nous châtier de nos demandes aux cieux!   (Garnier, *OE*, 38)

We are back to the fatalism of Diderot's earlier pages, in which we are asked to resign ourselves to the evils in life. Here (and this makes the novelistic/*drame sérieux* treatment of self-immolation so different from that in Greek or neoclassical tragedy) Richardson's works teach his readers to go back to life with renewed sociability. Once more, it is a sentimental education that we take with us from reading Richardson: we 'love', we 'pity', we 'commiserate', we 'venerate' in social life; we scorn existence. We have learned to perceive and understand suffering, though we go on no quests for truth, goodness or even change.

Though Diderot comes back to the didactic capabilities of art often in this essay, and in his discussions of the *drame sérieux* and painting, he is least interesting when he tries to describe the relationship between art and morality. Those who have attempted to find a way in which art can change behaviour (most notably Brecht, of course) have run into the same problems: the moral effects are always subsumed by the aesthetic ones. A critique or theory of judgment, to borrow from Kant, must always come first, even in the post-Romantic and anti-classicist twentieth century. While Diderot gives us a detailed and profound description of the absorption of the passive spectator or reader into the work of art, he never effectively reconciles the act of aesthetic contemplation with the infusion of virtue into the consciousness of the same spectator. We are left only with heightened awareness, which could be an effect of the aesthetic experience alone: the moral effects seem rather to be a kind of by-product.

Diderot, then, was neither the first nor the last to discover that a didactic intention could be at odds with aesthetic creation. The difficulty was exacerbated for him, as Dieckmann has also suggested, because the gap between illusion, the world created in a work of art, and empirical reality was hard enough to close; and the perception of a consistent reality was problematical without the addition of moral judgments.

Needless to say, this radical doubt even of empirical reality makes our task in trying to understand Diderot as a reader of Richardson yet more complex. The paradox which Dieckmann has seen in Diderot's commentary – how can an imitative reality be truer than empirical reality? – is still not the basic question. If, indeed, a work of art can be truer than the life we lead, should it imitate the details of ordinary existence, which are recognizable to all readers, or should it imitate the grander forms which are obscured by daily life? It is, of course, the difference between the neo-Aristotelian view of art still current among the neoclassical writers in France, and the neo-Platonic view of philosophers like Shaftesbury. We need only look at a passage from the *Éloge* to see how profound Diderot's mistrust of empirical reality (or historical reality, as he calls it) could be:

O Richardson! J'oserai dire que l'histoire la plus vraie est pleine de mensonges, et que ton roman est plein de vérités. L'histoire peint quelques individus; tu peins l'espèce humaine: l'histoire attribue à quelques individus ce qu'ils n'ont ni dit, ni fait; tout ce que tu attribues à l'homme, il l'a dit et fait: l'histoire n'embrasse qu'une portion de la durée, qu'un point de la surface du globe; tu as embrassé tous les lieux et tous les temps. Le coeur humain, qui a été, est et sera toujours le même, est le modèle d'après lequel tu copies. . . . Sous ce point de vue, j'oserai dire que souvent l'histoire est un mauvais roman; et que le roman, comme tu l'as fait, est une bonne histoire. O peintre de la nature! C'est toi qui ne mens jamais. (Garnier, *OE*, 39–40)

If this is an example of eighteenth-century ahistoricism at its purest, it does not arise because Diderot has a clear idea of a true reality to offer as an alternative to history. His praise of Richardson at the expense of historical reality seems literally (and unusually, for him) to pass over the essential point that the novels are *fiction*. But they are true to human nature (an underlying constant which, for the materialistic *philosophe*, seems to replace the Platonic notion of essence), and therefore imitate reality better than the mere chronicling of events can do. This is not, however, a very satisfying juxtaposition of history and fiction. It is almost as if the over-individuation in actual historical time, the constant occurrence of events which are so unlikely as to be *romanesque*, *invraisemblable*, is a kind of fiction gone mad – a fiction in which there are no rules.

In art, however, other principles must operate. It is no Romantic anachronism to attribute the notion of a shaping artistic consciousness to Diderot. For him, the imagination has not yet assumed the ascendancy it would enjoy in the theories of Coleridge and the German Idealists. But neither is the artist a slavish imitator of that confusing external reality which Diderot calls history; nor is he restricted to the conventions of neoclassical form (though Diderot is quite capable of playing with neoclassical concepts. See, for example, the opening of the 'Premier entretien' accompanying *Le Fils naturel*).[26] We have already discussed the dilemma in which Diderot places himself: what sort of realism does then belong to the artist; and if the province of art is the human spirit, what is the artist's obligation in the realm of ethics? If we are to judge by his exaltation of Richardson, we must conclude that the great artist is capable of creating a world at least as valid as, and certainly parallel to, the empirical world. Even vice and error have their place in art, but they are purified of the accidental qualities which they possess in real life, and are made into examples which guide rather than mislead.

The problem is, of course, that human nature is itself torn as much as is the empirical reality to which human beings belong. If history is full of *mensonges*, is the goblin in the cave, who is clearly there to deceive us, the bearer of truth? For Diderot, Richardson has raised the deepest questions of epistemology. Is the Moor true, or is he real? It is difficult to see how he can be both, since reality, in this context, seems to be the province of deception. Yet the imitation of reality in fiction somehow leads to a genuine perception of things. Similarly, we must ask ourselves about the relationship between *mensonge* and *illusion* in Diderot's work. It is obvious that *mensonge* is fundamentally an ethical term. We must consciously distort the truth in order to lie. But *illusion* is a distortion of the consciousness itself. Either we believe something to be true when it is not, or we deliberately create an appearance of truth. The material for our distortion comes either from empirical reality, itself an entity of dubious validity for Diderot, or from that *vérité, l'espèce humaine*. Nonetheless, illusion, when applied to human problems in art, preserves and clarifies the truths it finds, and there is the heart of the paradox.

Diderot has chosen an author as his model of truthful imitation in art whose greatest work is nothing but a portrayal of various sorts of distortion. The characters at Harlowe Place are either hypocritical or deluded. Lovelace himself is probably the most consummate liar in the history of fiction. Clarissa learns to understand herself only through violation and madness; her nobility of character does not give her clarity of vision. But it is the very duplicity – or, as modern critics might put it, the ambiguity – of the text which makes it a vehicle of truth for Diderot. Perhaps it is not surprising that a popular educator and rationalist should show such enthusiasm for Richardson's sombre and passionate books. What we have in all three of the novels, but particularly in *Clarissa*, is the unfolding of a process of self-education. As process, Richardson's vision is large enough to encompass the apparent contradictions in Diderot's estimation of him: a lying protagonist is true to life, if not truthful, because we never come to self-awareness without being shaken into questioning reality. We feel that Clarissa is triumphant because, in the end, she has used the hypocrisy and the lies to construct a new and braver reality: the sturdy integrity which grows outward from the self.

5
SEX AND THE *PHILOSOPHE*

Diderot and the critique of erotic decadence

The complexity of the struggles of the eighteenth century must not be oversimplified. But the contradictions, specifically in the work of Diderot, must be seen for what they are; and Diderot's enthusiasm for things English must be given a context. In the realm of morality, Diderot and his colleagues are indeed fighting a battle on two fronts. The two *infâmes*: religious excess, whether through individual practice or through institutionalized strangulation; and sexual licence, so closely related to that greater hypocrisy, are intertwined as they have not been in previous centuries, because they involve a language and ethical structure that have become emptied of meaning through constant but unquestioned use since the seventeenth century. A typical example of the attitude towards religion among the ladies who moved in the highest circles may be seen in the conduct of Mme de Geoffrin and Mme du Deffand. They were both unbelievers who practised the forms of religion for the sake of convention.[1]

Thus, we find Diderot and Rousseau working on the paradoxes which they saw at the root of a godless and worldly society that professed to honour both religion and virtue. Lucien Goldmann has observed this attraction to paradox in the two *philosophes* as well.[2] But, unlike the tragic writers of the seventeenth century, Diderot and his friends are able to make their *aperçus* the ground of action. Because these paradoxes are no longer seen as the source of primarily internal and personal struggles, they become susceptible to criticism (and, in the case of Diderot, to ridicule). They are dead weeds, as it were, which a healthy breath can blow away. Underneath there is new growth, and a new world.

The exploitation of this state of things in the eighteenth century is entertainingly various. Robert Darnton, for example, has shown how the illicit book trade of the century consisted of a mixture of subversive political propaganda and pornography, often combined in the same works.[3] The *Mémoires* of Casanova, whose real-life adventures afford occasional interesting parallels to those in French fiction of the same period, give us a clue to the ease with which the libertine could give a philosophical justification for sexual freedom. Though Casanova writes in a clumsy Italianate French, there are some echoes which suggest that he has surely read his Shaftesbury (or his Diderot, since he counted Voltaire and d'Alembert among his acquaintances):

Heureux ceux qui, sans nuire à personne, savent s'en procurer, et insensés ceux qui s'imaginent que le Grand-Être puisse jouir des douleurs, des peines et des abstinences qu'ils lui offrent en sacrifice, et qu'il ne chérisse que les extravagants qui se les imposent. Dieu ne peut exiger des ses créatures que l'exercice des vertus dont il a placé le germe dans leur âme, et il ne nous a rien donné qu'à dessein de nous rendre heureux; amour-propre, ambition d'éloges, sentiment d'émulation.[4]

Casanova opens the history of his exploits, in fact, with a credo: 'L'homme est libre, mais il cesse de l'être, s'il ne croit pas à sa liberté; et plus il suppose de force au destin, plus il se prive de celle que Dieu lui a donné en le douant de raison.'[5] Despite the gracelessness of the phrasing, it could serve as a credo for Lovelace, or for some of Diderot's heroes and heroines, particularly in *La Religieuse* and in *Jacques le fataliste*, for whom the question of freedom versus destiny (now that the will of God is not an acceptable excuse for an apparently relentless order in nature) is the more pressing in the shadow of scientific materialism. We might add that Casanova was, of course, imprisoned by the Inquisition; and that he was also, like a number of other Enlightenment figures, a freemason and student of the occult. The likenesses between the sociable secrecy of so many intellectuals, and the sociable but precarious reliance on convention of the women who frequented the salons, might make a profitable study.

In Diderot's own work, as in that of his contemporaries in all aspects of literary production, then, the two attacks on religious hypocrisy and sexual dishonesty go side by side. *La Promenade du sceptique*, for example, which was written in 1747 but confiscated before it could be published (A–T, I, 173), is a particularly clear case. There are three paths in Diderot's parabolic park. The first is filled with thorns, and is travelled by the pious; the second is covered with flowers, and is the broad road of pleasure and society; the third, lined with chestnut trees, is the way of philosophy. The religious fanatics of the thorny path are concerned with self-laceration and self-deprivation: they are blind, fervent and hypocritical. Significantly, Diderot gives us a description of their dress and accessories:

On trouve dans l'allée des épines des haires, des cilices, des disciplines, des masques, des recueils de pieuses rêveries, des colifichets mystiques, des recettes pour garantir sa robe de taches, ou pour la détacher, et je ne sais combien d'instructions pour porter fermement son bandeau, instructions qui sont toutes superflues pour les sots, et entre lesquels il n'y a pas une bonne pour les gens sensés. (A–T, I, 194)

This amusing description tells us that moral blindness and the obsessive concern with virginity lead to stupidity and hypocrisy. We are told later, in fact, that many of the walkers on the thorny path spend their nights among the flowers (A–T, I, 195). Should we miss the implication that any *taches* on clothing have something to do with the sins of sexuality, we can turn to the description of dress among the travellers on the path of flowers for a companion-piece in innuendo: 'Leur robe est dans un état pitoyable; ils la font savonner par intervalle; mais ce blanchissage dure peu; il n'est que de bienséance. On dirait que leur dessein principal soit de la chamarrer de tant de taches, qu'on n'en reconnaisse plus la couleur primitive' (A–T, I, 239).

The 'Allée des fleurs' is populated largely by women:

Ce qui donne le ton chez ce peuple léger; c'est un certain nombre de femmes charmantes par l'art et le désir qu'elles ont de plaire. L'une se glorifie d'un grand nombre d'adorateurs, et veut que le public en soit informé: l'autre se plaît à faire beaucoup d'heureux, mais il faut que leur bonheur soit ignoré. Telle promettra ses faveurs à mille galants, qui ne les accordera qu'à un seul; telle n'en bercera qu'un seul d'espérance, qui ne sera pas inhumaine à cent autres; et tout cela à la faveur d'un secret que personne ne garde; car il est ridicule d'ignorer les aventures d'une jolie femme, et il est de mode d'en enfler le nombre au besoin. (A–T, I, 238)

In this passage we are able to discern the true relics of the preciosity of past generations.[6] The ladies meet their friends in their boudoirs, from which only husbands are excluded. They are surrounded by the heirs to the *précieux* (the male habitués of the seventeenth-century salons), who in the eighteenth century are contemptuously called *petits-maîtres*. They are a degenerate race, and not at all courtly in the seventeenth-century sense. Instead, they are eager to gratify the physical desires of their mistresses, on the one hand, and the desire for amusement of the company they keep, on the other. Their language, correspondingly, is inflated out of proportion to the insignificant subjects of their patter:

Là s'assemblent des jeunes gens folâtres et quelquefois entreprenants, parlant de tout sans rien savoir, donnant à des riens un air de finesse, adroits à séduire une belle en déchirant ses rivales, passant d'un raisonnement sérieux qu'ils ont entamé, au récit d'une aventure galante, ou une circonstance les accroche et les jette, je ne sais comment, sur une ariette, qu'ils interrompent pour parler politique, et conclure par des réflexions profondes sur une coiffure, une robe, un magot de la Chine, une nudité de Clinschsted, une jatte de Saxe, une pantine de Boucher, quelque colifichet d'Hébert, ou une boîte de Juliette ou de Martin.   (A–T, I, 238)

This could be the world of Pope in *The Rape of the Lock*, or, even better, in *Epistle to a Lady*. The obsession with the small decorative objects with which aristocratic ladies surround themselves reminds us obliquely of Richardson's character, Lord G., the husband of the former Charlotte Grandison, who discusses china with the singlemindedness and passion which we now associate with small homeowners when they ponder the implications of leaky roofs and faulty drains.[7] Diderot's scenario shows us, by contrast, that Richardson could not have offered a faithful rendition of the aristocratic banter required for chat about the baubles of eighteenth-century upper-class life: the talk is wholly un-bourgeois and un-sober. It is revealing that Diderot is able to do so. As an intellectual, he has been accepted as an honorary member of the highest society: the days of such figures as the Duc de Rohan, who set his men on the youthful Voltaire, are rapidly declining. In fact, to return to our passage, the flightiness of the conversation (the *petits-maîtres* would perhaps have called it airiness), the pretentious 'lyricism' and careful turns of phrase about minutiae, are the logical consequences of the affectations in language which were cultivated in *précieux* circles in the seventeenth century. At the same time, Diderot's rather too defensively hearty descriptions of the behaviour of some of his aristocratic friends give us a hint that vulgarity was by no means excluded from the houses of the great.

There is the famous example of Mme d'Houdetot's *Hymne aux Tétons* (Roth, III, 107) but more significant is the account of life at Grandval, the Baron d'Holbach's country estate, which Diderot gives in a letter to Sophie (30 October 1759). In these pages, we are given an extremely lively rendition of the counterpoint of conversation in an informal setting. Diderot is holding forth on Mohammedanism (and with far too much perseverance for the taste of the company, as he scrupulously informs us). His sermon is interrupted incessantly by the ladies' teasing and gossip. The most outrageous of them is Mme d'Aine, the mother-in-law of the Baron, who keeps up a scabrous commentary on various subjects (Roth, II, 297). She spends most of the evening making coarse remarks about the ugliness of the *cul* of her lady's maid, who remains polite and docile despite it all (Roth, II, 298ff). She is ignorant, and a Mrs Malaprop into the bargain. Diderot describes her unique nomenclature with much amusement – she refers to the *Encyclopédie* as 'la Socoplie', for example (Roth, II, 306). Finally, he describes a particularly violent romp with a good-natured abbé which ends in a mutual loss of bladder control.

All of these escapades are seen by Diderot as endearing and entertaining moments in a life of aristocratic ease. There is no doubt that they are entertaining for a contemporary reader, if somewhat colourful, but one cannot help wondering about the enforced complaisance of the lady's maid and the abbé. Diderot seems to think Mme d'Aine the soul of generosity when she replaces the ruined clothes of the abbé: ' Madame d'Aine est honorable. Le petit prêtre est pauvre. Dès le lendemain, il y eut ordre d'acheter un habit complet. Comment trouverez vouz cela, mesdames de la ville? Pour nous, grossiers habitants du Grandval, il ne nous faut pas davantage pour nous amuser et le jour et le lendemain' (Roth, II, 307–8). There is a certain edgy obsessiveness with detail and apology here: one senses that Mme d'Aine's insensitivity to people of humble origin has not gone unnoticed by the *philosophe*, though he can include himself in the aristocratic *nous* at Grandval. It is interesting in any case to observe how the form of the *précieux* salon has been retained (even in this rather eccentric example), although it has become strongly flavoured with what writers of the period called *gauloiserie*, the infusion of what were perceived as Gallic high spirits.

When the women in *La Promenade du sceptique* speak, then, we have some idea of the range of subtlety of which they are capable. They use an inflated language, full of exaggerated adverbs and adjectives, but they are no more scrupulous than Mme d'Aine was in Diderot's anecdote. This inflation has already been the bane of the anti-*précieux* factions at the time of Mlle de Scudéry: Bray gives us an example in the overuse of the neological adverb *furieusement*.[8] In one of Diderot's little stories about life on the flowery path, a lady chatters in a similar conventional hyperbole. Bélise keeps hinting at improprieties in the behaviour of her best friend, who is about to marry the man to whom Bélise is speaking. When he, in horror, rephrases plainly each time what he thinks she has said, she answers repeatedly: 'Je ne dis pas cela . . .,' and she adds at one point: ' mais on a jasé, et je suis de la dernière surprise que vous ne soyez pas mieux informé . . . C'est quelque chose de terrible que ces premiers engagements . . .' (A–T, I, 245). She is full of exaggerations and overstatements; and the fluffiness of her diction increases the sinister implications of her meaning. This obliqueness is part of the aristocratic code of good breeding. As we shall see in 'Sur les femmes', it draws on an essentially feminine rhetoric. Indeed, when

Sterne, who became a warm friend of Diderot's, visited Paris in 1762, he did not fail to give a rendition of what appeared to him as a peculiarly feminine form of Gallic exaggeration. His own use of a diabolical reference for female sexuality is very English. We have seen it often in *Clarissa*:

> here everything is hyperbolized – and if a woman is but simply pleased – 'tis *Je suis charmée* – and if she is charmed 'tis nothing less, than that she is *ravi*-sh'd – and when ravi-sh'd (which may happen) there is nothing left for her but to fly to the other world for a metaphor, and swear, qu'elle étoit toute *extasiée* – which mode of speaking, is, by the bye, here creeping into use, and there is scarce a woman who understands the *bon ton*, but it is seven times in a day in downright extasy – that is, the devil's in her – by a small mistake of one world for the other –[9]

We cite at length from this early work because it gives us such a clear picture of Diderot's view of religious fanaticism and of aristocratic decadence. (Needless to say, the description of the path of chestnuts is placed midway between the description of the paths of thorns and of flowers, and its users are philosophers, all male, who neither care about the condition of their clothes, nor use unscrupulous language.) More specifically, the passages reflect the historical fact that women were considered primarily responsible for the social life of the salons – again, perhaps partially because they were the heiresses of *précieux* culture. The active lifetimes of Mme de Lambert and of Mme de Tencin, in fact, overlapped with the most successful years of the salon of Mme de Rambouillet, and with the lifetimes of such *philosophes* as Montesquieu and Voltaire (in the case of Mme de Tencin, with those of Diderot and Rousseau as well). Some suggestive aspects of these passages also lead us readily into a brief look at Diderot's *Bijoux indiscrets*, the pornographic novel which he published in 1748.

For one thing, there is a striking similarity between the talk at Mangogul's court and the conversation of the women and *petits-maîtres* in the *Promenade du sceptique*: an obsession with trinkets is given seriousness through the sheer volume of language devoted to it. We must not forget, indeed, the obvious point that the genitals are conventionally called 'bijoux' at this time: according to Lawrence Stone, in fact, a 'bijoux indiscret' was a dildo.[10] It follows, then, that *bijoutiers* are at one point summoned in to make muzzles for the loquacious vaginas. It is the sultan Mangogul's magic ring which is creating all the havoc among the women of his kingdom. And when the sultan places a bet with his favourite concubine, Mirzoza, that there is not a chaste woman to be found in his realm, the prize is significant. 'Je publierai,' says the sultan, '. . . que je suis enchanté de votre raisonnement sur la possibilité des femmes sages; j'accréditerai votre logique de tout mon pouvoir; et je vous donnerai mon château d'Amara, avec toutes les porcelaines de Saxe dont il est orné, sans en excepter le petit sapajou, en émail, et les autres colifichets précieux . . .' (DPV, III, 144). All of this suggests that sexuality is surrounded by artifice, *is* artifice, perhaps; that the decorative style of the period is not unrelated to a lack of candour and simplicity in sexual relations. One could even go so far as to suggest that the clockmaker God of the seventeenth century, now transformed into a trivialized deity of rococo jewellery and technology in the eighteenth, has created a new danger: the possibility that human beings and their emotions may be counterfeited too. Aram Vartanian, in his article entitled 'Érotisme et philosophie chez Diderot', has also suggested that the materialism of the period radically altered the notions of sexuality and sin: if human beings were susceptible to physical laws alone, then all the precepts of religion could be shown to be irrelevant. At the same time, for Diderot as for Shaftesbury, sexuality, with its pitfalls and pleasures, became a metaphor for the philosopher's quest for knowledge.[11] One might conclude that the striking obsession in the *Bijoux* with artifice and decoration, with technological innovation in objects both great and trivial, offers an early hint that Diderot was aware of the limits and the damaging effects of knowledge.

As for the novel itself, which Diderot wrote on a dare from Mme de Puisieux, his mistress at the time, we can let the reviewer from the *Correspondance littéraire* (then known as the *Nouvelles littéraires*) give us some background, as well as his judgment. The magazine in 1748 was in the hands of the Abbé Raynal, who was not yet acquainted with the *philosophe*. The reviewer puts the would-be pornographer in his place, even while giving him grudging credit for his talents:

Le succès de Crébillon a tourné la tête à mille sots qui ont voulu faire des romans de son genre. Nous venons d'en voir un, intitulé les *Bijoux indiscrets*. Le sujet est un prince qui, à l'aide d'une bague que lui a donnée un génie, force les bijoux de toutes les femmes à révéler leurs secrètes intrigues. Cette idée n'est pas neuve, et elle avait été traitée dans un autre ouvrage aussi licencieux, intitulé *Nocrion*. Les *Bijoux indiscrets* sont obscurs, mal écrits, dans un mauvais ton grossier et d'un homme qui connaît mal le monde qu'il a voulu peindre. L'auteur est M. Diderot, qui a des connaissances très-étendues, et beaucoup d'esprit, mais qui n'est pas fait pour le genre dans lequel il veut travailler.[12]

Although Naigeon claimed that Diderot was ashamed of the book until the end of his life, it has been shown that the *philosophe* added two chapters in 1757. He gained a certain amount of notoriety through this excursion into low forms,[13] but there is much of interest in it for the modern reader. We see the impact of Swift, for example, in the ludicrous meetings of the Académie de Banza, at which the scientists attempt to explain the mystery of the babbling *bijoux* (DPV, I, ch. 10). There is an overt reference to Swift, indeed, when Mangogul, in an excess of *ennui*, takes to the stables and turns his ring on his mare. The *bijou* speaks in horse-language, which has been translated, we are told, by Gulliver himself (DPV, III, 130). There are commentaries and satires on religion (throughout); on the state of French music (DPV, III, ch. 13); on one of Diderot's favourite subjects, the *clavecin oculaire* (DPV, III, vol. II, 275); on letters and the *Querelle des anciens et des modernes* (DPV, III, vol. II, ch. 5); and on the genre of the novel itself. One of the most interesting chapters consists of Mangogul's account of an allegorical dream he has had in which experimental science takes over from the old *esprit de système* – and as Diderot rightly adds in his subtitle, it is 'Le meilleur peut-être, et le moins lu de cette histoire' (DPV, III, 130). There are also some remarkably scabrous sections. In one, a well-travelled *bijou* talks in the languages which she spoke to her foreign lovers. She turns from English to Latin to Italian to a broken mixture of Spanish and Italian. The English fragment, at least, is far coarser than any French passage in the book. With the exception of the mysterious appellation of a part of the body called the 'Tarse', the grammar, idiomatic use and vocabulary are perfect, suggesting that Diderot had quite a considerable command of English (DPV, III, 219). (Robert Loyalty Cru, however, has pointed out that Diderot was capable of some hilarious mistranslations.)[14]

Female sexuality as a disease

When we turn our attention to the question of female sexuality, however, we find that one of the most interesting hints in the *Bijoux* is offered casually, almost in an aside. If sexual relations, and human relations in general, seem to suffer from the excessively self-conscious decorativeness of the rococo, female sexuality appears to be linked to a specific notion of disease. Diderot devotes a number of pages to the amorous adventures of the courtier Sélim, a thinly disguised version of the Duc de Richelieu, who was the most dashing and celebrated lover at the court of Louis XV. A striking characteristic of Sélim's first adventure is that it has one element – smallpox – in common with famous stories of sexual intrigue of the period. Sélim's first love is Émilie, a fourteen-year-old cousin. When it is discovered that she is pregnant, the young Sélim is packed off on the Grand Tour. The way in which he tells the court of the fate of Émile is chillingly revealing:

Je partis avec un gouverneur chargé de veiller attentivement sur ma conduite, et de ne la point gêner; et cinq mois après, j'appris par la gazette qu'Émilie était morte de la petite-vérole, et par une lettre de mon père, que la tendresse qu'elle avait eue pour moi, lui coûtait la vie. Le premier fruit de mes amours sert avec distinction dans les troupes du sultan: je l'ai toujours soutenu par mon crédit; et il ne me connaît encore que pour son protecteur [at the time of this account, Sélim is an old man]. (DPV, III, 201)

Émilie is passed over in one sentence, and the arrival of an illegitimate son in another; the next begins with Sélim's adventures in Tunisia. His listeners do not show surprise or dismay, and Sélim is not painted as a cruel man. His counsel is often wise, and his view of women, on the whole, is sympathetic; it is simply understood that he had to practise on someone. In any case, it is curious in itself that death by smallpox seems to serve as an acceptable euphemism for death as a result of sexual indiscretion.

One might perhaps call it coincidence that Casanova, a real-life lover, describes his first encounter in similar, though happier, terms. The fifteen-year-old girl with whom he is infatuated at the age of twelve is a sister of the priest who is the young Casanova's teacher and landlord. She first feigns possession by demons when she fears that she might be suspected of sexual delinquency (though she is in fact innocent). This is suggestive enough for a modern reader: exorcism doesn't help, but frank conversations with Casanova do. She never sleeps with him, but develops a terrible case of smallpox. Casanova nurses her safely through, though he contracts some pustules and involuntarily inoculates himself.[15] She is for some time in danger of permanent disfigurement. Casanova tells this tale with the rather touching artlessness that characterizes his style: he does not make judgments. Nevertheless, we feel that it was a narrow escape, and that the child's virginity may well have helped her.

When we recall Rousseau's Julie, we begin to wonder about coincidence as an explanation for these similarities. She, too, develops smallpox, though instead of dying she marries M. de Wolmar, against her own inclinations. Her lover, Saint-Preux, contracts the disease because he kisses her hand when he rushes in to see her during the crisis of her illness.[16] Perhaps Rousseau had heard this story through friends of friends who knew Casanova. Unlikely though it may seem, Casanova claims in his Mémoires that he actually met Rousseau at Mme d'Urfé's in 1757. He later refers to Rousseau's novel as 'l'infâme roman de la Nouvelle Héloïse'.[17] Julie, of course, is no virgin. The initial affair with Saint-Preux has no devastating repercussions, unless one counts the deadening purity of her married life as an effect of her youthful indiscretion. She dies a matron, and another man's wife, many years after her bout of smallpox. Yet after the very letter in which she confesses eternal love to Saint-Preux (having learned about his presence at her bedside from her cousin Claire), she marries Wolmar; and with her marriage comes conversion. In retrospect, the love which she feels for Saint-Preux in her convalescence is illusory: the illness itself has somehow prepared her for a marriage of convenience, and for the joyful fulfilment of duty. Her heart-rending last letter, included as it were posthumously in M. de Wolmar's account of her death, emphatically reaffirms her love for Saint-Preux, however: 'Je me suis longtemps fait illusion. Cette illusion me fut salutaire; elle se détruit au moment que je n'en ai plus besoin. Vous m'avez crue guérie, et j'ai cru l'être' (Garnier, *La Nouvelle Héloïse*, p. 728).

The most famous case of literary smallpox, after Julie's, is Mme de Merteuil's in *Les Liaisons dangereuses*. Here, smallpox has become a visitation from heaven. It is not a punishment for a first innocent lapse, as in the case of Sélim's Émilie; it ends neither in a complete cure nor in death. Instead, it takes on the character of a second Fall (lapsarian imagery abounds in the literature of sex). Mme de Merteuil is a woman who knows too much. The artifice of French society becomes a kind of innocence in comparison with the depth of her total control of its hypocrisies. Ladies are meant to flirt, to lie, to cover up: they are not meant to study the bibles of true feeling, such as *Clarissa*, in order to perfect their seeming. They are not supposed to become as fully ruthless as the code logically invites them to be; they are merely meant to dissemble and to suffer. Mme de Merteuil has become a tool-user, and her tools are other human beings. More essentially, she is very angry. She is a doer and user, on the one hand, and a person who expresses true and unpleasant feelings, on the other. She does so through the manipulation of convention. All of these strategies, except the last, in the eighteenth century as in the twentieth, are expected from men rather than from women. She is expelled from the Opéra, that tattered Eden of Paris society, for her transgression; and in true eighteenth-century fashion her humiliation is accompanied by the laughter of her peers, rather than by the thunder of the gods. The degree of wrath, however, is quite as relentless in Paris as it might have been in Paradise. The evening after her expulsion from the Opéra, she contracts the case of smallpox that disfigures her for ever.[18]

It would be pointless to try to force an evolutionary pattern out of the appearance of illness in these four disparate works, one of which is not, ostensibly, fiction at all. But it is curious that smallpox seems to be a conventional fate for sexually adventurous women in the eighteenth century. It is an illness which isolates and disfigures. It has all the properties of contagion which, emotionally, we associate with sexual taboos. While it has the power to make its victim temporarily an outcast from society, because it is so highly infectious, or permanently, through its scars, it can also serve as a test of true love. In this, again, it is like menstruation, pregnancy and childbirth. While women in stable relationships are likely to find that their husbands or lovers are able to overcome their possible repugnance at these overt marks of sexuality, unloved and licentious women are isolated by the same visible signs. In the cases of literary smallpox which we have just enumerated, the virtuous are helped by their lovers, and survive; the lost souls die, and the evil are tormented in the hellfires of ridicule and loneliness (in the case of Sélim's Émilie, of course, smallpox is the 'cover' for the real cause of death, childbirth itself). In all these examples, smallpox is the visible expression in women of their hidden sexual guilt. It seems to act as the public face of venereal disease (which, before it was properly understood, had a long history in male fantasy for what was hidden and destructive in womankind).[19] I am indebted to Dr Marian Jeanneret for reminding me that there is a clear linguistic connection in both English and French between the two maladies. In French, syphilis ('the pox') is *la vérole*, while smallpox is of course *la petite vérole*. When this destructiveness rebounds on a lady in literature, her true hideousness is exposed.[20] The degree of her suffering seems in direct proportion to the degree of her supposed transgression. As a lady says of Mme de Merteuil at the end of *Les Liaisons dangereuses*: 'la maladie l'avait retournée, et [à] présent son âme était sur sa figure'.[21]

This apparent epidemic of literary smallpox, then, may give us some understanding of the ambiguity with which sexual self-expression in women and, by no great extension, female self-expression in general, were regarded in the mid-eighteenth century. It is disconcerting to discover that even in the literature of such an overtly sexual society as that of upper-class France, women are still forced into self-immolation when their sexual knowledge becomes too great. We are reminded of Lovelace, who seeks to prove that Clarissa is 'mere body', and hence merely a woman. In our French examples, we see that women's bodies both define and destroy them: they are made to suffer physically as well as mentally for their sins.

When Diderot deals directly with the subject of female sexuality, on the other hand, there is no sense of sin. Diderot does not moralize: he is concerned with the influence of physiology and social expectation on sexual development and behaviour. But we are still given the portrait

of a pathology. The weakness of the sexual organs, as we shall
makes women susceptible to social weaknesses as well.

Diderot's views on the pathology of femininity

Much has been made of the definition of femininity as a kind of illness
in the nineteenth century, when doctors gradually replace priests as
the directors of women's lives. As is so often the case in intellectual
history, we discover that the *idée reçue* of woman as invalid is already
well established in the eighteenth century. Diderot's short essay, 'Sur
les femmes', is merely one example. It appeared in one of the
Correspondances littéraires of 1772 as a review of a book by a writer named
Thomas on the subject. Diderot reflects the uncertainty of the views of
his age in his volatile but incisive judgments. His materialism leads him
sometimes to see nature (defined, for him, as a physical predisposition)
as a forming principle, and sometimes education. The essay is full of
interleaved references to physical and social conditioning. When we
look at his description of menstruation and its consequences, for
instance, we can see that he indeed regards the monthly cycle as a
disease in essence. But he also mentions the 'despotism' of parents, and
writes in the strongest terms of the 'tyranny' of married life:

c'est à cet instant critique [the beginning of menstruation] qu'une jeune fille
devient ce qu'elle restera toute sa vie, pénétrante ou stupide, triste ou gaie,
sérieuse ou légère, bonne ou méchante, l'espérance de sa mère trompée ou
réalisée. Pendant une longue suite d'années, chaque lune ramènera le même
malaise. Le moment qui la délivrera du despotisme de ses parents est arrivé; son
imagination s'ouvre à un avenir plein de chimères; son coeur nage dans une
joie secrète. Réjouis-toi bien, malheureuse créature; le temps aurait sans cesse
affaibli la tyrannie sous laquelle tu vas passer. On lui choisit un époux. Elle
devient mère. L'état de grossesse est pénible presque pour toutes les femmes.
C'est dans les douleurs, au péril de leur vie, aux dépens de leurs charmes, et
souvent au détriment de leur santé, qu'elles donnent naissance à des enfants.
Le premier domicile de l'enfant et les deux reservoirs de sa nourriture, les
organes qui caractérisent le sexe, sont sujets à deux maladies incurables.

(A–T, II, 257–8)

The appearance of adult sexuality fixes the character of the young
girl. There is, needless to say, a certain contradiction between this
view, so misplaced and yet so close to the genetic determinism of the
twentieth century, and the rhapsodizing on the female personality
which we find both in this essay and elsewhere. Diderot criticizes
Thomas early in the review for relying on erudition, rather than on
feeling, when dealing with such a delicate subject: 'Cependant peu de

nos écrivains du jour auraient été capables d'un travail où l'on remarque de l'érudition, de la raison, de la finesse, du style, de l'harmonie; mais pas assez de variété, de cette souplesse propre à se prêter à l'infinie diversité d'un être extrême dans sa force et dans sa faiblesse, que la vue d'une souris ou d'une araignée fait tomber en syncope, et qui sait quelquefois braver les plus grandes terreurs de la vie' (A–T, II, 251–2). But the clever *philosophe* has not forgotten his determinism after all. What both fixes women and allows them latitude for their supposedly immense swings in emotion and behaviour is passion. The intensity of it distinguishes men from women: 'Les distractions d'une vie occupée et contentieuse rompent nos passions. La femme couve les siennes: c'est un point fixe, sur lequel son oisiveté ou la frivolité de ses fonctions tient son regard sans cesse attaché. Ce point s'étend sans mesure; et pour devenir folle, il ne manquerait à la femme passionnée que l'entière solitude qu'elle recherche' (A–T, II, 252).

Even the language of this passage suggests the sexual origins of this passion in women: Diderot uses the word 'couver' to describe the female tendency to gather her feelings inward. Diderot goes on to discuss female orgasm, and the difficulty many women have in achieving it, with a physiological and emotional sympathy so profound that it would be surprising to find a more perceptive analyst until our own century. Diderot is 'really' telling his readers that the uterus is the centre of repression, but that the social environment acts as an instrument of restraint or encouragement, oppression or liberation. In the description of menstruation, for example, we move from the monthly malaise to the moment which delivers the young girl from 'despotism' with such speed that it takes two readings to recognize that the despotism is not physiological, but parental.

Women, then, are formed and ruled by the sicknesses which define them: menstruation, childbirth, lactation, the menopause. Diderot holds the eighteenth-century view that hysteria is unique to women, and he does not question its etymology any more than would his contemporaries. The article 'Sensibilité, Sentiment (Médicine)' in the *Encyclopédie*, for example, is by one Dr Fouquet, and contains the following paragraph:

Quant aux femmes, leur constitution approche beaucoup, comme on sait, de celle des enfans; les passions sont chez elles extrêmement plus vives en général que chez les hommes. Leur grande *sensibilité*, dont un des principaux centres est l'utérus, les jette aussi dans des maladies que la nature sembloit avoir affecté uniquement aux femmes, mais dont le luxe et la mollesse ont fait présent aux hommes; je veux parler des vapeurs.[22]

Yet this sickness has its advantages: women are infinitely more susceptible to prophecy and to mystical experience than men. 'Jamais un homme s'est assis à Delphes, sur le sacré trépied', Diderot writes, not without a touch of envy (A–T, II, 252).

Diderot spends some pages on examples of divine possession, choosing indiscriminately from Racine, from mythology, from his knowledge about the *convulsionnaires* at the cemetery of Saint-Médard, and from contemporary accounts of a Prussian nun named Karsch. His description of the experience of the mystical German nun is orgasmic, but only because physical disappointment and frustration heighten her sensitivity to the spiritual equivalent of lovemaking: 'Rien de plus contigu que l'extase, la vision, la prophétie, la révélation, la poésie fougueuse et l'hystérisme', he tells us, and he goes on, in his typical way, to dramatize the scene in the Prussian nunnery: 'Cependant la recluse dans sa cellule se sent élever dans les airs; son âme se répand dans le sein de la Divinité; son essence se mêle à l'essence divine; elle se pâme; elle se meurt; sa poitrine s'élève et s'abaisse avec rapidité; ses compagnes, attroupées autour d'elle, coupent les lacets de son vêtement qui la serre.' And, he adds, 'Le quiétisme est l'hypocrisie de l'homme pervers, et la vraie religion de la femme tendre' (A–T, II, 255–6). The same ability to lose the self in the sublimated orgasm of mystical experience can make women susceptible to madness, both individually and collectively: one can almost hear Diderot making the connection between Delphi and the hillsides of Bacchus, between the nun Karsch and the maenads. Women do things in droves: they develop fainting fits or depression in their thousands, but they are easily shocked out of their follies, if the right method is employed. And the right method, for the post-Freudian reader, has an obvious character: a doctor waves a red-hot cauterizing iron in the faces of a crowd of epileptic girls; the lord mayor of a town where the women have been 'possessed of a disgust for living' declares that the first to kill herself will be exposed naked on the marketplace, 'et voilà les Milésiennes réconciliées avec la vie' (A–T, II, 257). Clearly a sexual organ must be spoken to in an appropriately sexual language.

The uterus, then, is not only the passive receptacle for children and male lust. It is an internal principle of change, one which allows philosophers, doctors and men in general to explain female inconsistency. It seems that Diderot regards femininity as a kind of permanent hypnosis. So suggestible is the hidden organ that women can be brought to believe and experience almost anything, as long as the method of suggestion speaks in some way to the womb. Perhaps quietism is seen by Diderot as the true religion of women, but the hypocrisy which rises from perversity, for men, because men have no uterus. Their sexual satisfaction is on the whole to be relied upon (one wonders whether the 'perverse' men are merely impotent or effeminate, or whether Diderot equates homosexuality and impotence). Men do not experience the frustration, whether physical or social, to which most energetic women are prey. A normal man who pretends to mystical experience, then, is symbolically faking an orgasm: he is crossing the borderline of gender if he makes himself into the vehicle of spiritual encounter.

But Diderot's notions on this point are implied, not stated. He seems unable to decide on any consistent view at all, though he is always frightened by the blurring of sexual boundaries: 'Il y a des femmes qui sont hommes, et des hommes qui sont femmes; et j'avoue que je ne ferais jamais mon ami d'un homme–femme' (A–T, II, 260). His fear in his own life that Sophie was engaged in a lesbian relationship with her sister is well known: he seemed to find homosexuality far more worrying than incest. In a letter to Sophie from La Chevrette (the residence of Mme d'Épinay) he writes: 'Mon amie, ne me louez pas trop votre soeur, je vous en prie. Cela me fait du mal . . .' and adds later: 'M'oubliez-vous dans le tumulte des fêtes et dans les bras de votre soeur?' In the same letter, he mentions *La Religieuse*, which he was working on at this time (September 1760); Roth's footnote tells us that the well-known Diderot scholar, Georges May, sees this anxiety about Sophie as closely linked to the portrayal of the lesbian abbess in the novel.[23]

We cite the following passages from 'Sur les femmes' at length, partially because this uncertainty about sexuality is so well reflected in the choppiness of the writing, and partially because the images and ideas which the *philosophe* summons up invite us to further pondering: 'Femmes, que je vous plains! Il n'y avait qu'un dédommagement à vos maux; et si j'avais été législateur, peut-être l'eussiez-vous obtenu. Affranchies de toute servitude, vous auriez été sacrées en quelque endroit que vous eussiez paru. Quand on écrit des femmes, il faut tremper sa plume dans l'arc-en-ciel et jeter sur la ligne la poussière des ailes du papillon . . .' (A–T, II, 260).

There is a slightly sinister conjunction between pity and terror in this bit of high-flown imagery. If women were not enslaved because of their sexuality, they would be revered as goddesses for the same reason. As soon as they are elevated in Diderot's imagination to the latter position, he uses fine language in a manner suspiciously like the soft-centred locutions in advertisements for unmentionable products in our own century. Our doubts are confirmed later in the passage, when we discover Diderot's true discomfort at the prospect of uterine supremacy. Unable, it seems, to get beyond imagery himself, he criticizes Thomas for not having presented his subject more 'scientifically'. At the same time, his own hypotheses are already formed. The uterus once more stands in the way: it seems to be a rock-hard core, impenetrable to ideas, yet subject to violent fluctuations, rather like the molten mass at the centre of the earth. Not surprisingly, there is an element of the geological in the next portion of fine writing:

Il ne suffit pas de parler des femmes, et d'en parler bien, monsieur Thomas, faites encore que j'en voie. Suspendez-les sous mes yeux, comme autant de thermomètres des moindres vicissitudes des moeurs et des usages. Fixez, avec le plus de justesse et d'impartialité que vous pourrez, les prérogatives de l'homme et de la femme; mais n'oubliez pas que, faute de réflexion et de principes, rien ne pénètre jusqu'à une certaine profondeur de conviction dans l'entendement des femmes; que les idées de justice, de vertu, de vice, de bonté, de méchanceté, nagent à la superficie de leur âme; qu'elles ont conservé l'amour-propre et l'intérêt personnel avec toute l'énergie de nature; et que, plus civilisées que nous en dehors, elles sont restées de vraies sauvages en dedans, toutes machiavélistes, du plus au moins. Le symbole des femmes en général est celle de l'Apocalypse, sur le front de laquelle il est écrit: MYSTÈRE. Où il y a un mur d'airain pour nous, il n'y a souvent qu'une toile d'araignée pour elles.

(A–T, II, 260)[24]

The lack of 'réflexion et principes' is obviously not the basic source of female inferiority in matters of intellect and morals. The terrifying power of womanly sexuality lies chained in uneasy subjugation, just as the Titans, an earlier stage of divinity, lie enslaved beneath the Olympian world in Greek mythology. Diderot is no enthusiast of Rousseau in this essay: self-interest, accompanied by prodigious primitive strength lost to civilized man, dominates the souls of savages and women. Elsewhere in the review, Diderot includes the confessions of an Indian woman from South America to show us that there are no utopias for women anywhere (A–T, II, 258–9). If women are unable to reason, they are at least able to take on the world directly, without the intervention of an educated consciousness. As Diderot adds later on:

Tandis que nous lisons dans des livres, elles lisent dans le grand livre du monde. Aussi leur ignorance les dispose-t-elle à recevoir promptement la vérité, quand on la leur montre. Aucune autorité ne les a subjuguées; au lieu que la vérité trouve à l'entrée de nos crânes un Platon, un Aristote, un Épicure, un Zénon, en sentinelles, et armés de piques pour la repousser. Elles sont rarement systématiques, toujours à la dictée du moment.   (A–T, II, 261)

The real 'mystère' for us, however, is not graven on the forehead of womankind. We have some difficulty in understanding how it comes about that this primeval woman, half priestess, half slave, half prophetess, half idiot, comes to be 'civilisée en dehors'. Diderot thinks that all of this veneer is merely part of the social armour which young girls need to protect their virginity: 'La seule chose qu'on leur ait apprise, c'est à bien porter la feuille de figuier qu'elles ont reçue de leur première aïeule. Tout ce qu'on leur a dit et répété dix-huit à dix-neuf ans de suite se réduit à ceci: Ma fille, prenez garde à votre feuille de figuier; votre feuille de figuier va bien, votre feuille de figuier va mal' (A–T, II, 260–1). We know that Diderot attacks exactly this attitude in his *Supplément au voyage de Bougainville*, written in the same year as the article on Thomas. But here, interestingly, he leaves what is clearly an important point until last. Even the hypocrisy surrounding female sexuality has its advantages for the man of letters:

Thomas ne dit pas un mot des avantages du commerce des femmes pour un homme de lettres; et c'est un ingrat. L'âme des femmes n'étant pas plus honnête que la nôtre, mais la décence ne leur permettant pas de s'expliquer avec notre franchise, elles se sont fait un ramage délicat, à l'aide duquel on dit honnêtement tout ce qu'on veut quand on a été soufflé dans leur volière. Ou les femmes se taisent, ou souvent elles ont l'air de n'oser dire ce qu'elles disent. On s'aperçoit aisément que Jean-Jacques a perdu bien des moments aux genoux des femmes, et que Marmontel en a beaucoup employé entre leurs bras. On soupçonnerait volontiers Thomas et D'Alembert d'avoir été trop sages. Elles nous accoutument encore à mettre de l'agrément et de la clarté dans les matières les plus sèches et les plus épineuses. On leur adresse sans cesse la parole; on veut en être écouté; on craint de les fatiguer ou de les ennuyer; et l'on prend une facilité particulière de s'exprimer, qui passe de la conversation dans le style.
(A–T, II, 261–2)

Femininity and enlightenment

The *philosophes* saw that religion, particularly quietist and ecstatic religion, a debased form of the seventeenth-century Jansenist intensity, was the last recourse of sexually disappointed or marginal women. But the vehicle of expression for this feminine piety was an essentially secular language, the inheritance of Mme de Rambouillet. And, as in England, though for very different reasons, its reliability varied. In the realms of religion and morals, it was seen, by Diderot and by his contemporaries, as hypocritical and empty: examples from *La Promenade du sceptique*, *Les Bijoux indiscrets* and the *Éloge* illustrate this point of view.

In matters of aesthetics and general expressiveness, on the other hand, Diderot recognized the influence that this same separation between intention and *bienséance* in language had on male writers and intellectuals. Unlike most English writers of the same period, he does not attribute greater sexual virtue to women (in this context, he uses the word 'honnêteté' very much as his English contemporaries would use its cognate); but he does see obliquity as a refining condition. As we have seen in other passages from Diderot, nothing could be more self-conscious than this feminine style, though the *philosophe* has also told us that female consciousness is peculiarly undeveloped. It is quite remarkable that the process of sublimation, as Diderot describes it, could so effectively channel the massive energies of uterine domination into the trivialized delicacy of the final image of little birds twittering in their gilded cage. Out of the primitive darkness of woman's nature come clarity, softness and tact: even so, we can see that this sublimation is at best partial. The repression of the greater part of female energy remains an inexhaustible source of destruction and illusion, but also of creativity and enlightenment.

Diderot seems to think that the more intimate the 'commerce' with women is, the more the *savant* will benefit. Intercourse itself, as in the case of Marmontel, confers some of that primitive energy upon the man who comes into contact with it. As Diderot has said already, women are able to be whole as men are not: they can read the book of Nature, *one* book, with all of themselves, and without the intervention of reasoned perception. Men, on the other hand, have only 'des livres', which may be but fragments of their own consciousness. In a sense, reflection is a painfully literal activity for men: they confront their own distortions and lack of integration when they look outward on the world. When Truth tries to enter their brains, it finds a phalanx of ancient philosophers, armed with their various systems, standing guard (as if Plato and his followers were Truth's implacable enemies). Women, on the other hand, are open to Truth because 'aucune autorité ne les a subjuguées' – an ironic way indeed of describing their ignorance. Whatever this mysterious 'Truth' may be, it is not to be found in philosophical systems, nor perhaps even in the reasoning of individuals, but in a harmony and dynamism in nature which a vaguely suggested intuitive faculty can alone apprehend. This is a notion that recurs in Diderot: it is held in solution, as it were, along with his deep convictions about popular education and personal cultivation.

When he begins to reflect upon the place of women, this physiologist of feeling is not very original: women feel, men think; women suffer, men enjoy, and so on. What is important for us, on the other hand, is a presumed moral equality, expressed negatively in Diderot's phrasing: 'L'âme des femmes n'étant pas plus honnête que la nôtre, mais la décence ne leur permettant pas de s'expliquer avec notre franchise, elles se sont fait un ramage délicat . . .' Women may be 'closelier fenced in' than men, as Allestree put it in his conduct book, but for Diderot this condition makes them able to approach *truth*, not grace.[25] Diderot usually sees religion and morality as suffocating, rather than elevating: the effect of the constant restraint on women's passions is to turn them too far inward. They are susceptible, as we have seen, to the various forms of madness, ranging from possibly enviable mystical states through to suicidal depression or mania. Allestree sees women's limitations in social life as a protection against the disturbances of sexuality; Diderot, more incisively, recognizes that passion goes underground when frustrated or denied. Even more interestingly, he is able to describe good effects as well as bad ones as a result of these restrictions: but the good effects help the men who live in female society, not the women themselves.

There is much here that anticipates Freud, of course. But we can never forget that femininity, for Diderot, is a disease, however positive some of its consequences may be: 'C'est de l'organe propre à son sexe que partent toutes ses idées extraordinaires. La femme, hystérique dans la jeunesse, se fait dévote dans l'âge avancé; la femme à qui il reste quelque énergie dans l'âge avancé, était hystérique dans sa jeunesse' (A–T, II, 255). Female passion, or libido, is essentially harmful: if repression itself is a bad thing, so is the object of that repression. There is no question of a cure for female misery, because women would cease to be themselves if it were ever discovered.

As we can see in the *Supplément au voyage de Bougainville*, on the other hand, Diderot places great weight on the evil effects of bad laws and customs:

Aussitôt que la femme devint la propriété de l'homme, et que la jouissance furtive d'une fille fut regardée comme un vol, on vit naître les termes *pudeur*, *retenue*, *bienséance*; des vertus et des vices imaginaires; en un mot, on voulut élever entre les deux sexes, des barrières qui les empêchassent de s'inviter réciproquement à la violation des lois qu'on leur avait imposées, et qui produisirent souvent un effet contraire, en échauffant l'imagination et en irritant les désirs. (A–T, II, 243)

His analysis of the relationship between sexual fears and frustrations (from the fear of pregnancy and loss of reputation to the failure to achieve orgasm) and the development of French culture is as candid and trenchant here as in 'Sur les femmes'. Indeed, the young Frenchman who must both adapt to and report on Tahitian sexual customs is himself a priest; so the link between sexuality and religion is constantly before our eyes. In fact the *Supplément* does not put forward a view of femaleness as pathological. It is still clear, however, though eminently predictable, that Diderot does not recognize some of his century's less enlightened attitudes in himself, though he sees them so clearly in French society at large. He tells us artlessly that children in Tahiti only belong to the mother until the child's father is named; that women must wear veils if they are sterile, old or menstruating; that the only criterion of beauty in a woman is fecundity (men are assumed to be potent); that the important characteristics in children seem to be inherited through the father (A–T, II, 231–2ff).

But, significantly, the major discussion in the *Supplément* is about the notion of naturalness itself; and sexuality, being that human quality most strangled by conflicting laws and customs, becomes the point of departure for the interlocutors' philosophizing:

B. . . . je croirais volontiers le peuple le plus sauvage de la terre, le Taïtien qui s'en est tenu scrupuleusement à la loi de la nature, plus voisin d'une bonne législation qu'aucun peuple civilisé.

A. Parce qu'il lui est plus facile de se défaire de son trop de rusticité, qu'à nous de revenir sur nos pas et de réformer nos abus.

B. Surtout ceux qui tiennent à l'union de l'homme et de la femme.

A. Cela se peut. Mais commençons par le commencement. Interrogeons bonnement la nature, et voyons sans partialité ce qu'elle nous répondra sur ce point.   (A–T, II, 241)

When nature is 'bonnement interrogée', we learn that she has several answers, as she does for all eighteenth-century questioners. On the one hand, 'Vice et vertu, tout est également dans la nature' (A–T, II, 243). The disinterested observer must not be shocked or blinded by his own prejudices into creating false categories which exclude any part of the full richness of the world. We can see a certain consistency in this attitude of Diderot's: it is to be found in other writings (*Le Rêve de d'Alembert*, *Lettre sur les aveugles*, *De l'Interprétation de la nature*, *Le Neveu de Rameau*) in which he considers monstrosities and defects merely as examples of nature's great fecundity. She is like an experimenter whose imagination creates new forms.

On the other hand, the 'vices' which are such an integral part of nature often turn out to be bad laws and customs. This disinclination to use terms like 'vice' and 'virtue', which imply too great a freedom of the will, is characteristic of Diderot. Sixteen years before 'Sur les femmes' and the *Supplément*, we find him making a similar point in a famous letter to Paul Landois (29 June 1756), though he comes to some rather harsh conclusions:

Mais s'il n'y a point de liberté, il n'y a point d'action qui mérite la louange ou le blâme. Il n'y a ni vice, ni vertu, rien dont il faille récompenser ou châtier.

Qu'est-ce qui distingue donc les hommes? La bienfaisance et la malfaisance. Le malfaisant est un homme qu'il faut détruire et non punir; la bienfaisance est une bonne fortune, et non une vertu.[26]

Jealousy, for example, is clearly such a socially created vice. Diderot defines it as follows: ' Passion d'un animal indigent et avare qui craint de manquer; sentiment injuste de l'homme; conséquence de nos fausses moeurs, et d'un droit de propriété étendu sur un objet sentant, pensant, voulant et libre' (A–T, II, 243). This generous and complex interpretation of sexual relationships still seems adventurous today.

But let us not forget two other powerful themes in Diderot's work: the conflict between an inner and outer person, and the notion of society as a paralysing form of technology. We have seen in 'Sur les femmes' that the natural woman lurks inside the individual, cradled like a permanent foetus in the womb: the female potential for energetic action and strong feeling must be contained, and is the cause of all her diseases. In the *Supplément*, Diderot gives us the male equivalent of this condition. To our surprise, we find the situation reversed:

B. Voulez-vous savoir l'histoire abrégée de presque toute notre misère? La voici. Il existait un homme naturel: on a introduit au dedans de cet homme un homme artificiel; et il s'est élevé dans la caverne une guerre civile qui dure toute la vie. Tantôt l'homme naturel est le plus fort; tantôt il est terrassé par l'homme moral et artificiel; et, dans l'un et l'autre cas, le triste monstre est tiraillé, tenaillé, tourmenté, étendu sur la roue; sans cesse gémissant, sans cesse malheureux, soit qu'un faux enthousiasme de gloire le transporte et l'enivre, ou qu'une fausse ignominie le courbe et l'abatte. (A–T, II, 246)

The interlocutor B. goes on to tell us that illness and poverty are the only two conditions, in the civilized state, which allow natural man to come unimpeded to the fore; but no sooner are convalescence or relief under way, than the artificial man resumes his tyranny. Indeed, artificiality seems to go with recovery, as if man is only healthy when he is internally fully divided. The very presence of the word 'monstre' tells us that the condition itself, agonizing as it is, is 'natural' and therefore to be accepted and studied. Perhaps we are meant to conclude that civilized man is himself a monster, possibly nature's mistake. We recall the hideous picture of the Moor in the cavern of motivation, from the 'Éloge', where the stripping away of hypocrisy only exposes greater horrors. Paradoxically, it is the *distance* from nature which lies at the heart of mankind; falseness is at the core of what appears an undisturbed creature, at one with his environment. If women have a womb, full of terrifying energy, but at least integrated with the forces outside themselves, men have consciousness, and consciousness is 'unnatural'. Strangely enough, however, both the primeval strength of women and the distancing consciousness of men are seen as essentially destructive. In both, a code of morality is originally superimposed from outside, and is a symptom that advanced societies are fatally susceptible to calcification (the 'on' of the passage is as impersonal a construction as the force of conventionality itself). Equally for both, the weight of classical imagery impels these descriptions: if women carry chained Titans within them, who murmur from time to time in threatened revolt, men are collectively the exposed Titan Prometheus, who is tortured endlessly by Olympian vultures.

It is curious, however, that in so sex-centred a society as that of France at mid-century, there are only obsessions and no candour: the vaginas in the *Bijoux* are full of surprises when they begin recounting their histories, though one is meant to see that any malicious gossip could have said as much of a neighbour in the days before the sultan had the ring without raising more than a chuckle. Only knowledge is devastating: innuendo is merely an expression of a collective anxiety. We can see glimpses in Lovelace of the same assumption that women are essentially lustful, even through his belief in Clarissa as purifier and redeemer. Clarissa's attempt to reject these terms altogether, by trying to create space for a personality among the prejudices which oppress her, can be seen as the defensive manoeuvre of middle-class morality, for which property and integrity are closely related concepts (we are here referring to the battle between Clarissa and Lovelace, in which the principles involved are different from those at Harlowe Place). But it is also a genuine step away from the obsessiveness of an aristocratic view of sexual character in women. Diderot, given his origins and a lifelong sentimentality about middle-class values (his plays, his writings on Greuze and other painters of domestic scenes, and his treatment of his daughter are all examples of it), is able to offer us one of his most profound insights when he contemplates the sexual fixations of high society in Paris and at court. He is able to expand the crude and anxious materialism of a small class into a principle for society at large, and having granted women some of the very sexual energy which aristocratic prejudice attributed to them, he can move beyond the obsession. He sees women as integrated, loving beings whose sexuality is only a reflection of an intensity of feeling, and not a moral attribute which can be socially imposed and controlled. One thinks of his portraits of Mlle de la Chaux and Mme de la Pommeraye, and his perception of his own mistress, Sophie Volland, as examples. The very style of his writing makes the connections between sexuality and every other aspect of culture: he learned to build on a vulnerability in himself, as in society, to give us a view of the artist exposed and at risk.

6

LA RELIGIEUSE AND *CLARISSA*: CONVENT AND BORDELLO

The 'Préface-Annexe': artifice and the feeling heart

One of the aspects of Richardson's work which Diderot most praised in his *Éloge* of 1762 was the transformation of ordinary events into an extraordinary and distilled reality through the power of fiction. But by the time Diderot came to write his farewell hymn to Richardson, he had himself been at the centre of a plot which must stand alone in the history of the novel: rarely has the impulse to transform lived experience into fiction taken quite such a literal form. We know the story from the account in the 'Préface-Annexe' appended to the main body of the novel. This 'Préface-Annexe' first appeared in Grimm's *Correspondance littéraire*, though *La Religieuse* was not published until 1796. We know that Diderot revised it himself. Herbert Dieckmann, who discovered the manuscript version of the 'Préface-Annexe' in the *fonds Vandeul*, reminds us of the significance of this fact: the 'Préface-Annexe' is no longer mere historical background, but a part of the novel.[1]

Suzanne Simonin was fabricated by Grimm, Diderot, Mme d'Épinay and their friends to lure the 'charmant marquis' de Croismare back to his circle in Paris from his castle in Normandy, where he had been living for fifteen months. She was slowly killed off as it became apparent that the tenderhearted marquis was indeed prepared to respond to her pleas for protection, but only by offering her a position as lady's maid to his daughter – in Normandy. He was on the point of arranging her trip when Diderot and his friends decided it was time to dispose of their unhappy nun, but it was all done in high spirits: 'Nous passions alors nos soupers à lire, au milieu des éclats de rire, les lettres qui devaient faire pleurer notre bon marquis; et nous y lisions, avec ces mêmes éclats de rire, les réponses honnêtes que ce digne et généreux ami lui faisait' (Garnier, *La Religieuse*, p. 210). Not until the marquis's return to Paris did he learn of the joke at his expense: 'il en a ri', Grimm assures us.

While the text itself is written as a memoir, this little history of the tale's origins tells us a great deal about the characters of the marquis de Croismare, of Grimm and, of course, of Diderot himself. Clearly, Diderot did most of the writing; and it was his idea to send Suzanne's first letter to the marquis's cousin of the same name, who was 'Gouverneur de l'École Royale Militaire'. This clever ploy gave a realistic air of virginal ignorance to the proceedings, and might possibly have helped to enlist the cousin's help in bringing the distant Croismare back to the capital (Garnier, *La Religieuse*, p. 212). What began as a hoax, however, soon became a serious matter for Suzanne's creator. Diderot's own story, told many years later as if Grimm were telling it, is quite deliberately revealing:

tandis que cette mystification échauffait la tête de notre ami en Normandie, celle de M. Diderot s'échauffait de son côté. Celui-ci, persuadé que le marquis ne donnerait pas un asile dans sa maison à une jeune personne sans la connaître, se mit à écrire en détail l'histoire de notre religieuse. Un jour qu'il était tout entier à ce travail, M. d'Alainville, un de nos amis communs, lui rendit visite et le trouva plongé dans la douleur et le visage inondé de larmes. 'Qu'avez-vous donc? lui dit M. d'Alainville; comme vous voilà! – Ce que j'ai? lui répondit M. Diderot, je me désole d'un conte que je me fais.'

(Garnier, *La Religieuse*, p. 210)

The intrusion of Diderot's own personality into the material characteristically leaves us in a shadowy land between fiction and autobiography. There are a number of celebrated *loci* in his work in which we are given a carefully edited portrait of Diderot the man succumbing to his own deep feelings. In the example from the 'Préface-Annexe', Diderot, as reader, is identified with his own creation to such an extent that he seems to have forgotten that he can dismantle her at will. He is in love, not with his nun, but with himself as embodied in the nun. He even says that the story is 'un conte que je *me* fais', a tale for himself alone. But of course Diderot never is quite alone. We know of the story (ostensibly) through Grimm, who had it told him by d'Alainville, who witnessed the scene, which arose out of a collective hoax; we know Diderot edited the story and, since we are reading it, we can hardly believe that Diderot was writing quite so purely for himself as his language suggests.

We immediately recall Diderot's description of himself in the *Éloge* after the death of Clarissa: his friends ask him if he has lost a relative or friend. Once more, the mourning eye is also a watchful one. Richardson's success as the creator of an artistic reality can be seen in the effect his characters have had on Diderot; but we are also invited to admire this superb reader, this man whose sensibility is so quick to respond to sublime moments in art. Like Richardson's correspondents in England, who chronicle every tear, every handful of desperately torn hair, for the benefit of the delighted author, Diderot makes sure that his melancholy is noted and remarked upon. We perhaps take too much for granted when we assume that eighteenth-century readers were like twentieth-century ones, who sit alone with their volumes: one senses the residual empire of theatre in the collective aspects of reading in this period. Even audiences, it seems, have audiences. When Diderot reads, he also performs: no one around him is unaware of what he has been thinking.

One of the most famous of such examples of feeling exposed comes from Diderot's essay on acting, *Paradoxe sur le comédien* (1773). The first sketch of his ideas appeared in the *Correspondance littéraire* of October, 1770, when Diderot attacked a pamphlet called *Garrick ou les acteurs anglais*. Though the *philosophe* developed his ideas considerably in the three years intervening between these two texts, his account of his identification with his acquaintance, Sedaine, appears in both. For the sake of brevity, I have selected the version from 'Observations sur Garrick', the earlier text:

Sedaine donne son *Philosophe sans le savoir*: la pièce chancelle à la première représentation, et j'en suis affligé; à la seconde, son succès va aux nues, et j'en suis transporté de joie. Le lendemain, je cours après Sedaine, il faisait le froid le plus rigoureux; je vais dans tous les endroits ou j'espère le trouver. J'apprends qu'il est à l'extrémité du faubourg Saint-Antoine; je m'y fais conduire: je l'aborde, je lui jette les bras autour du cou; la voix me manque et les larmes me coulent le long des joues: voilà l'homme sensible et médiocre. Sedaine froid, immobile, me regarde et me dit: *Ah! monsieur Diderot, que vous êtes beau!* Voilà l'observateur et l'homme de génie.   (A–T, VIII, 352)

It is impossible not to smile at the picture of Diderot giving gracious precedence to the now unknown Sedaine in the matter of genius. Diderot, after all, was obsessed with posterity. It is to be expected that he might sometimes misjudge his contemporaries, but we do not expect him to misallocate himself in this way; nor do we quite believe the image he projects. There is certainly some pride, as always in Diderot, in the exquisitely tuned pitch of his sensibility, but some notion of social risk as well. At worst, Sedaine is laughing at Diderot, though it is difficult to hazard a guess as to the degree of irony in the remark, since the eighteenth century had a high tolerance for effusiveness. At best, Diderot has painted himself as something of a buffoon, even if Sedaine is merely studying him, and not laughing. His very subjectivism has turned him into a thing, a dislocated self which others can contemplate. Though he himself began as a spectator of Sedaine's play, with the power to judge and criticize, he has ended up like a bad actor, with the playwright, who was originally the person at risk, as audience.

Diderot's tendency to identify with his friends has led to a misreading of the social situation, just as an actor misreads a role. The danger in this situation lies in letting oneself be taken over by what today's Kleinian psychologists would call external 'objects' – that is, other people, or in this case even literary works. We see Diderot as defenceless, whether he is shown in the role of creator, reader/critic, or friend. At the same time, of course, Diderot has given us an account of his humiliation, so that he has in fact regained control over his own incarnation as the foolish *homme médiocre*. The mixture of real pride and real self-contempt, of risk-taking and total control, is both striking and bewildering. Clearly, it reflects an ambivalence in Diderot's mind about the place of feeling in serious artistic effort. It would seem that one cannot be both good and productive; both a saint and a genius. What is curiously missing is the epic choice, the road which was chosen by the Romantics: Diderot never considers the persona of the artist as hero. His flaming ambition (for we know that he would be content with nothing less than the halo of sainthood or the laurels of genius) leans towards feeling in the content of the writing, where his pride manifests itself in emotional exhibitionism. But the fact that he is writing at all is a kind of containment: the man of feeling is made a specimen in the large, cool categories of the observant mind.

The artist as scientist

The imagery which I have instinctively selected to describe the Chinese-box effect of Diderot's exposure of himself in his writing tends to be scientistic; and indeed, it was probably suggested by Diderot's own fascination with the empirical process, particularly in medicine. He follows a policy of close observation in the description of himself and of others, and in a variety of contexts. We think of his clear-eyed view of somnambulism, offered by the celebrated Doctor Bordeu, in that infinitely suggestive text, *Le Rêve de d'Alembert* (1769). We have Diderot's frequent and meticulous descriptions of orgasm, several of which occur in *La Religieuse*. Even Diderot's original account of himself in tears over *Clarissa*, which appears four months before the publication of the *Éloge* in a letter to Sophie Volland (17 September 1761), contains an almost clinical enumeration of detail. It also shows enough self-possession to include an amused comment on the friend who has stumbled in upon Diderot's transports of emotion:

Ce que vous me dites de l'enterrement et du testament de Clarisse, je l'avois éprouvé. C'est seulement une preuve de plus de la ressemblance de nos âmes. Seulement encore mes yeux se remplirent de larmes; je ne pouvois plus lire; je me levai et je me mis à me désoler, à apostropher le frère, la soeur, le père, la mère et les oncles, et à parler tout haut, au grand étonnement de d'Amilaville qui n'entendoit rien ni à mon transport ni à mes discours, et qui me demandoit à qui j'en avois.

Certainly, Diderot shows himself as much of a 'genius' (by his own definition of the term) as the great actors whom he describes in the *Paradoxe*: the alterations in tone from deep feeling to wry observation are like Garrick's many changes of expression within two swings of a door (A–T, VIII, 352). But the careful attention to the detail of behaviour is not given so much for aesthetic reasons as to offer an accurate account of what happens to an organism under certain influences. In the very next sentence, after all, Diderot adds without any apparent sense of incongruity: ' Il est sûr que ces lectures sont très malsaines après le repas, et que vous choisissez mal votre moment; c'est avant la promenade qu'il faudroit prendre le livre' (Roth, III, 306). (Clearly Sophie, a lady of delicate health, has got indigestion through her involvement in Clarissa's fate.)

Even when Diderot is describing how an actor imitates a *modèle idéal*, he uses medical terminology:

On est soi de nature, on est un autre d'imitation; le coeur qu'on suppose n'est pas celui qu'on a. Quelle est donc la ressource en pareil cas? C'est de bien connaître les symptômes extérieurs de l'âme qu'on emprunte, de s'adresser à l'expérience de ceux qui nous voient, et de les tromper par l'imitation de ces symptômes d'emprunt, qui deviennent nécessairement la règle de leurs jugements; car il leur est impossible d'apprécier autrement ce qui se passe au dedans de nous. Celui qui connaît le mieux et qui rend plus parfaitement ces signes, d'après le modèle idéal le mieux conçu, est le plus grand comédien; celui qui laisse le moins à imaginer au grand comédien, est le plus grand des poëtes.

(A–T, VIII, 355)

Diderot writes not of ' characteristics', but of 'symptoms': the grand passions or great weaknesses of the stage are like a pathology.[2] The more one knows about the general complex of factors which constitute the ' disease', the better one is able to render the emotion or state of being. I do not intend to suggest that Diderot has a view of human nature as decadent; but we have seen numerous examples of his belief that it is essentially torn, off-balance, unharmonious: the disease of normality is not serious, or fatal, but it is part of the human condition.

The dialogue between 'Moi' and 'Lui' in *Le Neveu de Rameau* (written in 1762) is in part about this pathology. Rameau is a great eccentric, almost a great actor or great criminal, but since he has no unifying principles, no ethical *modèle idéal*, he can only act himself. The dialogue itself, where 'Moi' acts as the observer, the man who can write it all down, is the only means by which Rameau's efforts can become more than a mere collection of symptoms. His amorality is meant to shock: the will to survive alone – within this fictional context, of course – gives Rameau's character any continuity. Although he lives successively in time, as 'Moi' and the reader do, and seems to learn from experience, only the fragment of his character most immediately touched by that experience develops. It is possible, indeed, to say that opportunism at its purest is nothing but a series of reactions to chance events. The disease of ambition in the *Neveu*, for example, works directly on the will, leaving only an illusion of volition and a series of disintegrating selves in its wake.

When it comes to symptoms, in fact, Diderot is a master. Some writers have noted his clinical skills with admiration, even when they were applied to his own body; but the degree of specificity also suggests a tinge of hypochondriasis. 'Voici en quoi consiste mon mal à l'estomac:', he writes to the famous Genevan physician, Tronchin (31 March 1760), and the aptly chosen colon proves portentous. We are given a rush of data, the last of which suggests that he watches himself very closely indeed: 'À cette attaque dernière, il m'a semblé, quelques jours auparavant, que j'avais des mains engourdies et pesantes. – Les vents rendus, par haut surtout, me soulagent; mais ils se présentent pour sortir, et puis ils rentrent . . .' (Roth, III, 26–7).

It is unfair to make too much of Diderot's weaknesses. In this context, after all, hypochondriasis happens to form a felicitous alliance with the *philosophe*'s naturally acute eye for observation in all things, and with the sound methodology of the developing empirical sciences. Georges May, indeed, suggests that it is wrong even to consider Diderot a hypochondriac, because he was so pleased, rather than frightened, by his own diagnoses.[3]

For us, however, the importance of Diderot's fascination with symptoms lies in the intersection of public and private in his writing. A persona is evolved which seems to include both a doctor, who represents an institution, a method and a body of knowledge, and a patient, who is simply a suffering individual, a victim. We have seen one sort of exposure, the humiliation to which the man of feeling is susceptible in print. The Diderot of the 'Observations sur Garrick' and the *Paradoxe* is an *homme médiocre*; and though he shares a certain *mollesse* and extravagance of emotion with the Yorick of Sterne's *Sentimental Journey*, he is more clearly placed in a social world in which he is vulnerable to ridicule. Yet the very observing spirit, the *génie* in Diderot that has written about the whole incident, makes a significant example out of the foolish *philosophe* weeping on Sedaine's shoulder: not a moral example, but an aesthetic one. Diderot offers us a physiology of feeling in the act of writing itself. If one persona is the man who acts spontaneously, in response to the dictates of his heart, the other is the physician, noting the presenting symptoms and taking the pulse. When the observer happens to be a poet or an actor, rather than a physician, then the *modèle idéal* is not a textbook description of illness, but a perfect form to be imitated. In both situations, however, the observer exists in order to collect information.

Women, feeling and the paradoxes of individualism

Even within this model, which requires a sensitive but foolish person and a perceptive observer to generate its epistemological and aesthetic tensions, we find that there is a certain hierarchy in the degrees of feeling for Diderot. If the *philosophe* places himself in an inferior position to his friend Sedaine, because feeling has reduced the distance between consciousness and action in his own internal organization, women are put lower still in the theatre of society:

Voyez les femmes; elles nous surpassent certainement, et de fort loin, en sensibilité: quelle comparaison d'elles et de nous dans les instants de la passion! Mais autant nous le leur cédons quand elles agissent, autant elles restent au-dessous de nous quand elles imitent. Dans la grande comédie, la comédie du monde, celle à laquelle j'en reviens toujours, toutes les âmes chaudes occupent le théâtre; tous les hommes de génie sont au parterre. Les premiers s'appellent des fous; les seconds, qui s'occupent à copier leurs folies, s'appellent des sages. C'est l'oeil fixe du sage qui saisit le ridicule de tant de personnages divers, qui le peint, et qui vous fait rire ensuite et de ces fâcheux originaux dont vous avez été la victime, et de vous-même.   (Garnier, *OE*, 311)

This is an image of extreme complexity: there are eyes everywhere. Indeed, one is hard put to discover what anyone, man or woman, is supposed to be imitating in the 'comédie du monde'. It seems unlikely that Diderot means to suggest that women are always a little out of control, a little too prey to themselves ever to be great artists. The *philosophe* rarely puts forward quite so crude a notion, especially since he frequently cites Mlle Clairon, for example, as one of the great actresses of her time. Possibly Diderot is referring to the general quality of detachment, the ability to observe oneself from outside, which when applied to the world at large becomes the characteristic of genius. However, we interpret his idea of imitation, we cannot miss the sudden *bouleversement* in this passage. Quite abruptly, all these *âmes chaudes*, women and *hommes médiocres* like the Diderot who embraced Sedaine, are thrust upon the stage to be stared at. We think of the lunatics in the hospitals to which the fashionable world came out of curiosity: the *hommes sages*, if nothing else, are sane and observant.

Once again, there is a medical flavour to this theatre. The madness in normality comes from living too close to the source of feeling, in becoming a tissue of responses, a self passive and out of control. Only the genius, the physician of feeling who looks on from the outside, can make sense of the chaos. And indeed, the players and audience in this theatre seem to be in constant motion: some of the *âmes chaudes* in our paragraph appear to have come down from the stage as suddenly as they were put on it. In joining the *parterre* filled with *hommes sages*, they have been 'cured' and given the gift of clear sight through art. This secondary identification, which occurs through the transforming power of the vision of genius, has the opposite effect from the primary one, in which Diderot, the *âme chaude*, feels too deeply for his friend to remember his own boundaries. In this second case, the spectator remains as he was, a spectator; but he has been given distance and a perspective by losing himself in the work of art. One thinks of Diderot's comment on Greuze in the *Salon* of 1763:

C'est vraiment là mon homme que ce Greuze . . .

   D'abord le genre me plaît; c'est la peinture morale. Quoi donc! le pinceau n'a-t-il pas été assez et trop longtemps consacré à la débauche et au vice? Ne devons-nous pas être satisfaits de le voir concourir enfin avec la poésie dramatique à nous toucher, à nous instruire, à nous corriger et à nous inviter à la vertu?   (Garnier, *OE*, 524)

Diderot follows this reflection with pages showing exactly how the spectator can become entranced by Greuze's vision: in his art criticism particularly, he may be seen as the *homme sage* who understands the mechanisms of the effects which so enrapture the casual viewer (or reader). Even when he has achieved this admirable objectivity, however, Diderot rescues his warmer self from the rigours of too pure an intellectuality: 'Que . . . Et que mille diables emportent les critiques et moi tout le premier! Ce tableau est beau et très beau, et malheur à celui qui peut le considérer un moment de sangfroid!' he cries (Garnier, *OE*, 528). It is as if the aesthetic and ethical impulses were at last parting company for Diderot, but with great unease: sometimes Diderot seems to want to be seen as a *génie* himself, and sometimes as the tenderhearted and susceptible character whose very vulnerabilities make him the correct, perhaps the only, fitting audience for works of genius.

With the notion of audience, we return to our complicated theatrical passage from the *Paradoxe*. As if to confuse an already confusing situation still further, Diderot introduces a mysterious 'vous' into the welter of characters in the theatre. By now, indeed, the reader of this passage hardly knows, metaphorically at least, where to look. Diderot has not given *us* a role in this great 'comédie du monde' until the very end, when we are presented as victims, apparently, of the *fous* on stage, or perhaps of the *fou* that resides in all of us. Yet we know that we are really victims of the *génies*, because the rest of Diderot's essay draws us into his confidence, and Diderot plays the *homme médiocre* for the purposes of this experiment. We are all creatures of feeling, or we would not be able to be guided by art: we would not need to be educated by the perceptions of the *hommes sages*.

It is easy to get desperately entangled in apparent contradictions here, especially since this passage is genuinely obscure, in parts. But perhaps if we remember the 'as if', the playing with illusion in all of Diderot's work, we will not be so puzzled. The phrase 'pathology of normality', which sounds like a piece of nonsense, is made intelligible when we consider that Diderot really does see human nature as being like the monster in the cave, who wears masks even in the dark. Or we can recall the image of the creature who contains two personalities, the natural and the artificial, and whose health is defined by the degree of conflict between these two internal enemies. The more sensitively an individual is tuned (like the stringed instrument with which Diderot so often compares nervous organization),[4] the more isolated he or she is in individuality, and the more suffering is likely. One cannot look around oneself and generalize if the mass of energy is concentrated on living well. Indeed, this view of the hopeless entanglement in individualism became a real problem for Diderot, especially in later life.[5] There seemed to be a danger that the personality could be viewed as a mere series of responses, a stringed instrument indeed.

Nothing more perfectly exemplifies the passivity of individualism than the female sex. Diderot can bring a physiological perspective to this matter, as we have seen in 'Sur les femmes': since women are organized to bear children, their whole being centres around sexuality and its consequences. Childbirth, the most complete identification with natural processes, is a total annihilation of the self to create a new being. As every mythology has recognized, this is the perfect model of a successful work of art. But as mothers themselves can amply testify, it is only a very partial creativity, because the woman herself is a vehicle, a supremely involved spectator, but hardly an artist.

Perhaps we can extrapolate further. If a mother can never be an *homme sage*, a totally disinterested observer, she can be a *sage-femme* or midwife, an involved spectator who brings new life into the world. Whether women are virgins, mothers or midwives, it becomes apparent that they are a special case within the general category of feeling hearts. In a way, they can imitate only themselves: they are locked into a cycle of identification (with their children) and separation (through childbirth, lactation and childrearing) which is quite different from the male either/or of feeling versus the imitation of a *modèle idéal*. They cannot avoid this anatomical destiny which Diderot seems to have arranged for them. The mirror of the reproductive cycle is always before their eyes. To try to escape from it into the celibacy of a convent is to invite madness, the loss of any consciousness of self at all. Paradoxically enough, women who attempt to leave the wretched prison of their isolation in sexuality (by entering a convent, for example) condemn themselves to a far greater loneliness. The distortion of fundamental drives in themselves and others creates a false community, one which consists entirely of the vulnerable – a collection of victims, in fact.

Suzanne Simonin and the scientific 'gaze'

It is useful, particularly to the English reader whose expectations of fiction may have been formed in part by nineteenth-century realism, to think of *La Religieuse* as a mutation of the *conte philosophique* rather than as a fully fledged novel. Diderot doesn't attempt 'round' characters. His casual treatment of factual detail is a sign that characterization does not dominate. Every critic can point to inconsistencies in the story – Suzanne's age and sexual awareness undergo strange variations, for example.[6] Because the novel is written as a memoir, Suzanne is obliged to describe herself even when she is in a state of total abstraction, an admirable feat which has raised occasional snickers among readers who interpret the absence of *vraisemblance* as a weakness. There is an unavoidable and distinctly Pamela-like awkwardness about these passages: but in this narrative the difficulties of the form are left exposed, like pipework in a modern building. When Suzanne is found plunged in meditation during a vigil, for example, she has to tell us about her state through a description of the effect she has on others, and this sounds unpleasantly self-conscious, even conceited, for one so innocent. She has prostrated herself before the altar, and continues:

j'oubliai en un instant tout ce qui m'environnait. Je ne sais combien je restai dans cette position, ni combien j'y serais encore restée; mais je fus un spectacle bien touchant, il faut le croire . . . mon visage avait sans doute un caractère bien imposant, si j'en juge par l'effet qu'il produisit sur elles et par ce qu'elles ajoutèrent: que je ressemblais alors à notre ancienne supérieure, lorsqu'elle nous consolait, et que ma vue leur avait causé le même tressaillement.

(Garnier, La Religieuse, pp. 88–9)

When she lifts her veil before the archdeacon Hébert, who has come to Longchamp to exorcize demons, but learns instead of her tortures at the hands of the cruel superior Sainte-Christine, her description of herself is even more ludicrous:

J'ai la figure intéressante; la profonde douleur l'avait altérée, mais ne lui avait rien ôté de son caractère; j'ai un son de voix qui touche; on sent que mon expression est celle de la vérité. Ces qualites réunies firent une forte impression de piété sur les jeunes acolytes de l'archidiacre . . .

(Garnier, La Religieuse, p. 112)

Other examples abound, of course. Suzanne's unflinching eye never blinks or closes, even in sleep or trance. We have seen that this permanent awareness creates obvious stylistic problems. It also wreaks havoc among the other characters. For all Suzanne's sufferings, she prevails until her eyes are rather hastily shut in the 'Préface-Annexe'. In the meantime, she sees her mother, her stepfather and her saintly Superior, Mme de Moni, into their graves; she brings disgrace upon Mère Sainte-Christine, at least temporarily; and her rejection of the lesbian Superior's advances at the convent of Arpajon seems to be the direct cause of that lady's demise. Even her friend, Soeur Sainte-Ursule, succumbs to the disease which Suzanne doubtless transmits to her after her tortures at Longchamp.

Despite the many clear parallels to *Clarissa*, not the least of which is the construction of the novel around a seemingly endless series of trials, our heroine's virtue in this respect is too efficacious to compare with the slow martyrdom in Richardson. Clarissa dies before having had any discernible effect on her family or on Lovelace. Even Mother Sinclair's death owes nothing to her role in Clarissa's rape: it is effective because it is made to contrast with Clarissa's own flawless last moments. Only death releases Clarissa's power: she does not enjoy the fruits of her sufferings. But even then the richly deserved fates of her ravisher and 'friends' are unconvincing. We sense that Richardson could not bear to leave so raw a wound as an unrevenged innocent's death on the expectations of his readers. *La Religieuse*, on the other hand, operates on a truly Catholic system of rewards and punishments, though Diderot, perhaps following Richardson's lead, prefers vengeance to absolution when confessions are made: Diderot's atheism, as we know, had a very thoroughly orthodox background. Within the space of what is barely more than a novella, Suzanne gets through three convents and a horrific number of tortures. She is starved, beaten, trampled, humiliated, imprisoned, deprived of rest, whipped, slashed with broken glass and burned with hot irons, ostracized, encouraged towards madness and suicide, and left for dead after a funeral service. All this occurs before Suzanne even falls physically ill in response to maltreatment, and then we are only halfway through the novel.

But Suzanne's eye goes on mercilessly looking. The nuns' efforts sometimes appear to be frantic attempts to get that eye to look away. For what is brought under scrutiny in *La Religieuse* is not merely a conflict between fictional persons, but a pathology. If Clarissa has lived out the paradoxes of Christian belief in the most paradoxical of surroundings – a world which has renounced this belief without fully recognizing that it has done so – she at least emerges with an educated and integrated personality.

Diderot's Suzanne, instead, observes the distortions of personality in others. She has the precision and clarifying power of a microscope; and one would not think of trying to educate an optical instrument. She can undergo any amount of punishment without changing herself, though she brings, or rather inflicts, change on her closely scrutinized Superiors. Even the technical flaws in the novel may be seen as part of this *aliénation*, to use Suzanne's own word with a slightly different twist (Garnier, *La Religieuse*, p. 93). Suzanne refers to states of trance-like absorption. I mean to suggest social or even perceptual alienation; but the two conditions are related. Although Suzanne is the observer of events, she is at no distance from them: as a victim, she is in a morally powerful position. At the same time, little care is spent on her personal attributes, since they are not very important in this context.

Her very presence seems to be enough to make her three Superiors aware of their own failures. Each of them is harmed, even destroyed, by her steady gaze: 'Ah! chère enfant,' cries Mme de Moni when she tries to pray for Suzanne, 'quel effet cruel vous avez opéré sur moi! Voilà qui est fait, l'esprit s'est retiré, je le sens; allez, que Dieu vous parle lui-même, puisqu'il ne lui plaît pas de se faire entendre par ma bouche' (Garnier, *La Religieuse*, p. 66). Whether they are cruel or kind, or, like the Superior at Arpajon, somewhere confusedly in the middle, Suzanne's gaze penetrates to their essence.

Michel Foucault's notion of the 'gaze' is helpful in this context. In *The Birth of the Clinic*, he describes the passive stance of modern scientific inquiry. Our idea of rationality may be compared to an internal light which, when properly trained, makes us receptive to an open field of experience.[7] But Diderot himself stood between a Cartesian rationalism, whose model was of a world of transparent objects through which a unifying light of identity could shine, and our more familiar experimental rationalism, which consists partially of correct observation (the reading of nature) and partially of correct experimentation (the questioning of nature).[8] Foucault makes a telling comparison which perhaps helps us to make the distinction. He likens the 'gaze' of the eighteenth century to that of the gardener or botanist, who is required to 'recognize the specific essence in the variety of appearance'. The nineteenth-century 'gaze', on the other hand, is compared to the flame in a chemical operation: it actively works on the 'forms of relations of totalities' so that the 'essential purity of phenomena can emerge'.[9] (It might be added, incidentally, that the works of the *Naturphilosophen* and Goethe's late novel, *Die Wahlver-wandtschaften*, all from the first two decades of the nineteenth century, are permeated with these images of chemical change.)

As we can easily see, Suzanne's 'gaze' is somewhere on the border between these two kinds of perception. Within the convent, she is passive, but she allows us to study the various forms of illness which occur when sexuality is isolated and repressed. Whatever the ostensible differences in their characters, for example, the three Superiors all present certain symptoms of a unifying malady. On the other hand, Suzanne causes upheavals, chemical changes, as it were, in the objects of her gaze. Like Diderot's interpreter of nature in the scientific works, Suzanne forces her environment into giving up its secrets. The process of knowing is apparently violent. Although the sweep of Foucault's prose is sometimes altogether too daring, he is again suggestive when he writes:

the eye, which is akin to light, supports only the present. What allows man to resume contact with childhood and to rediscover the permanent birth of Truth is this bright, distant, open naivety of the gaze. Hence the two great mythical experiences on which the philosophy of the eighteenth century had wished to base its beginning: the foreign spectator in an unknown country, and the man born blind restored to light. But Pestalozzi and the *Bildungsromane* also belong to the great theme of Childhood-Gaze. The discourse of the world passes through open eyes, eyes open at every instant as for the first time.[10]

We may question this definition of *Bildung*, which is quite the opposite of that to which we are accustomed: education and develop-ment necessarily imply that the gaze cannot long view the world naively. But this description of a reliably virginal perspective does apply to *La Religieuse*. I use the word 'virginal' advisedly: for if Foucault gives us two eighteenth-century mythologies, he has no need in this book for a third, the trial of a young woman on the ground of sexuality as a test of the social world about her. Richardson gave the world this mythology, and it is a tribute to his genius that he was also one of the originators of the notion of *Bildung*. Clarissa grows out of exemplariness into myth, but becomes a person, too; and thus the novel, under Richardson's influence, at last came into its inheritance. Its characters could take on some of the power of figures of drama, while the form itself was free to offer as specific a vision of daily life as its author chose.

But Diderot, as I have suggested, wrote something closer to a *conte philosophique* than to a *Bildungsroman* in *La Religieuse*. As we have already seen, however, Diderot openly acknowledged his admiration for Richardson, and no critic doubts the Richardsonian influence on this work.[11] It is not difficult, indeed, to see the hand of imitation in this novel, and a few examples of it are not amiss. Suzanne far outshines her sisters, and attracts one of their lovers; she is forced into a marriage with Christ, rather than with a worldly suitor; she is imprisoned at home; she suffers a nosebleed in a scene which gives us the opportunity to revile her mother's hardheartedness. Mme de Moni dies a Clarissa-like death; the Superior at the convent of Arpajon, a Mother Sinclair-like one. There are two mad scenes; there is a close friend (Soeur Sainte-Ursule) who guards Suzanne's papers, as Anna Howe does in *Clarissa*; there are the flattery, cajoling and brutality which remind us so strongly of the attempts to force Clarissa to marry Solmes. Suzanne is even made to appear to be possessed by demons, so that the devil lurks again in the female sex. And Suzanne, like Clarissa, has a legalistic niceness of mind and an argumentative stamina that would do credit to any lawyer. But such similarities, which we would expect to find in mediocre writers of the period as well as in major ones, are not in themselves illuminating. They do help to justify the comparison between Richardson and Diderot, but do not tell us what Diderot did with Richardson's sexual mythology. Instead, we must study the general structure of the novel, and focus our gaze, in our turn, on the unblinking figure of Suzanne.

Clarissa, Suzanne and sexuality

Of Diderot's three extended narratives, *La Religieuse* alone is written in the form of a memoir. Only in the 'Préface-Annexe' is there any evidence of the authorial intrusion which is so slyly disruptive in

Jacques le fataliste; and though there is conversation, the dialogue is not a governing form, as in *Le Neveu de Rameau*. The use of a single narrative voice is anomalous for Diderot, and all the stranger when compared with *Clarissa*. The *philosophe*, who had borrowed so many lesser fictional strategies from Richardson, did not use the one major technique that to us seems the most congenial to his temperament: the interplay of several voices. In *Clarissa*, there are two protagonists. Both are equally powerful (in this, Richardson succeeded where even his illustrious predecessor, Milton, had failed in *Paradise Lost*). Their realization is impressive because they are clearly so deeply felt; and, as two separate personalities, Lovelace and Clarissa work out internal and societal conflicts on a battleground at the intersection of sex and religion. Their confidants occupy nearly as prominent a place as they do in the reader's attention, offering us information and perspectives which would be inappropriate to the hero and heroine. As in Diderot's dialogues, these secondary characters become more than foils to the protagonists; they take on a vitality of their own. It is no great wonder that Diderot admitted to Sophie Volland that he quite hoped Lovelace would attempt to ravish Anna Howe. He describes what might have happened with relish: ' Un beau jour, Lovelace auroit fait l'insolent, et Miss Hove lui auroit arraché la peau du visage avec ses ongles, et peut-être crevé un oeil avec la pointe de ses ciseaux.'[12]

Yet Diderot did not avail himself of this method in *La Religieuse*. Suzanne, like Clarissa, is isolated but not left alone. She is imprisoned, ostracized or cut off morally from anyone who might give her support. But it is quite striking that she does not seem particularly capable of strong feelings for others. In *Clarissa*, the cutting-off from relatives and friends is a constant source of pain. Clarissa's fundamentally loving nature is forced into an extreme loneliness which makes the eventual breakdown after the rape entirely plausible. Suzanne, in addition, as critics have pointed out, is singularly obtuse about sexual advances,[13] while Clarissa, like the Victorian ladies of fiction who owe so much to her, is vividly aware of sexual possibilities in everything. In fact, Diderot in life is closer to Clarissa in this respect than he is to his own heroine: Richardson's perception about sexual energy or libido was certainly much like his own, even if Diderot's moralizing on the subject followed quite a different line.

Suzanne's lack of awareness in sexual matters is in itself not particularly important. One could think that, like the high-pitched transvestite ladies of pantomime, Diderot may have simply got the tone wrong. On closer inspection, however, one must concede that there is a certain consistency in this lack of interest in others. ' Je suis née caressante', she writes (Garnier, *La Religieuse*, p. 185), but there is not much evidence to support this declaration. Even when her friend, Soeur Sainte-Ursule, dies (with the celerity characteristic of Diderot, especially when he is compared with Richardson, whose lingering death-scenes are sometimes almost novel-length), Suzanne does not skip the midday meal to be with the obviously moribund nun, and her tears are soon over. In fact, the vague appeal to the ineffable is closer to Prévost, who is fond of meaningless superlatives and protestations of inexpressible bliss or sorrow, than it is to the meticulous psychology of Richardson: 'Je ne saurais vous peindre ma douleur; cependant j'enviais son sort. Je m'approchai d'elle, je lui donnai des larmes, je la baisais plusieurs fois, et je tirai le drap sur son visage, dont les traits commençaient à s'altérer. Puis je songeai à exécuter ce qu'elle m'avait recommandé' (Garnier, *La Religieuse*, p. 134). It is all rather perfunctory. If one wanted to argue for the accuracy of Diderot's portrayal of character, one could always point to Suzanne's loveless background, with which this inability to love in adult life would be consistent.

But Suzanne is not a 'character' in this sense. She has no history and no future. Her life, after all, was conceived long after Diderot had constructed her death; and it was not written as an apology for that death, in the manner of works of religious instruction. One could say that Suzanne has no relationship with relationships. Her isolation is largely a function of her illegitimacy: the total consciousness which she has acquired as a result of her unfortunate origin is the same at the beginning of the novel as at the end. Surprisingly enough, indeed, there is some justification for the accusation of Jansenism which the cruel Mother Superior, Sainte-Christine, levels against Suzanne after the death of Mme de Moni (Garnier, *La Religieuse*, p. 73), though of course Diderot is using it at this point simply to attack the destructiveness of theological warfare. In truth, Suzanne is predestined to a life of victimization. She is the expiation for her mother's sin. Her lot in life has never been in question, though she has not always known this; and what is more, she seems to think that her parents' treatment of her has some justice: 'Je ne suis plus surprise des distinctions qu'on a mises entre mes soeurs et moi; j'en reconnais la justice, j'y souscris; mais je suis toujours votre enfant, vous m'avez portée dans votre sein, et j'espère que vous ne l'oublierez pas' (Garnier, *La Religieuse*, p. 57).

Indeed, her mother does not forget this fact. Suzanne is buried in the convent as an unpleasant memory is repressed in the unconscious. As is common with such memories, however, they (and Suzanne) have a way of obtruding themselves upon consciousness at inopportune moments. Suzanne protests at the first attempt to make her take the veil; is stunned into inarticulateness at the second, and of course, embarks upon the trial in order to get her vows rescinded. She begins life as the incarnation of a sin (though Diderot makes the sinfulness physical and individual, rather than spiritual and universal, as of course the Jansenists would) in the eyes of her parents, and soon enough becomes a financial obstacle to her sisters, and a source of money for the nuns. In selling Suzanne into the slavery of a convent, the Simonins are really trafficking in indulgences.

When Suzanne recalls the words of Mme de Moni during her persecutions at the hands of the Superior Sainte-Christine, one can see why she herself cannot be a good nun:

Entre toutes ces créatures que vous voyez autour de moi, si dociles, si innocentes, si douces, eh bien! mon enfant, il n'y en a presque pas une, non, presque pas une, dont je ne puisse faire une bête féroce; étrange métamorphose pour laquelle la disposition est d'autant plus grande, qu'on est entré plus jeune dans une cellule, et que l'on connaît moins la vie sociale. Ce discours vous étonne; Dieu vous préserve d'en éprouver la vérité. Soeur Suzanne, la bonne religieuse est celle qui apporte dans le cloître quelque grande faute à expier.

(Garnier, *La Religieuse*, p. 100)

Suzanne, after all, *is* the fault. But Diderot's materialism in science is significant here because, like any product in nature, she is in herself not in the least sinful. In the context of convent life, she is a kind of monster; but monstrosity appears out of the course of ordinary life only because we are socially conditioned to think it so. Her comment on the abnormality of the life of the recluse is itself an inverted view of her own position:

Dieu qui a créé l'homme sociable, approuve-t-il qu'il se renferme? Dieu qui l'a créé si inconstant, si fragile, peut-il autoriser la témérité des ses voeux? Ces voeux, qui heurtent la pente générale de la nature, peuvent-ils jamais être bien observés que par quelques créatures mal organisées, en qui les germes des passions sont flétris, et qu'on rangerait à bon droit parmi les monstres, si nos lumières nous permettaient de connaître aussi facilement et aussi bien la structure intérieure de l'homme que sa forme extérieure?

(Garnier, *La Religieuse*, p. 120)

Suzanne's innocence, then, is particularly unsullied, and allows her to view events with unnerving impartiality. It is the social aspect of religion which has so disrupted Suzanne's ties to her parents and which causes the distortions of personality in the other nuns that result in her persecutions. Mme de Moni's warning is once more illuminating. Suzanne is a still centre, the object of repression, the source of the transformation of the convent from an orderly society into a whirlwind of hysteria and cruelty. The convent is, in fact, another of those dark caverns that abound in Diderot's writing: sometimes we see the faces of angels, sometimes of Moors, but we never know which is the true one. Suzanne, as a visible reminder of sexual transgression, is disturbing enough in her very presence to be an effective figure, even without a sentimental education. It is we who are meant to be educated; and so we are given her eyes, if not her heart, to use an image of dismemberment appropriate both to the ferocious jealousy of a Lovelace and the anatomical curiosity of a Diderot.

What, then, of Suzanne's many tantalizing descriptions of herself at the hands of Sainte-Christine and the Superior at Sainte-Eutrope? There is no doubt that there is much in this novel that would have pleased Sade. It is easy enough to enumerate the scenes in which necks and breasts are exposed both to whips and to kisses. The nuns at Longchamp, like the lackeys in Buñuel's film *Belle de jour*, quite enjoy tying Suzanne with ropes and torturing her, and Suzanne's relationship with the Superior at Sainte-Eutrope is represented almost entirely by escalating moments of seduction. There is more than a little of the flavour of Mother Sinclair's brothel in *La Religieuse*: one has the impression, indeed, that this frightening, all-female world has become the model for Diderot's convent. But this seductiveness, though it clearly owes much to contemporary pornography and to Diderot's own pleasure in fantasies involving helpless women (his continuing commentary on Vernet in the *Salon de 1767* is one example)[14] is also a convenient way of testing some of the *philosophe*'s ideas about female sexuality.

The notion of Suzanne as an all-seeing eye is not incompatible with her inviting physical nakedness; it is rather as if the corpse on the dissecting table were also the doctor doing the dissection. Ludi Jordanova has described the penetrating gaze of the eighteenth-century and nineteenth-century anatomist as metaphorically male: she cites the medical engravings and wax models of the time as evidence of the highly sexual nature of dissection. If hairless male anatomical models stride forward to reveal their musculature but not their sexual organs (clutching mathematical instruments in a purposeful hand), female models recline, their waist-length hair streaming, to reveal breasts, ovaries and womb, but none of the organs common to both sexes.[15] Lawrence Stone's book, *The Family, Sex and Marriage in England 1500–1800*, in fact contains a late-eighteenth-century illustration (Plate 36) of such a wax model. It is surrounded by a group of women who are clearly fascinated by this excursion into sex education. Examples of such double vision occur quite often in Diderot. Rather like a Cubist nude, Suzanne is able to look upon her own body and out upon the world, even if the planes of her own existence as a character are thereby fatally realigned.

Indeed, the coolness with which she observes her family, fellow nuns and Superiors is like the Sultan Mangogul's in the *Bijoux indiscrets*. The Sultan is a voyeur who moves about under a cloak of invisibility, while Suzanne's very visibility and resulting vulnerability, give us the opportunity for insight. The convent and the boudoir are the undersides of another, civilized feminine world, that of the *cercle* in Mirzoza's harem: as in 'Sur les femmes', each world has its own language. Mirzoza's world is that of the *salons*: the convents of *La Religieuse* and the boudoirs of the *Bijoux* are but *loci* for the expression of sexuality in varying degrees of primitiveness.

As we can see, this novel is resonant. We can refer both to works which Diderot had already written and to works which were not yet produced, such as 'Sur les femmes'. There is a certain resonance, too, between the *Promenade du sceptique* and *La Religieuse*. In both, three visions of life are offered, in approximately similar relation to one another.

Curiously enough, the parallelism between the path of chestnuts in the *Promenade* and the sympathetically rendered view of life under the direction of Mme de Moni is not particularly close except that both are seen with a fundamentally favourable if critical eye. It is striking that Mme de Moni's reign is so short: fewer than nine pages of the novel are devoted to an account of Suzanne's relationship with her, and then she dies. But her influence is powerful. Suzanne appeals often to her memory, and compares both herself and Mère Sainte-Christine to the saintly woman. One of the cruellest of Mère Sainte-Christine's actions (when Suzanne thinks she is on the point of being hanged) is to snatch away the portrait of Mme de Moni which Suzanne carries next to her heart. Mme de Moni is presented first, so that the reader can always compare the brief perfection of her example to the massive flaws of her successors.

She is, of course, no philosopher; and if we remember Diderot's analysis of the female character, this comes as no surprise. Women, after all, are not educated to reason, and in any case their mysterious inner organs pull them away from rational processes. But Mme de Moni is the female equivalent of Diderot's philosophic idols: she cannot be a Seneca, but she can attain states of mystical transport which allow her access to realms of experience beyond the limitations of self: 'En vérité', writes Suzanne, 'cette femme était née pour être prophétesse, elle en avait le visage et le caractère' (Garnier, *La Religieuse*, p. 68). The general interest in the powers of apprehension, as opposed to those of ratiocination, gives weight to the eighteenth-century notion of female experience. It is almost as if Lockean epistemology has required a new, materially fixed version of the act of faith.

In Mme de Moni, we have faith incarnate – but, as we have seen, even this spiritual confidence is no match for Suzanne's unwillingness to enter into the religious state. We are never allowed to forget the sexual roots of the most elevated religious utterances. Suzanne describes the effects which Mme de Moni's states of inspired prayer have on her charges:

Ses pensées, ses expressions, ses images pénétraient jusqu'au fond du coeur; d'abord on l'écoutait; peu à peu on était entrainée, on s'unissait à elle, l'âme tressaillait, et l'on partageait ses transports. Son dessein n'était pas de séduire, mais certainement c'est ce qu'elle faisait: on sortait de chez elle avec un coeur ardent, la joie et l'extase étaient peintes sur le visage, on versait des larmes si douces! . . . Ce n'est pas à ma seule expérience que je m'en rapporte. C'est à celle de toutes les religieuses. Quelques-unes m'ont dit qu'elles sentaient naître en elles le besoin d'être consolées comme celui d'un très grand plaisir; et je crois qu'il ne m'a manqué qu'un peu plus d'habitude, pour en venir là.

(Garnier, *La Religieuse*, p. 65)

Even in this portrait of disinterested goodness, there is, again, a hint of the pornographic novels of initiation to which *La Religieuse* probably owes some of its structure: spiritual virginity, too, can be lost, and mystical pleasure, too, takes practice. But Mme de Moni's motives are unimpeachable, whatever the charms of her powerful personality. The scene at Suzanne's bedside, the morning of the day on which the young postulant is to take the veil for ever, stands in sharp contrast to the ludicrous nocturnal scene at Sainte-Eutrope, when the lesbian Superior gets into bed with Suzanne. Mme de Moni, in fact, here becomes something of a spiritual physician. She has spent the night interceding with God, even whipping herself before the altar, in the hope that divine comfort will germinate directly in Suzanne's troubled soul. When she enters, she seats herself by the bed, puts a hand on Suzanne's forehead, watches her attentively, and finally asks a series of questions: 'N'avez-vous pensé à rien pendant la nuit? . . . Vous n'avez fait aucun rêve? . . . Qu'est-ce qui se passe à présent dans votre âme?' (Garnier, *La Religieuse*, p. 67). Indeed, Suzanne tells us something of Mme de Moni's extraordinary gaze. Only she, of all the characters in the novel, shares Suzanne's gift for observation, which she uses actively and incisively, like a surgical beam of light: 'Elle avait les yeux petits, mais ils semblaient ou regarder en elle-même, ou traverser les objets voisins, et démêler au-delà, à une grande distance, toujours dans le passé ou dans l'avenir' (Garnier, *La Religieuse*, p. 68).

In a word, her gaze is *penetrating*. It has all the qualities which we associate with male sexuality. There may be an autobiographical reason for this. Diderot has Bordeu, in *Le Rêve de d'Alembert*, tell the story of a priest called 'Le Moni ou de Moni' from the *philosophe*'s own home town of Langres whose absolute religious faith keeps him from feeling pain during a surgical operation.[16] The phallic precision of medical diagnosis and the spiritual exactness of reading souls through the eyes are not far apart. As Peter Brooks would certainly suggest, the emphasis on penetrating glances and on the fixing of another person's essence reminds us that *La Religieuse* owes much to the preciosity of the seventeenth century;[17] but the sexual and scientific implications of the glance are introduced and developed in the eighteenth century.

When Mme de Moni tries to fill herself up with spiritual energy before the struggle with Mme de Simonin over the fate of the unfortunate Suzanne, she describes the intensity of her need to observe deeply in order to enter into meditation, and then uses unquestionably male orgasmic imagery about the nature of her eloquence:

Je ne suis pas venue pour vous entretenir, mais pour vous voir et vous écouter. J'attends votre mère. Tâchez de ne pas m'émouvoir; laissez les sentiments s'accumuler dans mon âme; quand elle en sera pleine, je vous quitterai. Il faut que je me taise, je me connais, je n'ai qu'un jet, mais il est violent, et ce n'est pas avec vous qu'il doit s'exhaler. (Garnier, *La Religieuse*, p. 68)

Even Mme de Moni, then, is tied to Suzanne by implicitly sexual links. She uses the power of her gaze and meditations to imprint Suzanne's image upon her own heart and, indeed, looking and reflecting are as effective for her in fixing this internal portrait as lovemaking would be in the world. Then the Superior goes forth, like the disguised and faithful lovers in operas, to give herself to another (Mme Simonin) in the interest of her beloved. Mme de Moni, charismatic and strong, in a sense takes on the disguise of a man when she closets herself with Mme de Simonin: her encounter with Suzanne's mother seems to be a spiritual parallel to the original lapse which brought Suzanne into the world. In a life without victims, this second orgasm, so chastely rhetorical, rather than physical, would surely cancel out the evil effects of Mme de Simonin's error. Instead, Mme de Moni is herself diminished, and Suzanne is left to her suffering.

If we continue to draw parallels between the *Promenade* and *La Religieuse*, there is little doubt that the way of thorns of the earlier work has been considerably lengthened, if not widened, in this novel. In Mère Sainte-Christine, the portrait of religious fanaticism is rendered in every detail:

Celle-ci avait le caractère petit, une tête étroite et brouillée de superstitions; elle donnait dans les opinions nouvelles; elle conférait avec des sulpiciens, des jésuites . . . [Elle] renvoya à chaque religieuse son cilice et sa discipline, et fit retirer l'Ancien et le Nouveau Testament.

(Garnier, *La Religieuse*, pp. 72–3)

This inauspicious beginning is followed, as we know, by a staggering list of Suzanne's tortures. There is a great deal of quite literal emphasis on the narrowness of the path of religious fanaticism, even in these sadistically titillating scenes. Suzanne is constantly being dragged through corridors, or is forced to walk through them in the dark. The scene in which she is required to make *amende honorable* is particularly revealing:

Le soir, lorsque je fus retirée dans ma cellule, j'entendis qu'on s'en approchait en chantant des litanies; c'était toute la maison rangée sur deux lignes . . . On me passa une corde au cou; on me mit dans la main une torche allumée et une discipline dans l'autre. Une religieuse prit la corde par un bout, me tira entre les deux lignes, et la procession prit son chemin . . .

(Garnier, *La Religieuse*, p. 128)

On the same occasion, the nuns sow her path with bits of broken glass, and earlier in her persecutions, when they are trying to drive her into madness, the corridor is made even more dangerous. Besides glass, they leave red-hot tongs in her path, and make the narrow corridors nearly impassable (Garnier, *La Religieuse*, p. 107). When she is ostracized by the community, the corridors once more become part of the arena of her sufferings: 'nos corridors sont étroits; deux personnes ont, en quelques endroits, de la peine à passer de front: si j'allais, et qu'une religieuse vint à moi, ou elle retournait sur ses pas, ou elle se collait contre le mur, tenant son voile et son vêtement, de crainte qu'il ne frottât contre le mien' (Garnier, *La Religieuse*, p. 99).

The incident in which an impressionable novice interprets Suzanne's appearance as an attempted sexual attack also occurs in the corridor (Garnier, *La Religieuse*, pp. 153–4). And when Suzanne is awaiting the outcome of her trial, she can tell by the disorder in the corridors that she has lost:

Mais l'après-midi, le bruit et le mouvement reprirent subitement de tout côté; j'entendis des portes s'ouvrir, se refermer, des religieuses aller et venir, le murmure de personnes qui se parlent bas. Je mis l'oreille à ma serrure; mais il

me parut qu'on se taisait en passant, et qu'on marchait sur la pointe des pieds.
Je pressentis que j'avais perdu mon procès; je n'en doutai pas un instant.

(Garnier, *La Religieuse*, p. 123)

It is hardly necessary to add, of course, that as many distressing
scenes occur in places other than hallways. But the rather startling
descriptions of actual comings and goings from one point to another
suggest the imbalance of community life in a subtle way. Like an
organism which is not in a state of health, the convent is full of hectic
and overheated activity. The corridors, like the blood vessels of a sick
animal, throb with poisonous life. And like a prison, which could
perhaps be seen as an organism entirely dominated by infection and
the battle against it, every location in the convent becomes an excuse
for oppression and torture. Metaphorically, Suzanne is not at home.
She is being pushed, through physical need or the brutality of others,
away from her cell, and a bounded and orderly individuality, into
physical and spiritual exile. We cannot forget the parallel to *Clarissa* in
this skilful rendering of a claustrophobic existence: Mrs Sinclair's
house, too, is a warren of little rooms full of busy women on errands of
malice. In *Clarissa*, however, the inability of one person to understand
another and the sexual nature of the struggle between Clarissa and
Lovelace are emphasized in the proliferation of locked rooms.

Although the episodes involving the bigoted Mother Superior,
Sainte-Christine, form the central panel of this triptych, equal space is
devoted to the last panel. Diderot's adapted version of the flowery path
in the *Promenade du sceptique* is the description of life at the convent of
Sainte-Eutrope. If much of the action during Mère Sainte-Christine's
ascendancy at Longchamp takes place between one room and
another, there is no doubt that at Sainte-Eutrope life revolves around
the bedroom. From the first day, the Superior educates Suzanne to the
importance of beds (Garnier, *La Religieuse*, p. 143); the cells become
little *boudoirs*; and the Mother Superior's, in particular, is a parody of a
great lady's. Suzanne describes one of many such scenes: 'On parla des
oiseaux de la mère celle-ci, des tics de la soeur celle-là, de tous les petits
ridicules des absentes; on se mit en gaieté. Il y avait une épinette dans
un coin de la cellule, j'y posai les doigts par distraction . . .' (Garnier,
La Religieuse, p. 145). When Suzanne plays sacred music, she is told by
the Superior that there is enough of that in church, and Suzanne
accordingly chooses something livelier:

Je chantai donc une chansonnette assez délicate, et toutes battirent des mains,
me louèrent, m'embrassèrent, me caressèrent, m'en demandèrent une seconde: petites minauderies fausses, dictées par la réponse de la supérieure; il n'y

avait presque pas une là qui ne m'eût ôté ma voix et rompu les doigts, si elle l'avait pu. Celles qui n'avaient peut-être entendu de musique de leur vie, s'avisèrent de jeter sur mon chant des mots aussi ridicules que déplaisants, qui ne prirent point auprès la supérieure.

'Taisez-vous, leur dit-elle, elle joue et chante comme un ange, et je veux qu'elle vienne ici tous les jours; j'ai su un peu de clavecin autrefois, et je veux qu'elle m'y remette.'   (Garnier, *La Religieuse*, pp. 145–6)

We have seen examples of this exaggerated and hypocritical language in the story of Bélise, in the *Promenade*, and in the convent scene in the *Bijoux indiscrets*. In these examples, Diderot uses the conventional language of society ladies to tell us something about the degrees of transparency in a social code. The *double entendre* works only when a member of the group in which it is uttered does not have full knowledge of its meaning. This kind of language is transparent to everyone except the uninitiated, who are made open to ridicule automatically, since ignorance always means social disgrace.[18] The appetite for novelty, for social virgins, is a kind of libertinism: society women, like rakes, can also be on the prowl for women less sophisticated than themselves. A *ruelle*, then, can reflect the male world of sexual pursuit very closely. If the nuns sound like flattering lovers when they are at their most vicious, it is because they are part of a female universe which may have originated the language of sexual subtlety. Suzanne, in this case, does not recognize that the Mother Superior has declared her sexual interest to the rest of the group when she announces her intention to polish her musical skills.

On the other hand, of course, Suzanne herself offers us a different sort of transparency. Like Montesquieu's Usbek in the *Lettres persanes*, or Candide, or the innumerable virgins of eighteenth-century pornography, among many other contemporary literary innocents, Suzanne tells us everything. As Foucault has put it, her eyes are always open as if for the first time. Though she is not unthinking (she describes her occasional wriggles of irritation, as well as her confused moments of sexual arousal), she is uncomprehending. Through the very process of being manipulated, she gains a certain control over her social environment. Because she doesn't understand the double language at Sainte-Eutrope, she is not susceptible to its power. That invincible purity, instead, is a moral juggernaut, causing a veritable *sauve-qui-peut* among the nuns. One can perhaps think of *La Religieuse* and other *contes philosophiques* as the parents of nineteenth- and twentieth-century muckraking journalism. Underneath both forms lies an unshakeable belief in the power of the word to bring down unjust institutions: if one observes well and reports faithfully, Nature will do the rest.

As we can see, Suzanne's purity serves a very different function from Clarissa's. *Clarissa* is a hymn to individualism: the heroine learns to know herself. The Harlowes' hypocrisy and Lovelace's sexual desires are never in doubt; and though Clarissa is duped by the masks Lovelace puts up all around her, her basic perception of the motives of the people whom she encounters is not changed. Mother Sinclair and her nymphs are destructive mainly because their images become part of Clarissa's frightening inner life. They take on the quality of hallucinations, and stand in the way of a clear perception of self and of mental health. I would hardly care to argue, of course, that a social world is not deeply involved in this education of the self. Indeed, Clarissa's development and ultimate fate are a condemnation of the conventional and unreflecting life around her. If, however, we compare Clarissa to Suzanne, the difference in perspective will, I hope, become plain.

Clarissa, for one thing, is the greater rhetorician of the pair. She recognizes the travesty of a common moral language at Harlowe Place, and she can match Lovelace's rants with an equivalently dramatic Christian eloquence. If anyone resorts to *double entendre*, it is she: the famous letter to Lovelace, in which she tells him that she is travelling to her father's house, is but the most striking example in the novel. But her *mots à double entente* always refer to a spiritual sphere: they are the exact opposite of those which we encounter repeatedly in French novels of the same period, where a spiritual or cultural reference has a physical second meaning. Since Clarissa is not our only source of information about events and characters, we are always aware of how others regard her. Consequently, her moments of self-doubt have a flavour of authenticity: others, too, think that she has spiritual pride, or too many scruples, or too little knowledge of her own heart. Most of all, her purity is almost entirely moral: she is not ignorant about sex, money or the social life around her. She has a complicated system of inner checks and balances, a machinery of emotional restraint and intellectual rigour, to which she has increasing recourse as her persecutions mount.

Suzanne's purity, on the other hand, could be called primarily epistemological. Her sexual naïvety, as we have said, is not convincing unless we see it as another aspect of the transparency to which I referred earlier. The famous scene in which Suzanne listens at the keyhole to the lesbian Mother Superior's confession, for example, has often been remarked upon, because Suzanne, having assured us throughout her memoir that she remains unaware of the nature of the Superior's advances, now writes: 'J'écoutais, le voile qui jusqu'alors m'avait dérobé le péril que j'avais couru se déchirait, lorsqu'on m'appella. Il fallut aller, j'allai donc; mais, hélas! je n'avais que trop entendu. Quelle femme, monsieur le marquis, quelle abominable femme!' (Garnier, *La Religieuse*, p. 198).

We must, in fact, think of this epistemological transparency of Suzanne's in quite literal terms. Medical analogies are never inappropriate for Diderot: we have already compared Suzanne to a watchful corpse on the dissection table, a synthesis of experimenter and experimented-on. Because Suzanne's acquisition of knowledge is entirely about the world outside herself, she shows no signs either of development or of education. When Mère Sainte-Christine locks her into a dreadful little dungeon, complete with dripping walls and skull, for example, she reacts with distress. But her expressions of despair are quite different from Clarissa's. Clarissa is being observed by others, and we learn of her breakdown only through the reports of Lovelace and the servants. Suzanne, on the other hand, is made to do all this work herself. The effect of making her report on the amusing dance of gesture in this scene might be to make us aware that there *is*, for Diderot, a convention for expressing such sentiments. Suzanne, again, is an instrument:

Mon premier mouvement fut de me détruire; je portai mes mains à ma gorge; je déchirai mon vêtement avec mes dents; je poussai des cris affreux; je hurlais comme une bête féroce; je me frappai la tête contre les murs; je me mis toute en sang; je cherchai à me détruire jusqu'à ce que les forces me manquassent, ce qui ne tarda pas. (Garnier, *La Religieuse*, p. 83)

As I have several times suggested, it would be a mistake to expect much in the way of a Richardsonian personality from Diderot's Suzanne. Her function in the novel is instead rather like that of a membrane or tissue of feeling, so finely spread out that the reader receives all impulses through it. This is the sense in which Suzanne's transparency seems so literal; she is a *réseau*, a webby organization of nerves and sensations, and all her sufferings serve to prove a point. Since she is a narrator rather than a character, she can heap the catalogue of bodily insult onto page after page, without suffering much apparent damage. Even her death has a physical, rather than a spiritual or moral cause: it is the result of an inflammation of the leg which she bruised while escaping from the convent. Through her, the evidence comes in, and we are invited to draw conclusions: institutions are always destructive, but most so when the reasons for their existence have disappeared or become corrupted; sexuality is distorted whenever it is not given full expression; the will to freedom is inextinguishable, and ought not to be suppressed (Garnier, *La Religieuse*, pp. 153–4). It is somewhat ironic that we cannot draw these sorts of concise lessons from Richardson, who had after all set out to be didactic in just this way.

Diderot and his characters

However we regard Suzanne, it is worth remembering that her relationship with Mme de Moni sets a pattern for the rest of the novel. *La Religieuse* could be called a Gothic novel in quite a commonsensical way, if one were inclined to talk fashionably about its 'architecture': its structure is as vertical as that of any cathedral spire. Suzanne has only one friend of her own age, Soeur Sainte-Ursule, who serves as a contact to the outside world and then dies. Otherwise, her absorbing relationships are entirely with women much older than she, and who exercise authority over her. The control which the three Superiors exert is always highly sexual; each of them has a language and imagery peculiar to her own character. Mme de Moni's words are strong and simple, and she is as often silent as transported with holy eloquence; Soeur Sainte-Christine, as one might expect, sounds like a menacing police agent with a penchant for sadistic exercises in the nude; and the lesbian Superior, as we have seen, mentions religion only by accident or necessity. She is far closer in spirit to the most licentious ladies of secular society than she is to Mme de Moni, and we are meant to recognize the contrasts between them. Suzanne makes the comparison herself: 'Je ne pouvais la comparer à ma première supérieure; quelle différence! Ce n'était ni la même piété, ni la même gravité, ni la même dignité, ni la même ferveur, ni le même esprit, ni le même goût de l'ordre' (Garnier, *La Religieuse*, p. 187).

We can compare the direction of the lesbian Superior's cross-examination of Suzanne to Mme de Moni's, even though some of the questions are identical:

Suzanne, dormez-vous bien? – Vous endormez-vous tout de suite? – Mais quand vous ne vous endormez pas tout de suite, à quoi pensez-vous? – Et le matin, quand vous vous éveillez de bonne heure? – . . . Vous n'aimez pas à rêver? – A vous reposer sur votre oreiller? – A jouir de la douce chaleur du lit? – Jamais vous n'avez été tentée de regarder, avec complaisance, combien vous êtes belle?   (Garnier, *La Religieuse*, pp. 164–5)

Both Superiors are searching for a pattern of symptoms. Mme de Moni, however, wants to know if the spiritual medicine she has administered through her self-mutilation at the altar has had any discernible effect. The Superior of Sainte-Eutrope, like a good *tronchiniste*, attempts to learn about Suzanne's habits. She is more interested in her character, her predispositions, than she is in any extraordinary manifestations: like Casanova, she is a student of the physiology of seduction. But we learn a great deal about her physiology as well: Suzanne observes her so clearly that there is some doubt about which of the pair is more the victim of the other.

One can point out the similarities between a famous description in one of Diderot's letters of the character of a native of Langres, where Diderot himself was born, and the portrait of the Superior of Sainte-Eutrope. 'Les habitants de ce païs ont beaucoup d'esprit, trop de vivacité, une inconstance de girouettes', he writes to Sophie in the letter. '. . . La tête d'un Langrois est sur les épaules comme un coq d'église au haut d'un clocher.'[19] When Suzanne recounts her arrival at Sainte-Eutrope, she soon tells us about the appearance and behaviour of her new Superior:

C'est une petite femme toute ronde, cependant prompte et vive dans ses mouvements; sa tête n'est jamais rassise sur ses épaules; il y a toujours quelque chose qui cloche dans sa vêtement; sa figure est plutôt bien que mal; ses yeux, dont l'un, c'est le droit, est plus haut et plus grand que l'autre, sont pleins de feu et distraits . . . Sa figure décomposée marque tout le décousu de son esprit et toute l'inégalité de son caractère . . .

(Garnier, *La Religieuse*, pp. 139–40)

This is not the only point of implicit comparison between the lesbian Superior and Diderot himself. One discovers quickly that Diderot tended to identify himself with victims;[20] and it is easy enough to observe this tendency in some of his earlier works. *La Religieuse* is a curious document in this respect, because the lesbian Superior, that bundle of contradictions, has so many of Diderot's own characteristics. She is inconsistent, lively and sexed so highly that the slightest stimulus apparently brings her to orgasm. Diderot may have held the common eighteenth-century view that lesbianism and nymphomania, or indeed homosexuality and satyriasis, were related (indeed, it is a view that prevails in popular prejudice today). But we also know that Diderot's own sexual feeling was easily inflamed, and served as an essential part both of the creative process (in the act of composition) and the educative process for the reader (through the vividness of style and example).

The sexual scenes are often ludicrous. While the process of arriving at a climax is carefully observed, as always in Diderot, the means of satisfaction are laughable: the Superior needs only to lift Suzanne's neck-linen, which she does with the mechanical regularity of a wind-up toy, and she is almost at the point of consummation. We can attribute part of this excessively responsive sexuality to a mixture of ignorance and distaste on Diderot's part. But since there is also considerable evidence that the Superior of Sainte-Eutrope is an expression of some of Diderot's own tendencies, we cannot explain her actions quite so simply. Suzanne describes the Superior's recovery after a particularly violent orgasm in interesting terms: 'Cependant cette bonne supérieure, car il est impossible d'être si sensible et de n'être pas bonne, me parut revenir à elle . . .' (Garnier, *La Religieuse*, p. 156). We recall Diderot's earlier enthusiasm for Shaftesbury, who maintained that a good man is one who feels deeply. We may also suspect that there is a touch of the scientific heroism of the eighteenth and nineteenth centuries, when the model doctor experimented dangerously on himself first of all and carefully observed the results of his efforts.

Another example of the Superior's volatile sexuality, related with amusing naïvety by Suzanne, occurs when the Superior, with her hand inevitably under the young nun's neck-linen, seems to faint away with pleasure at the *clavecin*:

Je fis d'abord des accords, ensuite je jouai quelques pièces de Couperin, de Rameau, de Scarlatti; cependant elle avait levé un coin de mon linge de cou, sa main était placée sur mon épaule nue, et l'extrémité de ses doigts posée sur ma gorge. Elle soupirait, elle paraissait oppressée, son haleine s'embarrassait; la main qu'elle tenait sur mon épaule d'abord la pressait fortement, puis elle ne la pressait plus du tout comme si elle eût été sans force et sans vie, et sa tête tombait sur la mienne. En vérité cette folle-là était d'une sensibilité incroyable, et avait le goût le plus vif pour la musique; je n'ai jamais connu personne sur qui elle eût produit des effets aussi singuliers.

(Garnier, *La Religieuse*, p. 152)

It is hardly necessary to reiterate that Diderot often describes himself as reacting in just this strong and sexual way to aesthetic or philosophic stimuli, even though Suzanne's ignorance creates an additional irony, based on misunderstanding.

As in the case of Mme de Moni, the lesbian Superior's sexuality has an essentially male cast. She is politically powerful, and she is the aggressor and the seeker: she wants to know everything about Suzanne – and knowledge itself creates more desire, as we can see when Suzanne recounts the tale of her sufferings at Longchamp (Garnier, *La Religieuse*, pp. 159–60). Her sexual desire is so easily stimulated that we are meant to think of it as a kind of disease. It is too close to Diderot's experience of phallic arousal to be in any way acceptable to him. Her perpetually unsuccessful groping in Suzanne's linen reminds us of Mr B.'s entertaining efforts in *Pamela*. While Mr B. engages in transvestism at one point in an attempt to trick Pamela into compliance, the lesbian Superior is tied into her disguise for ever. She is, in fact, an example of the dreaded *homme–femme*, with the desires of a man and the body and supposed emotional weakness of a woman.

But it is difficult to tease out exactly where the sexual line should be drawn. In the scene which has just been mentioned, in which Suzanne tells the story of her persecutions, the Superior reacts in a manner almost indistinguishable from some of Diderot's own moments of sensuously melting sympathy. 'Ne crains rien,' she tells Suzanne:

'j'aime à pleurer, c'est un état délicieux pour une âme tendre que celui de verser des larmes. Tu dois aimer à pleurer aussi, tu essuieras mes larmes, j'essuierai les tiennes, et peut-être nous serons heureuses au milieu du récit de tes souffrances; qui sait jusqu'où l'attendrissement peut nous mener? . . . Raconte, mon enfant, dit-elle; j'attends, je me sens les dispositions les plus pressantes à m'attendrir; je ne pense pas avoir eu de ma vie un jour plus compatissant et plus affectueux . . .'   (Garnier, *La Religieuse*, p. 159)

Especially in his earlier days, as we have seen in Chapter 4, the *philosophe* had been quite capable of this sort of complacency at the idea of his own sensibility. But by 1760, we can detect the beginning of substantial self-criticism. The Superior's character may have some goodness in it, but her charity is sensual to the core: she luxuriates in her tears as she luxuriates in the cushions that fill her cell. By the time Diderot came to the subject of virtuous tears in his *Salon de 1767*, he had fully worked out his suspicions about motivation:

La Rochefoucauld a dit que, *dans les plus grands malheurs des personnes qui nous sont le* [sic] *plus chères, il y a toujours quelque chose qui ne nous déplaît pas.*
. . . N'y aurait-il pas à cette idée un côté vrai et moins affligeant pour l'espèce humaine? Il est beau, il est doux de compatir aux malheureux; il est beau, il est doux de se sacrifier pour eux. C'est à leur infortune que nous devons la connaissance flatteuse de l'énergie de notre âme.   (A–T, XI, 117)[21]

The lesbian Superior, then, is ethically suspect because she is too responsive. Her precise consciousness of the effect that Suzanne's story will have on her makes her a perfect aesthete, but a very poor moralist. Suzanne's misfortunes only reinforce the Superior's own awareness of herself: her relationship with the young nun is omnivorous, but not properly tender. The fact that Suzanne is unwilling does not keep her from making her attempts: here, again, she reminds us somewhat of Richardson's Mr B. Instead of the loss of the sense of self which we associate with love, we see a constant aggrandizement, an overwhelming drive toward self-affirmation, in which Suzanne's ignorance is enlisted *malgré elle*. In Soeur Thérèse, we see the effects of this same passion when it is extinguished. Thérèse has been sucked out, and is left without strength of will. Her life force seems to fade in direct proportion to the Superior's: there is a degree of vampirism implied in Diderot's account of a rapacious sexual drive.

When Suzanne rejects her advances, in fact, the Superior's fragile organization of feeling breaks down entirely, and she must recognize the emptiness of her isolated life. Unlike Suzanne, the Superior really is a woman possessed, though it is her own desire that inhabits her: like all vampires, she cannot be said to enjoy the restless excess of a vitality which depends on parasitism. When Suzanne, echoing the little novice who shrank from her at Longchamp, mutters, 'Satana, vade retro, apage Satana,' she shows a characteristic lack of empathy; for when *she* turns away from the Superior, confession, madness and death follow with devastating rapidity. The development of the Superior's insanity obviously follows a prescribed pattern. We can turn to the description of the mad nun at the beginning of the novel, before Suzanne has even renounced her vows the first time:

Elle était échevelée et presque sans vêtement; elle traînait des chaînes de fer; ses yeux étaient égarés; elle s'arrachait les cheveux; elle se frappait la poitrine avec les poings; elle courait, elle hurlait; elle se chargeait elle-même, et les autres, des plus terribles imprécations . . .

Suzanne is told, among other things, that the nun thinks herself surrounded by demons, flaming abysses, and other hellish contraptions (Garnier, *La Religieuse*, pp. 45–6). The Superior's madness and death parallel this description closely:

On ne tarda pas à la séquestrer, mais sa prison ne fut pas si bien gardée, qu'elle ne réussît un jour à s'en échapper. Elle avait déchiré ses vêtements, elle parcourait les corridors toute nue, seulement deux bouts de corde rompue pendaient de ses deux bras; elle criait: 'Je suis votre supérieure, vous en avez toutes fait le serment, qu'on m'obéisse. . . . Au feu! . . . Au meurtre! . . . Au voleur! . . . A mon secours! . . . A moi, soeur Thérèse . . . A moi, soeur Suzanne . . .'

. . . Quelle mort, monsieur le marquis! Je l'ai vue, je l'ai vue la terrible image du désespoir et du crime à sa dernière heure. Elle se croyait entourée d'esprits infernaux; ils attendaient son âme pour s'en saisir . . . La soeur Thérèse la suivit de près . . . (Garnier, *La Religieuse*, p. 202)

There is a hint of the violence of this madness even in some of the description of the Superior's orgasms: in one case, for instance, she actually appears to foam at the mouth (Garnier, *La Religieuse*, p. 155).

Orgasm, madness, death: this seems the predictable progression of an ambiguous sexuality which, for all its social haziness, takes over the whole person in its excessive vitality. It is a kind of priapism, most unbecoming to women. Perhaps there is more than coincidence in the fact that the two characters who suffer from this disease in the novels, Mother Sinclair and the lesbian Mother Superior, are mother-figures, sexually mature and even past maturity. These portraits of meno-pausal women are quite devastating in their implications: it appears that there is something quite immoral about women who concentrate on their own fear of mortality, once they have moved beyond childbearing age. Both authors are very severe about these older women, even though it is quite clear that the aged harlot and the middle-aged virgin have never been suitable, or even likely, candi-dates for maternity. Mother Sinclair and the lesbian Superior find how very strong the life-force has become. They die ungracefully, strug-gling as if in the grip of one last diabolical orgasm, while Clarissa and Suzanne, who are neither mothers nor impostor mothers nor leaders nor manipulators of virgin souls, succumb with dignity. Their bodies are unawakened, despite the different sorts of knowledge they acquire. They are, according to their creators, true women.

Madness, of course, is not uniquely the province of these dangerous mother-figures. Suzanne and especially Clarissa also come close to experiencing real derangement. Both for the evil and the virtuous, states of madness continue to deepen and amplify what we know of the characters of the sufferers. It is interesting that Suzanne almost gives in to suicidal despair ('il y a des puits partout'), while Clarissa is plunged deeper into the forms of religious meditation. Even when these meditations no longer follow a pattern of logical expectation, they are still far from being nonsensical ravings. They even move us, in the same way that Ophelia's disconnected bursts of song move us: we recognize a tragic poetry of suffering in them, though the actual experience of the massive disjunction of personality may be unfamiliar to us.

We can oppose the quietest madness or near-madness to which Suzanne and Clarissa are susceptible to the mania which characterizes the two *hommes–femmes*. Like Satan in *Paradise Lost*, Mother Sinclair and the Superior of Sainte-Eutrope are always incapable of insight. Given a chance to peer into the noumenal world, they see only hallucinations. The Moor in the cavern remains forever masked. Clarissa, on the other hand, perceives the world (including Mother Sinclair) as part of a waking nightmare because that is precisely what it has become, and her madness is therefore a way of seeing beneath the masks of daily perception. The best sorts of breakdown (and I don't think that it is a Romantic anachronism to attribute a respect for madness to either Richardson or Diderot) allow for clear sight and reorganization. They are not so total that the core of an essentially sturdy personality is lost from sight. This is the kind of breakdown which Clarissa experiences; while Suzanne's despair is a consequence (and not the final one) of insight itself.

Richardson and the feminization of knowing

What, then, can we finally say about Diderot's debt to Richardson? There has been some evidence that Diderot did not imitate his contemporary in technical matters to any great extent; and if we look at Suzanne alone, we would find it difficult to make a serious comparison between her and Clarissa on moral or aesthetic grounds. But if we study Diderot's fictional convents as a whole, we can see the outlines of a by now familiar sexual mythology. Diderot has taken the battle between Clarissa and Lovelace into an entirely female realm. Sexuality, as in Richardson's brothel, serves as background and motive, but both the seducer and the seduced are women.

The male figures who interrupt the daily round of brutality or depravity seem mostly to be the representatives of the rationalistic and compassionate society to which Diderot himself would have belonged, but they are singularly ineffectual. M. Manouri loses the trial which he has undertaken on behalf of Suzanne, partially through rhetorical incompetence; the archdeacon Hébert can only control the immediate injustice done to Suzanne at the hands of Mère Sainte-Christine, but does not appear again after her transferral to the convent of Sainte-Eutrope; Suzanne's first confessor, Père Lemoine, does succeed in getting her out of the clutches of the Superior, but he is quickly replaced, while the second, Dom Morel, shares so much of Suzanne's disaffection with monastic life that he, too, finds himself in a similar position: 'Le nouveau directeur est également persécuté par ses supérieurs, et me persuade de me sauver de la maison' (Garnier, *La Religieuse*, p. 203).

The forces of irrationalism, represented by the kindly mysticism of Mme de Moni, but more commonly by the sadism and excess of the nuns who succeed her, seem to be winning against the forces of Enlightenment. Recent feminist interpretations of Mozart's *Magic Flute* (performed in 1791) have emphasized that the libretto is, among other things, a parable about the triumph of the light of patriarchy over the darkness of matriarchy.[22] In this novel, one could say that the Church, the Queen of the Night herself, still exercises unscrupulous power. The narrow-mindedness and bigotry of religious attitudes have an exact parallel in the perversion of sexuality among the priestesses of Catholicism.

But if we cling to this almost allegorical interpretation of *La Religieuse*, we are doing both Richardson and Diderot an injustice. A more significant point about this work is its uneasy androgyny. If the three Superiors are all, in one way or another, *hommes–femmes*, only the lesbian Superior has been portrayed as such consciously enough to merit a violent end. As we have seen in the case of Mme de Moni, the imagery and the notion of efficacy with which this strong character is imbued suggest a certain rather conventional picture of masculinity: Diderot is unique neither among his contemporaries nor among his sex in granting honorary manhood to deserving women. We are attempting to tease out an ideology, a certain pattern of eighteenth-century clichés, when we refer to such qualities as strength and incisiveness as male. On the other hand, Mme de Moni has certain talents (for prophecy, deep feeling and empathy) which show her to be particularly feminine by Diderot's standards; and her death, much like Clarissa's, is noble and peaceful.

Suzanne, of course, is an *homme–femme* in much the same way. She has a rationalist's eye, and her scrutiny, so like a steadily illuminated lens, has an active effect on the darkness of the Catholic womb (to mix a metaphor) in which she finds herself trapped. She is the only nun of her sisterhood to make connections to the outside world and, when she does so, it is always with men. But what is so curiously Richardsonian about her position is her purity. Clarissa is pure too, but hers is the purity of a full human being. Suzanne is a medium, a life lived rather than the person who lives it. Clarissa looks inward. She develops an identity out of the shattered expectations of her family, her seducer, her society and her class. The fact that her suffering and death have profound social (and literary) consequences is almost incidental to her destiny. Suzanne looks outward: even the descriptions of her own despair are reports, rather than the musings of a troubled mind.

Nonetheless, Suzanne does succeed in moving us. Perhaps the criticism in these pages appears unfairly harsh. It is not meant to be. After all our reservations and mockeries have been disposed of, we must admit that Suzanne can bring tears to our eyes, as she did to those of her creator. Yet her double birth – in the laughter of the group gathered around Mme d'Épinay's dinner table, and in the sensibility of the *philosophe* alone in his study – may be seen as an emblem of the complexity of her history. We can offer an almost purely epistemological interpretation of her function as a character – as indeed we have done – because there is little doubt that the very process of the acquisition of knowledge, whether through perception or intuition, is being brought under observation in this novel. Despite the coltishness of language and gesture in some parts of the work, however, there is a genuine charm about some of the more powerful scenes. The *cri de coeur* when Suzanne flings herself before the Archdeacon after her supposed exorcism, for example, is entirely convincing:

Je fis quelques pas, puis je revins, et je me prosternai aux pieds de la supérieure et de l'archidiacre.

'Eh bien, me dit-il, qu'est-ce qu'il y a?'

Je lui dis, en lui montrant ma tête meurtrie en plusieurs endroits, mes pieds ensanglantés, mes bras livides et sans chair, mon vêtement sale et déchiré:

'Vous voyez!' (Garnier, *La Religieuse*, p. 116)

The debt to Richardson in such a passage is quite clear. Gesture and costume offer mute testimony to Suzanne's suffering, and she has no need for long speeches. The quality of her suffering, however, differs in essentials from Clarissa's. It is used as proof or evidence of injustice: the courtroom, even if an ecclesiastical one, is not located in the hereafter, but in the present, on earth. Suzanne is no martyr, and her patience does not extend to silence when a golden opportunity to reveal all arises. She is in the convent against her will; she collects her data methodically, faces the consequences bravely, and flees without a feeling that she has done wrong. If we think of Clarissa during her flight to Hampstead, by contrast, when she makes no attempt to contradict Lovelace upon his visit to reclaim her, or if we remember her cheerful and smiling as death closes in, we can see that Suzanne serves quite a different fictional purpose.

Suzanne, indeed, may be seen as an embattled philosopher, fighting for the right to know and to act freely in a world where the exercising of these faculties is by no means yet perceived as God-given. It is instructive to reflect on the two environments of hypocrisy in *Clarissa* and *La Religieuse*. At Harlowe Place, in *Clarissa*, a crass materialism wears pious clothes; in *La Religieuse*, the hypocrisy is of exactly the same kind, even if the Harlowes are greedy landowners and the nuns are supposedly religious recluses. But the two heroines are fighting quite different battles: Clarissa seeks the restoration of spiritual meaning in life, while Suzanne offers a humanistic secularism which is neither inconsistent with her professions of faith nor dependent on them.

Like the Superior of Sainte-Eutrope, Suzanne has a great deal of her creator in her. Richardson has made the space, as it were, for Diderot to express his notions about perception, feeling and development in a significant literary form. He has provided an imagery for Diderot's art and, more important, a new view of the self. When Diderot makes

Suzanne an instrument of knowledge, he is perhaps giving us a general metaphor. Her very purity allows her to be both mother and midwife to knowledge, the Virgin Mary of a secular world. But there is no escaping the commentary that Diderot must be providing on himself as well: he, too, is a midwife at the birth of knowledge, a stringed instrument, the weeping Encyclopedist who points helplessly at his own scars. Since he does not believe in a hereafter, he can hardly subscribe to Clarissa's lesson that the integrity of the self (including an immortal soul) is power; after all, earthly rewards become insignificant by such a standard. But does he believe, with the rest of the *côterie Holbachique*, that knowledge is power? Does Kant's *Sapere aude* really apply?

One leaves *La Religieuse* with the distinct impression that Suzanne's femininity, and the passivity which is so prominent in the chronicles of her sufferings, weaken the case for Enlightenment. When we consider the Superior of Sainte-Eutrope, with her frightening imbalances, her agility in moving toward and away from social expectation, we are even more puzzled. Her sexuality is very close to Diderot's own as he wrote about it, at least: and she is certainly condemned for it. Her sexual energy, and the pursuit of the special kind of knowledge which it brings, seem deliberately to be placed in the 'wrong' body. There are no triumphs in *La Religieuse*: only the rejection of one social role after another. Diderot chooses to practise a sort of fictional transvestism which will doubtless leave readers mystified for some time to come. It is difficult for us to understand why the blurring of sexual distinctions holds such terror and fascination for him (indeed, a comparison with *Sir Charles Grandison* might be illuminating from this point of view). But it is easy to see a certain degree of self-condemnation in these portraits of women who, in one way or another, are failures. Richardson's mythology has helped Diderot to consider the moral and philosophical aspects of sexuality, and to restore a certain dignity both to women and to sexual self-expression. It has, surprisingly enough, become a means of self-analysis for the *philosophe* as well. The mistrust of feeling (especially the submission to quasi-sexual impulse as a substitute for moral action), never leaves him after the writing of this novel. Though the connection may at times seem hidden, both the *Éloge* and *La Religieuse* suggest that Diderot read and learned from Richardson better than any of his contemporaries (with, of course, the exception of Rousseau). He was perhaps the only reader who saw that Clarissa never submitted to feeling and impulse either. Richardson would have fared better in his own and succeeding centuries if lesser readers had seen as much.

AFTERWORD

The exaltation of women in fiction really began with *Clarissa*; and the cult of tears reached its height in the decades after the novel's publication in 1748. But women were not the only clientele for the new form and its emphasis on feeling, though its impact on them was great. As male readers came under the sway of the new heroines, they too in a sense *became* the women under attack in literature. This process of identification, unique to its time, has been neither perceived properly nor understood properly. It is easier to study the most literal aspects of the problem of 'influence' – what writers read, the conditions of publication, readership figures, and so on – than it is to write with precision about a diffused sensibility. Yet it is also clear that Richardson, Diderot, Prévost, Sterne and the German critics and writers of the same period shared an emotional climate. A 'feminization of culture' (a term I borrow from the title of the brilliant book by Ann Douglas) began in eighteenth-century England and France. Richardson provided a necessary moment of recognition, a tragic myth that in its way and time was as powerful as any our culture has evolved.

This book is proposed as one case study among the many that would be required for any real understanding of such a development. I have attempted simply to answer this question: what is the nature of the myth, and how did it arise? In Richardson's novel, the trial of Clarissa involves both her sexuality and her religion. We are given the exploration of a secularized passion which puts all of mid-century morality on trial. In the end, *Clarissa* provides the model for a sexualization of religion; and the story of the heroine's fall and rise, as it were, is the mythic narrative of that process. There is a distinct shift of sexual responsibility in this novel. Men become the evil sexual force in culture and women become suffering servants, guardians and emblems of a property-centred and individualistic moral universe. The profane and secular have become, in a word, sacred.

Conveniently for the scholar, Richardson himself was relatively ill-read. It is easy to recognize that his own vocabulary and interests are not themselves deeply rooted in literary tradition, but at the same time it is possible to make grand claims for his effect on literary posterity. *Clarissa* is one of the few works of art which has had a really profound effect on both learned and popular culture. After the first few enthusiastic decades, novels of its length and its leisurely eighteenth-century pace were no longer tolerated by the reading public, and it became the exclusive province of specialists who spent most of their time (as I suggested in my Introduction) squabbling with one another about its literary merits. The very reason for the constant bickering was probably its peculiar influence on the culture of the West. On the one hand, it contributed substantially to the 'mainstream' view of women and their place in society. In most Victorian novels, strong women pay for their strength, either through death or through some other sort of martyrdom in unhappy marriages or secret undeclared loves. The good girl languishes too, but has accepted the condition of suffering as essential to her female identity (we may think of the heroines of Wilkie Collins's *Woman in White* as well as of the women in the novels of George Eliot and Elizabeth Gaskell). There are no bouncing Fieldingesque heroines or women who exert any control at all over their fates in the vast bulk of popular literature, and very few even in the major novels of the nineteenth century. The exceptions are so rare that they spring to mind instantly: opportunists like Becky Sharp, rebels like the heroines of *Jane Eyre* or *Wuthering Heights*. We know also that by the nineteenth century, novels of the Richardsonian type had become firmly entrenched as mirrors of society: they were meant to reflect social and psychological realities. We are still grappling with the implications of such an aesthetic today.

On the other hand, there is a way in which *Clarissa* went distinctly underground. It is the sort of novel which filters through the roots of consciousness, like a subterranean stream. Writers may have read Richardson (and I am sure that even in Victorian times the number that did so declined steadily), but the ordinary reader did not. Richardson's profoundly subversive critique of his society antagonized the educated men of the nineteenth century and yet became the model for an essentially 'feminine' fiction. In attacking Richardson, the Victorians were attacking that part of themselves which rejected the sexual myth in *Clarissa*, even though the dominant culture subscribed to a partly misapprehended version of it.

The readers of *Clarissa* were not, of course, confined to England. When we come to writers in other countries, our criteria change slightly. A true myth on this scale will cross national boundaries, but will have to be readily assimilable into a variety of cultural traditions.

In my close reading of Diderot, himself a close reader of Richardson, I have tried to show that Diderot indeed recognized what Richardson's novels, and in particular *Clarissa*, were all about. He was even able to criticize other French writers such as Prévost and Rousseau for their failure or success as imitators of the Richardsonian model. His interest in Richardson was linked to specific aesthetic concerns – the relationship of drama to the novel, the nature of heroes and heroines in contemporary literary forms, the imitation of reality in general – and to political, religious and even scientific preoccupations which I have tried at least briefly to expose. But if we are to believe the *Éloge*, Richardson was most important to Diderot as a measure of the moral sensitivity and ultimate worth of the people around him. Even from his anti-Catholic and anti-clerical perspective, Diderot recognized that a certain transformation of religious impulse had occurred. And as it happened, the relationship between sexuality and religion was one of his own obsessions.

A scholar who wanted to continue this sort of work could profitably spend considerable time linking *Clarissa* with national traditions in a more specific way: with the *préciosité* of seventeenth-century France, for example. That is another period in which language was examined and eroticized in the service of a peculiarly feminine rhetoric. Or one might consider *Clarissa* as an early *Bildungsroman*, antedating the German movement at the end of the eighteenth century and beginning of the nineteenth, which concentrated on the education of young men. *Clarissa*, after all, is an extended study of the evolution of the single person in a society apparently inimical to the development of individuals, but ultimately deeply dependent on the ideology of individualism.

Perhaps most interesting of all in a history of readings of a major text is the history of misreadings which accompanies it. Though the study of misreading has been the life work of Harold Bloom, it doesn't take a Bloomian world-view to recognize the importance of this essentially irrational process. Characters misread each other even within *Clarissa* itself. All readers, and not only those with a vocation, are called into some sort of creative dialogue with a significant text; not only with the text itself, but with what they learn of it at second hand in their daily experience (through hearsay, gossip, reviews or letters, for example). Certainly that is how novels, films and television operate. At the same time, we must remember that the strongest readers of fiction read their predecessors very precisely indeed, as we can see in the case of Richardson and Diderot. From a creative point of view, such a precise reading is not necessarily the best. Diderot's *Religieuse* doesn't compare in complexity with *Clarissa*. But since some aspects of *Clarissa* were understood by very few readers indeed, it is worth examining the criticism of a brilliant and empathetic admirer. Even so, Diderot used the myth he understood so well in a special way in his novel. The gap between his criticism of Richardson and his own efforts at absorption or emulation is great enough to allow us to say that if he was not a misreader, he was still a miswriter, as indeed all writers of any consequence must be.

The really significant history of misreading has yet to be compiled. From Rousseau to Sade, from the Gothic novels of Mrs Radcliffe to the Perils of Pauline, from Jane Austen to Virginia Woolf, there are enough texts which misunderstand, rework and sometimes challenge the doctrine of transcendence in *Clarissa*. The 'religion of sex', as Leslie Fiedler has put it, has been potent indeed, making converts in every European culture from the eighteenth century to our own. This study is offered as a beginning. I have tried to understand the source of Richardson's originality by looking closely at the mythology to which he somehow managed to give expression; and I have studied one of his most faithful and intelligent readers in another culture. The fact that Diderot's sensibility, education and interests were so radically different from Richardson's strengthens the argument, I think, for the existence and apprehension of a deep mythic structure of belief about sexuality. The story of subsequent misunderstandings will then, I hope, be made easier to tell.

NOTES

Introduction

1 T. C. Duncan Eaves and Ben D. Kimpel, *Samuel Richardson: A Biography* (Oxford: The Clarendon Press, 1971). This biography gives an excellent summary of the quarrels between Pamelists and anti-Pamelists, and is a good source generally on subsequent debates. See ch. VI, 'The Pamela Vogue; *Pamela* Part II, 1740–1742', pp. 119–53. I shall cite this work hereafter as Eaves and Kimpel.

2 Mme Le Prince de Beaumont, *Contes Moraux* (Lyon: Pierre Bruyset Ponthos, 1774), p. 97.

3 Jean-Jacques Rousseau, *Julie, ou La Nouvelle Héloïse*, ed. René Pomeau (Paris: Éditions Garnier Frères, 1960), p. 4.

4 For an excellent discussion of the claims to realism of early fiction, see Arthur Jerrold Tieje, 'A Peculiar Phase of the Theory of Realism in Pre-Richardsonian Fiction', *PMLA*, 28 (1913), 213–52.

5 Vivienne Mylne, *The Eighteenth-Century French Novel: Techniques of Illusion*, 2nd edn (Cambridge, England: Cambridge University Press, 1981), p. 221.

6 Pierre Choderlos de Laclos, 'De l'éducation des femmes', in *Oeuvres complètes* (Paris: Bibliothèque de la Pléiade, 1944).

7 Tony Tanner, *Adultery in the Novel: Contract and Transgression* (Baltimore and London: The Johns Hopkins University Press, 1979).

8 Mylne, *The Eighteenth-Century French Novel*, p. 222.

9 Leslie Stephen, *English Literature and Society in the Eighteenth Century* (London: Duckworth & Co., 1904), pp. 161–2.

10 Cited in Eaves and Kimpel, p. 1. Original source is S. T. Coleridge, *Anima Poetae*, ed. Ernest Hartley Coleridge (London: 1895), p. 166.

11 Ian Watt, *The Rise of the Novel* (Berkeley and Los Angeles: University of California Press, 1967), p. 153, hereafter cited as Watt.

12 Story told and citations included in Eaves and Kimpel, p. 352.

13 The reader may make judgments about the worth of recent criticism independently. Two such works are Nancy K. Miller, *The Heroine's Text: Readings in the French and English Novel, 1722–82* (New York: Columbia University Press, 1980), and Janet Todd, *Women's Friendship in Literature* (New York: Columbia University Press, 1980). A critical exchange on

Richardson and Fielding took place in the pages of the journal *Novel*. Cf. Antony J. Hassall, 'Women in Richardson and Fielding', *Novel* (Winter 1981), in reply to Katherine M. Rogers, 'Sensitive Feminism versus Conventional Sympathy: Richardson and Fielding on Women', *Novel* (Spring 1976).

14 See especially Michel Foucault, *The History of Sexuality, Volume I: An Introduction*, trans. Robert Hurley (London: Allen Lane, 1978).

15 Mark Kinkead-Weekes, *Samuel Richardson: Dramatic Novelist* (London: Eyre Methuen Press, 1973), hereafter cited as Kinkead-Weekes.

16 Margaret Anne Doody, *A Natural Passion: A Study of the Novels of Samuel Richardson* (Oxford: Oxford University Press, 1974), hereafter cited as Doody.

17 Kinkead-Weekes, p. 397.

18 Ibid., pp. 402–3.

19 Ibid., p. 419.

20 Ibid., pp. 424–5.

21 Another recent work in this tradition is by Carol Houlihan Flynn, *Samuel Richardson: A Man of Letters* (Princeton, NJ: Princeton University Press, 1982).

22 William Beatty Warner, *Reading Clarissa: The Struggles of Interpretation* (New Haven and London: Yale University Press, 1979), hereafter cited as Warner.

23 Ibid., p. 39.

24 Ibid., p. 57.

25 Ibid., p. 260.

26 Recently published by Cornell University Press, Ithaca, New York (1982), under the title *Clarissa's Ciphers: Meaning and Disruption in Richardson's Novels*. I have not yet seen a copy of the book.

27 Samuel Johnson, 'The Preface to Shakespeare' (1765), excerpted in *The Restoration and the Eighteenth Century* (vol. 3 of *The Oxford Anthology of English Literature*), ed. Martin Price (New York and London: Oxford University Press, 1973), pp. 566–7.

28 Robert Palfrey Utter and Gwendolyn Needham, *Pamela's Daughters* (New York: Macmillan, 1936).

29 Some of the works by these authors which have been consulted include Ernst Cassirer, *The Philosophy of Symbolic Forms, vol. 2: Mythical Thought* (New Haven: Yale University Press, 1955, 1965), and *Language and Myth*, trans. Suzanne K. Langer (New York: Dover Publications Inc., 1946); Sigmund Freud, *Totem and Taboo* (London: Routledge & Kegan Paul, 1975); Claude Lévi-Strauss, *The Raw and the Crooked*, vol. I of *An Introduction to a Science of Mythology*, trans. John and Doreen Weightman (New York and Evanston: Harper & Row, 1969); Edmund Leach, *Culture and Communication* (Cambridge, England: Cambridge University Press, 1979); Roy Wagner, *Lethal Speech: Daribi Myth as Symbolic Obviation* (Ithaca and London: Cornell University Press, 1978), and *The Invention of Culture* (Chicago and London: The University of Chicago Press, 1981).

30 Roland Barthes, *Mythologies* (St Albans, Herts.: Granada Publishing, 1973).

31 Ibid., p. 116; also see Barthes on mythic language, p. 110.

32 Paul Ricoeur, *De l'interprétation: essai sur Freud* (Paris: Éditions du Seuil, 1965), pp. 49–50.

33 Roy Wagner, *The Invention of Culture*, p. 66.

34 According to scientists to whom I've spoken, however, taxonomy belongs to the infancy of science, when explanatory models are not yet very sophisticated.

35 K. K. Ruthven, *Myth*, no. 31 in the series *The Critical Idiom* (London: Methuen & Co., 1976), pp. 72ff.

36 Northrop Frye, *Anatomy of Criticism* (New York: Atheneum, 1969).

37 Jonathan Culler, *The Pursuit of Signs: Semiotics, Literature, Deconstruction* (London: Routledge & Kegan Paul, 1981).

38 See Culler's discussion, ibid., pp. 54ff, and Hans Robert Jauss, 'Literaturgeschichte als Provokation der Literaturwissenschaft', in *Literaturgeschichte als Provokation* (Frankfurt am Main: Suhrkamp Verlag, 1970), pp. 144–207.

1 *Clarissa* and the Puritan conduct books

1 Anna Laetitia Barbauld, ed., *The Correspondence of Samuel Richardson* (London, 1804), IV, 187 – hereafter cited as 'Barbauld', with volume and page number. The letter is dated 6 October 1748 (?), and Lady Bradshaigh still uses the pseudonym 'Mrs Belfour' at this early stage in her acquaintance with Richardson.

2 Eaves and Kimpel, p. 286.

3 Fuller discussions may be found in: Katherine Hornbeak, 'Richardson's *Familiar Letters* and the Domestic Conduct Books', *Smith College Studies in Modern Languages*, 19, no. 2 (January 1938), 1–29; Herbert Schöffler, *Protestantismus und Literatur: Neue Wege zur Englischen Literatur des 18. Jahrhunderts* (Göttingen: Vandenhoeck & Ruprecht, 1958), pp. 151–80; Cynthia Griffin Wolff, *Samuel Richardson and the Eighteenth-Century Puritan Character* (Hamden, Conn.: Archon Books, 1972), pp. 4–54; John A. Dussinger, 'Conscience and the Pattern of Christian Perfection in *Clarissa*', *PMLA*, 81.1 (1966), 236–45; Doody, chs II and VII. A very complete survey of conduct books and texts on the education of women involved in the *Ladies Library* may be found in Rae Blanchard, 'Richard Steele and the Status of Women', *Studies in Philology*, 26 (1929), 325–55, but it takes no account of Puritan influences or attitudes in these works. Also see (for a general account) Levin L. Schücking, *The Puritan Family: A Social Study from the Literary Sources*, trans. Brian Battershaw, 1929 (rpt London: Routledge & Kegan Paul, 1969). William Sale tells us, in his classic *Samuel Richardson: Master Printer* (Ithaca, NY: Cornell University Press, 1950), that Richardson actually printed Defoe's *Family Instructor* in 1727, and his *Religious Courtship* in 1729 (p. 162).

4 I, 367 (hereafter abbreviated to *CH*).

5 Wolff, *Samuel Richardson and the Puritan Character*, p. 18; also *CH*, II, 194–5.

6 Erich Poetzsche, 'Samuel Richardsons Belesenheit: Eine literarische Untersuchung', *Kieler Studien zur englischen Philologie*, NF I–IV, 1908, cites two quotations from Richardson's letters in which the novelist comments on 'Bishop Fleetwood', p. 56. The work itself is William Fleetwood, *The Relative Duties of Parents and Children . . . etc* (London: 1705), hereafter cited as Fleetwood.

7 Joanna Clare Dales, 'The Novel as Domestic Conduct Book: Richardson to Jane Austen' Diss. Cambridge, 1970, p. 54.

8 Jeremy Taylor, *The Rule and Exercise of Holy Living . . . [and Holy Dying]*, 10th edn (London: 1674), p. 50, hereafter cited as Taylor, and abbreviated to *HL* and *HD* respectively. See the *CBEL* and the Catalogue of the British Museum for a list of editions.

9 Richard Allestree, *The Whole Duty of Man* (London: 1751), hereafter cited as Allestree. First edition, 1658–60.

10 William Gouge, *Of Domesticall Duties, Eight Treatises* (3rd edn) (London: 1634), pp. 447–8, hereafter cited as W. Gouge.

11 Schöffler, *Protestantismus und Literatur*, pp. 183ff; Watt, pp. 36, 49–50.

12 Thomas Gouge, *Christian Directions, shewing How to walk with GOD All the Day long*, (London: 1661), ch. 3, 'Of Ejaculatory Prayers', hereafter cited as T. Gouge.

13 Kinkead-Weekes, pp. 123ff. See also Frederick W. Hilles, 'The Plan of *Clarissa*, *PQ*, 45 (1966), 236–48.

14 I am indebted to Professor Theodore Ziolkowski, of Princeton University, for the terms 'framework' and 'core'. I have borrowed them from his analysis of the structure of the German elegy.

15 See, for example, *Pamela, or Virtue Rewarded* (London: J. M. Dent & Sons, 1938), II, Letter XXXVII, 185ff.

16 John Carroll, ed., *Selected Letters of Samuel Richardson* (Oxford: The Clarendon Press, 1964), pp. 141–2, hereafter cited as Carroll.

17 For an interesting view of the strained and even short-sighted over-attentiveness of the letter-reader in an epistolary novel, see John Preston, *The Created Self: The Reader's Role in Eighteenth-Century Fiction* (London: Heinemann, 1970), pp. 38–40.

18 T. Gouge, ch. 3, p. 5, 'Of Secret Prayer in the Morning'.

19 Schöffler, *Protestantismus und Literatur*, p. 153.

20 Ann Douglas, *The Feminization of American Culture* (New York: Alfred A. Knopf, 1977).

21 Joanna C. Dales, 'The Novel as Domestic Conduct Book', pp. 99–100.

22 Raymond Williams, *The Country and the City* (St Albans, Herts.: Paladin, 1975), p. 84.

23 I am indebted to Jean L'Espérance, a social historian formerly at the University of Essex and one of the founders of the Women's Research and Resources Centre in London, for alerting me to the change in attitudes

towards sex in the conduct books, and for her enormously helpful guidance on Puritanism in general.

24 See, for example, Paul Kluckhohn, *Die Auffassung der Liebe in der Literatur des 18. Jahrhunderts und in der deutschen Romantik* (Halle: Verlag von Max Niemeyer, 1922), pp. 68–74; Christopher Hill, 'Clarissa Harlowe and her Times', *Essays in Criticism*, 5 (1955), 315–40, but especially pp. 330–2; William H. Haller, *The Rise of Puritanism* (Philadelphia: University of Pennsylvania, 1972), pp. 120ff; and, of course, the inevitable Schücking and Schöffler, whose relevant pages have been cited elsewhere in these Notes.

25 W. Gouge, pp. 179–268.

26 Joanna C. Dales, 'The Novel as Domestic Conduct Book', pp. 56–62.

27 *The Ladies Library*, p. 173.

28 Ibid., Introduction, pp. 5–6.

29 For another view (though I think it untenable on the basis of evidence), see Watt, pp. 144ff, on female chastity and unmarried women.

30 Allestree, *The Ladies Calling*, p. 158; also cited in Watt, p. 144.

31 H. J. Habakkuk, 'Marriage Settlements in the Eighteenth Century', *Transactions of the Royal Historical Society*, XXXII (1949), 15–30.

32 A roughly contemporary account of this process at work may be found in Patrick Colquhoun, *A Treatise on the Police of the Metropolis* (London: 1796).

33 Williams, *The Country and the City*, pp. 68–71.

34 Stone, *The Family, Sex and Marriage*, pp. 272–5.

35 *The Ladies Library*, pp. 40–2.

36 *The Poems of Alexander Pope*, ed. John Butt (London: Methuen & Co., 1975), p. 562, lines 61–8. Pope's famous line, '. . . ev'ry Woman is at heart a Rake', comes from this poem as well (line 216).

37 *Pamela*, II, 263, 288.

38 Samuel Richardson, *The History of Sir Charles Grandison*, ed. Jocelyn Harris (Oxford: Oxford University Press, 1972), p. 143, hereafter cited as *Grandison*.

39 For a description of life at these two retreats, see Eaves and Kimpel, pp. 65, 496ff. Also see Dorothy Marshall, *Dr Johnson's London* (London, New York and Sydney: John Wiley & Sons, 1968), p. 35.

40 *Grandison*, I, 131, 188.

41 Mark Kinkead-Weekes, 'Defoe and Richardson: Novelists of the City', in *The Sphere History of Literature in the English Language*, vol. IV, ed. R. Lonsdale (London: Sphere Inc., 1971), p. 254.

42 Dorothy Marshall, *Dr Johnson's London*, pp. 55–6, 125–7, 124. See also E. N. Williams, *Life in Georgian England* (London: Batsford, 1963), pp. 31, 51–3, 58–9, 72–3, 74–5. For a more contemporary account, see Tobias Smollett, *Humphry Clinker* (1771), also cited by Marshall.

43 Cited in Eaves and Kimpel, p. 539. The phrase appears in a letter to Mrs Delany, 14 March 1753.

44 Barbauld, I, 'Introduction', p. 114.

45 All quotations from Allestree, *The Ladies Calling*, Preface.

46 I am indebted to Ruth Perry, Associate Professor of English in the Department of the Humanities, MIT, for pointing this out.

47 Mary Astell, *The Christian Religion, as Profess'd by a Daughter of the Church of England* (London: 1705), pp. 35–6.

48 Ibid., p. 37.

49 Ibid., p. 34.

2 The moral struggle at Harlowe Place

1 John Milton, *Comus*, lines 329–30. Also Gillian Beer, 'Richardson, Milton and the Status of Evil', *RES*, NS 19, no. 75 (1968), 262; John A. Dussinger, 'Conscience and the Pattern of Christian Perfection in *Clarissa*'; Cynthia Griffin Wolff, *Samuel Richardson and the Eighteenth-Century Puritan Character*, p. 103.

2 Paul E. Parnell, 'The Sentimental Mask', *PMLA*, 78 (1963), 532.

3 Cynthia Griffin Wolff, *Samuel Richardson and the Eighteenth-Century Puritan Character*, p. 131.

4 Cited in Patricia M. Spacks, 'Ev'ry Woman is at Heart a Rake', *Eighteenth-Century Studies*, 8 (Fall 1974), 36.

5 *OED*, 'Honour'.

6 John Locke, *Essay Concerning Human Understanding* (1690; facsimile rpt Menston, Yorkshire, England: The Scolar Press, 1970), bk. III, ch. 10, sect. 34, p. 251. Misquoted in Watt, p. 28.

7 *OED*, 'Honesty'.

8 See, for example, two of Richardson's letters to Hester Mulso in Carroll, pp. 185, 217.

9 For more on Richardson's debt to Milton, see William Marks Sowell, 'The Novel as Puritan Romance: A Comparative Study of Samuel Richardson, the Brontës, Thomas Hardy and D. H. Lawrence', Diss. Stanford University, 1964, pp. 1–30.

10 William Wycherley, *Plays*, ed. Gerald Weales (New York: New York University Press, 1967), pp. 259, 319.

11 *The Works of Sir George Etherege: Containing his Plays and Poems* (London: 1715), p. 197.

12. Ibid., p. 194.

13 See, for example, Cynthia Griffin Wolff, *Samuel Richardson and the Eighteenth-Century Puritan Character*, pp. 102–3.

14 On witchcraft, see Keith Thomas, *Religion and the Decline of Magic: Studies in Popular Beliefs in Sixteenth- and Seventeenth-Century England* (London: Weidenfeld & Nicolson, 1971); Alan Macfarlane, *Witchcraft in Tudor and Stuart England: A Regional and Comparative Study* (London: Routledge & Kegan Paul, 1970); H. R. Trevor-Roper, 'The European Witch-Craze', in *The Crisis of the Seventeenth Century: Religion, the Reformation and Social Change* (New York: Harper & Row, 1968), pp. 110, 127.

15 Leslie Fiedler, *Love and Death in the American Novel* (New York: Criterion Books, 1960), chs 1–3.
16 Joseph Glanvill, *Saducismus Triumphatus: or, Full and Plain Evidence Concerning Witches and Apparitions*, ed. Coleman O. Parsons (1689; facsimile rpt Gainesville, Fla: Scholars' Facsimiles and Reprints, 1966), Parsons's Introduction.
17 Erich Poetzsche, 'Samuel Richardsons Belesenheit: Eine literarische Untersuchung', p. 54.
18 Glanvill, *Saducismus Triumphatus*, 'The Postscript', p. 29.
19 Ibid., p. 362.
20 Kinkead-Weekes, pp. 230–1.

3 'Clarissa lives: LET THIS EXPIATE!'

1 James Boswell, *Life of Johnson*, ed. R. W. Chapman and J. D. Fleeman (London: Oxford University Press, 1970), p. 480.
2 Watt, p. 232.
3 My discussion here is based on an undergraduate seminar on medieval literature conducted in 1968–9 by John Freccero, then Professor in the Department of Romance Literature at Cornell University, and now at Stanford. There was nothing elementary about this introduction to Dante and Petrarch. I have been much influenced by his discussion of biblical criticism and theology and their relationship to literature. See also Frank Kermode, *The Sense of an Ending: Studies in the Theory of Fiction* (London: Oxford University Press, 1967), p. 25.
4 *Dante's Inferno*, ed. and trans. John D. Sinclair (New York: Oxford University Press, 1969), p. 75.
5 René Girard, *Deceit, Desire and the Novel: The Self and Other in Literary Structure*, trans. Yvonne Freccero (Baltimore, Md, and London: Johns Hopkins University Press, 1965).
6 Francis Ferguson, however, uses the terms 'logic' and 'rhythm' interchangeably in his analysis of tragedy. See *The Idea of a Theater* (Princeton, NJ: Princeton University Press, 1972), pp. 40–1.
7 Linda K. Kerber, 'The Politicks of Housework', *Signs*, 4 (2), 402–6.
8 J. E. Cirlot, *A Dictionary of Symbols* (2nd ed.), trans. Jack Sage (London: Routledge & Kegan Paul, 1971), pp. 358, 152–3, 71, 286–7.

4 Diderot's *Éloge de Richardson* and the problem of realism

1 Eaves and Kimpel, p. 493.
2 Ibid., p. 583.
3 *Grandison*, 3, 400.
4 Letter to Warburton, 14 April 1748; cited in Eaves and Kimpel, p. 583.
5 Ibid., pp. 318–19.
6 Ibid., p. 494.
7 Cf. Anita Brookner, *Greuze: The Rise and Fall of an Eighteenth-Century Phenomenon* (London: Elek, 1972), pp. 21–2, 25.

8   A somewhat dated and inaccurate account of Diderot's impact on drama
    is to be found in J. Assézat and Maurice Tourneux, *Oeuvres complètes de
    Diderot* (Paris: Garnier Frères, 1875–7), VII, Assézat's 'Notices pré-
    liminaires', 6–9 and 171–3. Hereafter cited as A–T, followed by vol. no.
    and page. Jacques and Anne-Marie Chouillet, who have edited vol. X (*Le
    Drame bourgeois, Fiction II*) of the authoritative new edition of the *Oeuvres*
    (Paris: Hermann, Éditeurs des Sciences et des Arts, 1980), have pointed
    to the immediate and considerable influence of Diderot's drama in
    France, xviii. This edition, which will be used in my discussion where
    appropriate, will be known by its abbreviation DPV for its three editors,
    Professors Dieckmann, Proust and Varloot. For more on the performance
    of Diderot's plays, especially *Le Fils naturel*, see Jacques Proust, 'Le
    Paradoxe du *Fils naturel*', *Diderot Studies*, 4 (1963), pp. 209–20; and
    Marian Hobson, 'Notes pour les "Entretiens sur *Le Fils naturel*"', *Revue
    d'Histoire littéraire de la France*, 74, no. 2 (March–April, 1974), pp. 203–13.
9   DPV, X, xviii–xix.
10 Leo Spitzer, 'The Style of Diderot', in *Linguistics and Literary History:
    Essays in Stylistics* (Princeton, NJ: Princeton University Press, 1948), pp.
    135–92.
11 Georges Roth, ed., *Correspondance de Diderot* (Paris: Les Éditions de Minuit,
    1955), 2 (18 November 1758), 88. Hereafter cited as Roth, followed by
    vol. no. and page.
12 Ibid., (27 November 1758), 96.
13 Ibid., 89.
14 A–T, VII, 7, 173.
15 Cf. Alice Green Fredman, *Diderot and Sterne* (New York: Columbia
    University Press, 1955).
16 A–T, VIII, 344–5.
17 *Dictionary of National Biography* (London: pub. since 1917 by Oxford
    University Press), 21, 1284.
18 Roger Kempf, *Diderot et le roman: ou le démon de la présence* (Paris: Éditions
    du Seuil, 1964), p. 20, hereafter cited as Kempf.
19 A–T, IV, 100–1.
20 J.-J. Rousseau, *Les Confessions* (Paris: Editions Garnier Frères, 1964),
    p. 645; see also Kempf, p. 21.
21 Denis Diderot, *Oeuvres esthétiques*, ed. Paul Vernière (Paris: Éditions
    Garnier Frères, 1968), pp. 25, 37 hereafter cited as Garnier, *OE*.
22 Kempf, p. 22, thinks that Diderot knew *Pamela* in English as early as 1742.
    See also June Sigler Siegel, 'Diderot and Richardson: A Confluence of
    Opposites', Diss. Columbia, 1963, p. 33. For more detail on the changes
    in Diderot's philosophy, cf. Robert Loyalty Cru, *Diderot as a Disciple of
    English Thought* (1913; rpt New York: Columbia University Studies in
    Romance Philology and Literature, 1966), pp. 125ff.
23 Kempf, pp. 33–4.
24 Ibid., p. 34.

25 Denis Diderot, *Oeuvres philosophiques*, ed. Paul Vernière (Paris: Éditions Garnier Frères, 1964), pp. 310–11, hereafter cited as Garnier, *OP*.
26 DPV, X, 85.

5 Sex and the *philosophe*

1 Roger Picard, *Les Salons littéraires et la société française, 1610–1789* (New York: Brentano's, 1943), pp. 237–8.

2 Lucien Goldmann, *The Philosophy of the Enlightenment: The Christian Burgess and the Enlightenment*, trans. Henry Maas (London: Routledge & Kegan Paul, 1973), pp. 41–2.

3 Robert Darnton, 'Trade in the Taboo: The Life of a Clandestine Book Dealer in Pre-revolutionary France', in *The Widening Circle: Essays on the Circulation of Literature in the Eighteenth-Century Europe*, ed. Paul J. Korshin (Philadelphia: University of Pennsylvania Press, 1977), pp. 11–83.

4 Giacomo Casanova, *Mémoires*, I (Paris: Gallimard, 1958), p. 7.

5 Ibid., p. 1.

6 There are some extremely interesting sources on *précieux* language. The evolution of typically *précieux* words like *galant, honnêteté* and *estime* from the seventeenth to the eighteenth centuries is fascinating. One can begin by looking at the article 'Galant' in Littré, *Dictionnaire de la langue francaise*. See also the articles 'Galant' and 'Galanterie' (written by Voltaire and cited by Littré) in Denis Diderot *et al.*, *Encyclopédie* ('Neufchastel' [Paris]: 1765), VII, 427–8. Another work on language is Ferdinand Brunot, *Histoire de la langue française des origines à 1900, vol. IV: La Langue classique, 1610–1715* (Paris: Librairie Armand Colin, 1930), 280–95. Other works include Peter Brooks, *The Novel of Worldliness: Crébillon, Marivaux, Laclos, Stendhal* (Princeton, NJ: Princeton University Press, 1969); René Bray, *La Préciosité et les précieux de Thibault de Champagne à Jean Giraudoux* (Paris: Éditions Albin Michel, 1948); Frank J. Warnke, *European Metaphysical Poetry* (New Haven and London: Yale University Press, 1961), pp. 29–31; Carolyn C. Lougee, *Le Paradis des femmes: Women, Salons and Social Stratification in Seventeenth-Century France* (Princeton, NJ: Princeton University Press, 1976). There is an old-fashioned but useful history, Paul Kluckhohn, *Die Auffassung der Liebe in der Literatur des 18. Jahrhunderts und in der deutschen Romantik* (Halle: Verlag von Max Niemeyer, 1922); see also Lucien Goldmann, *The Hidden God*, trans. Philip Thody (London: Routledge & Kegan Paul, 1964).

7 *Grandison*, II, 417–18.

8 Bray, *La Préciosité*, p. 173. Other examples may be found in Brunot, IV, 221ff, and in his vol. VI, part 2 (*Le Dix-huitième siècle: La Langue post-classique*), ch. 3, 1078ff. See also Picard, *Les Salons littéraires et la société française*, pp. 86–100.

9 Cited in Alice Green Fredman, *Diderot and Sterne*, pp. 10–11; from Sterne's *Letters*, ed. L. P. Curtis (Oxford: The Clarendon Press, 1935), pp. 161–2.

10 Lawrence Stone, *The Family, Sex and Marriage in England*, p. 537.

11 Aram Vartanian, 'Érotisme et philosophie chez Diderot', *Cahiers de l'Association Internationale des Études Françaises*, 12–13 (1961), 371–2.

12 Grimm, Diderot, Raynal, Meister, etc., *Correspondance littéraire*, ed. Maurice Tourneux (Paris: Garnier Frères, 1877), I, no. 16, 139.

13 Arthur M. Wilson, *Diderot* (New York: Oxford University Press, 1972), pp. 86–7.

14 Cru, *Diderot as a Disciple of English Thought*, p. 314. According to Lawrence Stone, 'tarse' was a contemporary word for penis. Cf. *The Family, Sex and Marriage in England*, p. 538.

15 Casanova, *Mémoires*, I, 56.

16 Rousseau, *Julie, ou La Nouvelle Héloïse*, pp. 307–18.

17 Casanova, *Mémoires*, II, 231ff, 1167.

18 Choderlos de Laclos, *Les Liaisons dangereuses*, ed. René Pomeau (1782: rpt Paris: Garnier Flammarion, 1964), pp. 375–6, 378.

19 R. S. Morton, *Venereal Diseases*, 2nd edn (London: Penguin Books, 1972), p. 32.

20 A profitable study could be made of the same trend in German literature of the *Sturm und Drang* and Romantic periods: one thinks of Kleist's *Käthchen von Heilbronn*, Goethe's *Götz von Berlichingen*, and some of the Romantic *Märchen*.

21 Laclos, *Les Liaisons dangereuses*, p. 378.

22 *Encyclopédie*, XV, Article 'Sensibilité, Sentiment (Médecine)', 47.

23 Roth, II, 63, 69.

24 Diderot obviously liked the comparison between women and the symbol of the Apocalypse. He used it in letters to Sophie and to Grimm in 1759 (Roth, II, 138, 140).

25 See ch. 1 for a discussion of Allestree.

26 Roth, I, 214.

6 *La Religieuse* and *Clarissa*: convent and bordello

1 Herbert Dieckmann, 'The Préface-Annexe of *La Religieuse*', *Diderot Studies*, II (1952), 31.

2 For a view of the eighteenth-century attitude towards medicine, see Michel Foucault, *The Birth of the Clinic: An Archaeology of Medical Perception*, trans. A. M. Sheridan Smith (London: Tavistock Publications, 1973), pp. 90ff.

3 Georges May, *Diderot et 'La Religieuse': Étude historique et littéraire* (Paris: Presses Universitaires de France, and New Haven, Conn.: Yale University Press, 1954), p. 98.

4 See, for example, *Entretien entre d'Alembert et Diderot* and *Le Rêve de d'Alembert*, in Garnier, *OP*, 271–4, 368.

5 Carol Blum, *Diderot: The Virtue of a Philosopher* (New York: The Viking Press, 1974), pp. 73–4, hereafter cited as Blum.

6 For a detailed account of these inconsistencies see Vivienne Mylne, *The Eighteenth-Century French Novel*, pp. 199–202, hereafter cited as Mylne.

7   Foucault, *The Birth of the Clinic*, p. 98.

8   Ibid., pp. xiv, 108.

9   Ibid., pp. 119–20.

10 Ibid., p. 65.

11 One can cite Diderot's own letter to Mme d'Épinay in early November 1760 (Roth, III, 221). See also Joseph Texte, *Jean-Jacques Rousseau and the Cosmopolitan Spirit in Literature: A Study of the Literary Relations between France and England during the Eighteenth Century* (London: Duckworth & Co., and New York: The Macmillan Co., 1899), p. 225; Dieckmann, 'The Préface-Annexe of *La Religieuse*', 32, 34; May, *Diderot et 'La Religieuse'*, pp. 12–15, and (by the same author) *Le Dilemme du roman au dix-huitième siècle* (Paris: Presses Universitaires de France, and New Haven, Conn.: Yale University Press, 1963), p. 129.

12 Roth, III, 310–11.

13 Blum, p. 73.

14 A–T, XI, 143.

15 From a talk by Ludi Jordanova, of the Wellcome Unit for the History of Medicine, Oxford University, given at the Women in Society Research Seminar, King's College, Cambridge, on 18 January 1979.

16 Garnier, *OP*, 351. Also Georges May, *Diderot et 'La Religieuse'*, p. 159.

17 Brooks, *The Novel of Worldliness*, pp. 50, 63ff and esp. pp. 72–6 (on *La Princesse de Clèves*).

18 For another discussion of the *double entendre*, see Mylne, p. 201.

19 Roth, II, 207.

20 Blum, p. 78, is one of many critics who note this tendency.

21 A note by Jacques Voisine, in his edition of Rousseau's *Confessions* (Paris: Éditions Garnier Frères, 1964), discusses a passage from one of Rousseau's favourite authors, La Bruyère, which Jean-Jacques used in his *Lettre à d'Alembert* (1758). Diderot's own suspicion of motivation echoes both La Bruyère and Rousseau at many points.

22 Ludi Jordanova discussed this point in her seminar at King's College, Cambridge; a more developed and formal argument may be found in Rose Laub Coser, 'The Principle of Patriarchy: The Case of *The Magic Flute*', *Signs*, 4, no. 2 (Winter 1978), 337–48.

BIBLIOGRAPHY

I. Primary sources

Addison, Joseph, and Richard Steele. *The Spectator*, ed. Donald F. Bond. Oxford: Oxford University Press, 1965.

Allestree, Richard. *The Ladies Calling in Two Parts*. The Fourth Impression. Oxford: 1676.

The Causes of the Decay of Christian Piety. London: 1704.

The Whole Duty of Man. London: 1751.

Astell, Mary. *An Essay in Defence of the Female Sex*. London: 1696.

The Christian Religion, As Profess'd by a Daughter of the Church of England. London: 1705.

Bayly, Lewis. *The Practice of Piety: Directing a Christian how to Walk, that he may please God*. The Fifty-First Edition. London: 1714.

Boswell, James. *Life of Johnson*, ed. R. W. Chapman and J. D. Fleeman. London: Oxford University Press, 1970.

Bunyan, John. *Grace Abounding to the Chief of Sinners*, ed. Roger Sharrock. Oxford: The Clarendon Press, 1962.

Casanova, Giacomo. *Mémoires*. Paris: Gallimard, 1958.

Choderlos de Laclos, Pierre. *Oeuvres complètes*. Paris: Bibliothèque de la Pléiade, 1944.

Les Liaisons dangereuses (1782), ed. René Pomeau. Paris: Garnier Flammarion, 1964.

Collier, Jane. *Essay on the Art of Ingeniously Tormenting*. London: 1753.

Colquhoun, Patrick. *A Treatise on the Police of the Metropolis*. The Second Edition, Revised and Enlarged. London: 1796.

Dante's Inferno, ed. and trans. John D. Sinclair. New York: Oxford University Press, 1969.

Defoe, Daniel. *Good Advice to the Ladies: shewing, that as the World goes, and is like to go, the best way for them is to keep unmarried* [pamphlet]. London: 1702.

The Family Instructor, in Three Parts. London: 1715.

Religious Courtship. London: 1729.

Diderot, Denis. *Oeuvres complètes*, ed. J. Assézat and Maurice Tourneux. Paris: Garnier Frères, 1875–7.

Correspondance, ed. Georges Roth. Paris: Les Éditions de Minuit, 1955.

Oeuvres philosophiques, ed. Paul Vernière. Paris: Éditions Garnier Frères, 1964.

Bibliography

La Religieuse. Paris: Garnier Flammarion, 1968.

Oeuvres esthétiques, ed. Paul Vernière. Paris: Éditions Garnier Frères, 1968.

Oeuvres, ed. H. Dieckmann, J. Proust and J. Varloot. Paris: Hermann, Éditeurs des Sciences et des Arts, 1975.

et al., eds. *Encyclopédie*. 'Neufchastel' [Paris]: 1765.

Duclos, Charles Pinot. 'Considérations sur les moeurs de ce siècle', *Oeuvres complètes de Duclos*. Paris: Janet et Cotelle, 1820.

ed. *Grammaire générale et raisonnée du Port-Royal*. 1846; rpt Geneva: Droz, 1968.

Etherege, George. *The Works of Sir George Etherege: Containing his Plays and Poems*. London: 1715.

Fleetwood, William. *The Relative Duties of Parents and Children, Husbands and Wives, Masters and Servants*. London: 1705.

Foxe, John. *The Book of Martyrs: Containing an Account of the Sufferings and Death of the Protestants in the Reign of Queen Mary the First*. London: 1732.

Glanvill, Joseph. *Saducismus Triumphatus: or, Full and Plain Evidence Concerning Witches and Apparitions* (1689), ed. Coleman O. Parsons. Gainesville, Fla: Scholars' Facsimiles and Reprints, 1966.

Gouge, Thomas. *Christian Directions, shewing How to walk with GOD All the Day long*. London: 1661.

Gouge, William. *Of Domesticall Duties, Eight Treatises*. The Third Edition. London: 1634.

Grimm, Diderot, Raynal, Meister, etc. *Correspondance littéraire*, ed. Maurice Tourneux. Paris: Garnier Frères, 1877.

Halifax, George Savile (First Marquis of). *The Lady's New-years Gift: or, Advice to a Daughter*. London: 1688.

Hervey, James. *Meditations and Contemplations. In Two Volumes*. The Seventh Edition. London: 1750.

Johnson, Samuel. 'The Preface to Shakespeare' (1765), excerpted in *The Restoration and the Eighteenth Century* (vol. 3 of *The Oxford Anthology of English Literature*), ed. Martin Price. New York and London: Oxford University Press, 1973, pp. 566–7.

Law, William. *Practical Treatise upon Christian Perfection*. London: 1726.

A Serious Call to a Devout and Holy Life. London: 1729.

Le Prince de Beaumont, Marie. *Contes moraux*. Lyon: Pierre Bruyset Ponthos, 1774.

Lillo, George. *The London Merchant, or The history of George Barnwell*. Second Edition. London: 1731.

Locke, John. *Essay Concerning Human Understanding*. 1690; Menston, Yorkshire, England: The Scolar Press, facsimile 1970.

Mackenzie, Henry. *The Man of Feeling*, ed. Brian Vickers. London: Oxford University Press, 1970.

Otway, Thomas. *Venice Preserv'd; or, a Plot Discover'd. A Tragedy*. Dublin: 1762.

Pope, Alexander. *The Poems of Alexander Pope*, ed. John Butt. London: Methuen & Co., 1975.

Richardson, Samuel. *The Apprentice's Vade Mecum: or, Young Man's Pocket-Companion, in three parts*. London: 1734.

Bibliography

A Collection of the Moral and Instructive Sentiments, Maxims, Cautions, and Reflexions, Contained in the Histories of Pamela, Clarissa, and Sir Charles Grandison. Digested under Proper HEADS . . . London: Printed for S. Richardson, 1755.

Correspondence, ed. Anna Laetitia Barbauld. London: 1804.

The Works of Samuel Richardson, ed. Leslie Stephen. London: Henry Sotheran & Co., 1883.

Familiar Letters on Important Occasions, ed. J. Isaacs. London: George Routledge & Sons, 1928.

Pamela, or Virtue Rewarded. London: J. M. Dent & Sons (New York: E. P. Dutton & Co. Inc.), 1938. In 2 vols. Introduction by George Saintsbury.

Selected Letters of Samuel Richardson, ed. John Carroll. Oxford: The Clarendon Press, 1964.

The History of Sir Charles Grandison, ed. Jocelyn Harris. Oxford: Oxford University Press, 1972.

Clarissa, in 4 volumes, ed. John Butt. London, Melbourne and Toronto: Dent Everyman's Library, 1978.

Rousseau, Jean-Jacques. *Émile, ou de l'éducation*, ed. F. and P. Richard. Paris: Garnier, 1951.

Julie, ou La Nouvelle Héloïse, ed. René Pomeau. Paris: Éditions Garnier Frères, 1960.

Les Confessions, ed. Jacques Voisine. Paris: Éditions Garnier Frères, 1964.

Discours sur l'origine et les fondements de l'inégalité parmi les hommes (avec: *Discours sur les sciences et les arts*), ed. Jacques Roger. Paris: Garnier Flammarion, 1971.

Shaftesbury, Anthony Ashley Cooper (Third Earl of). *Characteristicks of men, manners, opinions, times*. Second Edition. London: 1714.

Steele, Richard, ed. (?). *The Ladies-Library*. London: 1714.

Sterne, Laurence. *A Sentimental Journey through France and Italy*. 1768; rpt London: Penguin Books, 1967.

Taylor, Jeremy. *The Rule and Exercise of Holy Living*. [includes . . . *of Holy Dying*]. The Tenth Edition. London: 1674.

Temple, Sir William. *Works in Two Volumes*. The Fourth Edition. London: 1750.

Thomas à Kempis. *The Christian's Exercise: or, Rules to Live above the World while we are in it*. London: 1717.

Voltaire, *Lettres sur La Nouvelle Héloïse*. Paris: 1761.

Dictionnaire philosophique. Paris: 1764.

Wycherley, William. *Plays*, ed. Gerald Weales. New York University Press, 1967.

Young, Edward. *Conjectures on Original Composition*. London: 1759.

II. Secondary sources

Abensour, Léon. *La Femme et le féminisme avant la révolution*. Paris: Éditions Ernest Leroux, 1923.

Bibliography

Adam, Antoine (ed.). *Les Libertins au XVII⁰ siècle*. Paris: Buchet Chastel, 1964.

Allen, Walter. *The English Novel*. London: Pelican Books, 1954.

Ariès, Philippe. *Western Attitudes toward Death: From the Middle Ages to the Present*. Baltimore, Md, and London: The Johns Hopkins University Press, 1974.

Ascoli, Georges. 'Essai sur l'histoire des idées féministes en France, du XVI⁰ siècle à la Révolution'. *Revue de Synthèse historique*, XIII (1906).

Auerbach, Erich. *Vier Untersuchungen zur Geschichte der französischen Bildung*. Bern: A. Francke A. G. Verlag, 1951.

Barber, Elinor G. *The Bourgeoisie in Eighteenth-Century France*. Princeton, NJ: Princeton University Press, 1955.

Barthes, Roland. *Mythologies*. St Albans, Herts: Granada Publishing, 1973.

Bayley, John. *The Characters of Love*. London: Chatto & Windus, 1968.

Bayne-Powell, Rosamond. *Eighteenth-Century London Life*. London: John Murray, 1937.

Housekeeping in the Eighteenth Century. London: John Murray, 1956.

Beauvoir, Simone de. 'Faut-il brûler Sade?', *Temps modernes*, VII (1952), 1208.

Beer, Gillian. 'Richardson, Milton and the Status of Evil', *RES*, NS 19, no. 75 (1968), 261–70.

Beer, Patricia. *Reader, I Married Him*. London: Macmillan, 1974.

Belaval, Yvon. *L'Esthétique sans paradoxe de Diderot*. Paris: Bibliothèque des idées, 1950.

Beljame, Alexandre. *Men of Letters and the English Public in the Eighteenth Century, 1660–1774*, ed. Bonamy Dobrée. London: Kegan Paul, 1978.

Bertaut, Jules. *La Jeune Fille dans la littérature française*. Paris: Michaud, 1910.

Blanchard, Rae. 'Richard Steele and the Status of Women', *Studies in Philology*, 26 (1929), 325–55.

Bloom, Harold. *A Map of Misreading*. New York: Oxford University Press, 1975.

Blum, Carol. *Diderot: The Virtue of a Philosopher*. New York: The Viking Press, 1974.

Boas, Frederick S. 'Richardson's Novels and their Influence', *Essays and Studies by Members of the English Association, II*. Oxford: The Clarendon Press, 1911, 37–70.

From Richardson to Pinero. London: John Murray, 1936.

Bray, René. *La Préciosité et les précieux de Thibault de Champagne à Giraudoux*. Paris: Éditions Albin Michel, 1948.

Bredvold, Louis I. *The Natural History of Sensibility*. Detroit: Wayne State University Press, 1962.

Brissenden, R. F. *Samuel Richardson*. London, New York, Toronto: Longman, Green & Co., 1958.

Virtue in Distress: Studies in the Novel of Sentiment from Richardson to Sade. London and Basingstoke: The Macmillan Press, 1974.

ed. *Studies in the Eighteenth Century: Papers Presented at the David Nichol Smith Memorial Seminar, Canberra, 1966* (in 2 vols). Canberra: Australian National University Press, 1968, 1973.

Bibliography

Brookner, Anita. *Greuze: The Rise and Fall of an Eighteenth-Century Phenomenon*. London: Elek, 1972.

Brooks, Peter Preston. *The Novel of Worldliness: Crébillon, Marivaux, Laclos, Stendhal*. Princeton, NJ: Princeton University Press, 1969.

Brunel, Lucien. 'Diderot et les encyclopédistes', in vol. VI of L. Petit de Julleville, ed., *Histoire de la langue et de la littérature française*. Paris: Colin, 1909, 316–85.

Brunot, Ferdinand. *Histoire de la langue française des origines à 1900*. Paris: Librairie Armand Colin, 1913–.

Carter, Angela. *The Sadeian Woman: An Exercise in Cultural History*. London: Virago, 1979.

Cassirer, Ernst. *The Philosophy of the Enlightenment*. Princeton, NJ: Princeton University Press, 1951.

   The Philosophy of Symbolic Forms, vol. 2: Mythical Thought. New Haven: Yale University Press, 1955, 1965.

   Language and Myth, trans. Suzanne K. Langer. New York: Dover Publications Inc., 1946.

Castle, Terry. 'The Insistence of the Letter: Fiction and Experience in the Novels of Samuel Richardson', Diss. University of Minnesota, 1980.

Catrysse, Jean. *Diderot et la mystification*. Paris: Éditions A. G. Nizet, 1970.

Cecil, Mirable. *Heroines in Love, 1750–1974*. London: Michael Joseph, 1974.

Cirlot, J. E. *A Dictionary of Symbols* (2nd edn), trans. Jack Sage. London: Routledge & Kegan Paul, 1971.

Cockshut, A. O. J. *Man and Woman: A Study of Love and the Novel*. New York: Oxford University Press, 1978.

Copeland, Edward. 'Allegory and Analogy in *Clarissa*: The "Plan" and the "No-Plan"', *ELH*, 39 (1972), 254–65.

Coser, Rose Laub. 'The Principle of Patriarchy: The Case of *The Magic Flute*'. *Signs*, 4, no. 2 (Winter 1978), 337–48.

Cowler, Rosemary, ed. *Twentieth-Century Interpretations of Pamela: A Collection of Critical Essays*. Englewood Cliffs, NJ: Prentice-Hall Inc., 1969.

Craig, David. *The Real Foundations: Literature and Social Change*. London: Chatto & Windus, 1973.

Crane, R. S. 'Suggestions toward a Genealogy of the "Man of Feeling"', *ELH*, 1 (1934), 205ff.

Creed, John Martin and John Sandwith Boys Smith. *Religious Thought in the Eighteenth Century: Illustrated from writers of the period*. Cambridge: The University Press, 1934.

Cru, Robert Loyalty. *Diderot as a Disciple of English Thought*, 1913; rpt New York: Columbia University Studies in Romance Philology and Literature, 1966.

Culler, Jonathan. *The Pursuit of Signs: Semiotics, Literature, Deconstruction*. London: Routledge & Kegan Paul, 1981.

Dales, Joanna Clare. 'The Novel as Domestic Conduct Book: Richardson to Jane Austen'. Diss. Cambridge, 1970.

Bibliography

Darnton, Robert. 'Trade in the Taboo: The Life of a Clandestine Book Dealer in Pre-revolutionary France', in *The Widening Circle: Essays on the Circulation of Literature in Eighteenth-Century Europe*, ed. Paul J. Korshin. Philadelphia: University of Pennsylvania Press, 1977.

Day, Robert Adams. *Told in Letters: Epistolary Fiction before Richardson*. Ann Arbor, Mich.: University of Michigan Press, 1966.

Dieckmann, Herbert. 'The Préface-Annexe of *La Religieuse*', *Diderot Studies*, II (1952), 21–147.

  Cinq leçons sur Diderot. Geneva and Paris: Librairie E. Droz and Librairie Minard, 1959.

  'Religiöse und metaphysische Elemente im Denken der Aufklärung', *Wort und Text: Festschrift für Fritz Schalk*, ed. Harri Meier. Frankfurt am Main: Vittorio Klostermann, 1963, pp. 334–54.

  'Philosophy and Literature in Eighteenth-Century France', *Comparative Literature Studies*, VIII, no. 1 (March 1971), 21–41.

  Studien zur Europäischen Aufklärung. Munich: Wilhelm Fink Verlag, 1974.

Donovan, Robert. 'The Problem of Pamela, or, Virtue Unrewarded', *SEL*, III (1963), 377–95.

Doody, Margaret Anne. *A Natural Passion: A Study of the Novels of Samuel Richardson*. Oxford: Oxford University Press, 1974.

Douglas, Ann. *The Feminization of American Culture*. New York: Alfred A. Knopf, 1977.

Downs, Brian W. *Richardson*. London: George Routledge & Sons, 1928.

Dussinger, John A. 'Conscience and the Pattern of Christian Perfection in *Clarissa*', *PMLA*, 81.1 (1966), 236–45.

  'Richardson's "Christian Vocation"', *Papers on Language and Literature*, III (1967), 3–19.

Eagleton, Terry. *The Rape of Clarissa*. Oxford: Basil Blackwell, 1982.

Eaves, T. C. Duncan and Ben D. Kimpel. *Samuel Richardson: A Biography*. Oxford: The Clarendon Press, 1971.

Ehrenpreis, Irvin, and Robert Halsband. *The Lady of Letters in the Eighteenth Century*. Los Angeles: William Andrews Clark Memorial Library, University of California, 1969.

Elioseff, Lee Andrew. *The Cultural Milieu of Addison's Literary Criticism*. Austin, Texas: University of Texas Press, 1963.

Ellrich, Robert J. 'The Rhetoric of *La Religieuse* and Eighteenth-Century Forensic Rhetoric', *Diderot Studies*, III (1961), 129–54.

  'The Structure of Diderot's *Les Bijoux indiscrets*', *RR*, 52 (1961), 279–89.

Fargher, Richard, ed. *Life and Letters in France: Volume II, The Eighteenth Century*. London: Thomas Nelson & Sons, 1970.

Farrell, William J. 'The Style and the Action in *Clarissa*', *SEL*, III (1963), 365–75.

Fauchery, Pierre. *La Destinée féminine dans le roman européen du dix-huitième siècle, 1713–1807: Essai de gynécomythie romanesque*. Paris: Librairie Armand Colin, 1972.

Bibliography

Ferguson, Francis. *The Idea of a Theater*. Princeton, NJ: Princeton University Press, 1972.

Fiedler, Leslie. *Love and Death in the American Novel*. New York: Criterion Books, 1960.

Flynn, Carol Houlihan. *Samuel Richardson: A Man of Letters*. Princeton, NJ: Princeton University Press, 1982.

Forno, Lawrence J. 'The Cosmic Mysticism of Diderot', *Studies on Voltaire and the Eighteenth Century*, 143 (1975), 113–40.

Foucault, Michel. *The Birth of the Clinic: An Archaeology of Medical Perception*, trans. A. M. Sheridan Smith. London: Tavistock Publications, 1973.

  The History of Sexuality, Volume I: An Introduction, trans. Robert Hurley. London: Allen Lane, 1978.

Fredman, Alice Green. *Diderot and Sterne*. New York: Columbia University Press, 1955.

Freud, Sigmund. *Totem and Taboo*. London: Routledge & Kegan Paul, 1975.

Frye, Northrop. *Fables of Identity: Studies in Poetic Mythology*. New York: Harcourt, Brace & World Inc., 1963.

  Anatomy of Criticism. New York: Atheneum, 1969.

Gay, Peter. *The Science of Freedom* (vol. 2 of *The Enlightenment: An Interpretation*). London: Wildwood House, 1973.

Gillie, Christopher. *Character in English Literature*. London: Chatto & Windus, 1965.

Girard, René. *Deceit, Desire and the Novel: The Self and Other in Literary Structure*, trans. Yvonne Freccero. Baltimore, Md, and London: The Johns Hopkins University Press, 1965.

Godenne, René. 'Les Nouvellistes des années 1680–1750 et *La Religieuse*', *Diderot Studies*, 16 (1973), 55–68.

Golden, Morris. *Richardson's Characters*. Ann Arbor, Mich.: The University of Michigan Press, 1963.

Goldmann, Lucien. *The Hidden God*, trans. Philip Thody. London: Routledge and Kegan Paul, 1964.

  The Philosophy of the Enlightenment: The Christian Burgess and the Enlightenment, trans. Henry Maas. London: Routledge & Kegan Paul, 1973.

Green, F. C. *Literary Ideas in Eighteenth-Century France and England: A Critical Survey*. New York: Frederick Ungar Publishing Co., 1966.

Gutwirth, M. 'Mme de Staël, Rousseau and the Woman Question', *PMLA*, 86 (1971), 100–9.

Habakkuk, H. J. 'Marriage Settlements in the Eighteenth Century', *Transactions of the Royal Historical Society*, XXXII (1949), 15–30.

Haller, William H. *The Rise of Puritanism*. Philadelphia: University of Pennsylvania, 1972.

Hardwick, Elizabeth. *Seduction and Betrayal: Women and Literature*. New York: Random House, 1974.

Harris, R. W. *Reason and Nature in the Eighteenth Century: 1714–1780*. London: Blandford Press, 1968.

Bibliography

Hassall, Antony J. 'Women in Richardson and Fielding', *Novel* (Winter 1981).

Hazard, Paul. *Quatre études*. New York: Oxford University Press, 1940.

Hill, Christopher. 'Clarissa Harlowe and her Times', *Essays in Criticism*, 5 (1955), 315–40.

Hilles, Frederick W. 'The Plan of *Clarissa*', *PQ*, 45 (1966), 236–48.

Hilles, Frederick W. and Harold Bloom, eds. *From Sensibility to Romanticism: Essays Presented to Frederick A. Pottle*. New York: Oxford University Press, 1965.

Hobson, Marian. 'Notes pour les "Entretiens sur *Le Fils naturel*"', *Revue d'Histoire littéraire de la France*, 74, no. 2 (March–April 1974), 203–13.

Hornbeak, Katherine. 'Richardson's *Familiar Letters* and the Domestic Conduct Books', *Smith College Studies in Modern Languages*, 19, 2 (1938), 1–29.

'The Complete Letter Writer in English, 1568–1800', *Smith College Studies in Modern Languages*, 15, 3–4 (1934).

Hufton, Olwen. 'Women in Revolution 1789–1796', *Past and Present*, 53 (1971), 90–108.

Hughes, Leon. 'Theatrical Convention in Richardson', in *Restoration and Eighteenth-Century Literature, Essays in Honor of Alan Dugald McKillop*, ed. Carroll Camden. Chicago: University of Chicago Press, 1963, pp. 239–70.

Humphreys, A. R. *The Augustan World: Life and Letters in Eighteenth-Century England*. London: Methuen & Co., 1964.

Huxley, Julian. 'A Factor Overlooked by the Philosophes: The Population Explosion', *Studies on Voltaire and the Eighteenth Century*, 25 (1963), 861–83.

Jauss, Hans Robert. *Literaturgeschichte als Provokation*. Frankfurt am Main: Suhrkamp Verlag, 1970.

Jones, Louis Clark. *The Clubs of the Georgian Rakes*. New York: Columbia University Studies in English and Comparative Literature, 1941.

Kearney, Anthony. '*Clarissa* and the Epistolary Form', *Essays in Criticism*, 16 (1966), 44–56.

Kempf, Roger. *Diderot et le roman: ou le démon de la présence*. Paris: Éditions du Seuil, 1964.

Sur le corps romanesque. Paris: Éditions du Seuil, 1968.

Kerber, Linda K. 'The Politicks of Housework', *Signs*, 4 (2), 402–6.

Kermode, Frank. *The Sense of an Ending: Studies in the Theory of Fiction*. London: Oxford University Press, 1967.

Kinkead-Weekes, Mark. '*Clarissa* Restored?', *RES*, NS 10 (1959), 156–71.

'Defoe and Richardson – Novelists of the City', in *The Sphere History of Literature in the English Language, vol. IV*, ed. R. Lonsdale. London: Sphere Inc., 1971, 226–58.

Samuel Richardson: Dramatic Novelist. London: Eyre Methuen, 1973.

Kluckhohn, Paul. *Die Auffassung der Liebe in der Literatur des 18. Jahrhunderts und in der deutschen Romantik*. Halle: Verlag von Max Niemeyer, 1922.

Bibliography

Konigsberg, Ira. *Samuel Richardson and the Dramatic Novel*. Lexington, Ky: University of Kentucky Press, 1968.

Kors, Alan Charles. *D'Holbach's Coterie: An Enlightenment in Paris*. Princeton, NJ: Princeton University Press, 1976.

Korshin, Paul J., ed. *The Widening Circle: Essays on the Circulation of Literature in Eighteenth-Century Europe*. Philadelphia: University of Pennsylvania Press, 1977.

Krauss, Werner. *Perspektiven und Probleme, zur französischen und deutschen Auflärung und andere Aufsätze*. Berlin: Luchterhand, 1965.

 ed. *Die französische Aufklärung im Spiegel der deutschen Literatur des 18. Jahrhunderts*. Berlin: Akademie-Verlag, 1963.

 ed. *Neue Beiträge zur Literatur der Aufklärung*. Berlin: Rutten, 1964.

Kreiser, B. Robert. *Miracles, Convulsions and Ecclesiastical Politics in Early Eighteenth-Century Paris*. Princeton: Princeton University Press, 1978.

Krutch, Joseph Wood. *Five Masks: A Study in the Mutations of the Novel*. New York: Jonathan Cape and Harrison Smith, 1930.

Larnac, Jean. *Histoire de la littérature féminine en France*. Paris: Éditions KRA, 1929.

Lathuillère, Roger. *La Préciosité: Étude historique et linguistique, I*. Geneva: Librairie Droz, 1966.

Laurenson, Diana, and Alan Swingewood. *The Sociology of Literature*. London: Paladin, 1972.

Leach, Edmund. *Culture and Communication*. Cambridge, England: Cambridge University Press, 1979.

Leavis, F. R. *The Great Tradition*. New York: Doubleday & Co. Inc., 1954.

Leavis, Q. D. *Fiction and the Reading Public*. London: Chatto & Windus, 1965.

Lee, Vera. 'Innocence and Initiation in the Eighteenth-Century French Novel', *Studies in Voltaire and the Eighteenth Century*, 153 (1976), 1307–12.

Lesser, Simon O. 'A Note on *Pamela*', *College English*, XIV (1952), 13–17.

Lévi-Strauss, Claude. *The Raw and the Cooked*, vol. I of *An Introduction to a Science of Mythology*, trans. John and Doreen Weightman. New York and Evanston: Harper & Row, 1969.

Lewinter, Roger. 'L'Exaltation de la vertu dans le théâtre de Diderot', *Diderot Studies*, 8 (1966), 119–69.

Lougee, Carolyn C. *Le Paradis des femmes: Women, Salons and Social Stratification in Seventeenth-Century France*. Princeton, NJ: Princeton University Press, 1976.

Lough, John. *An Introduction to Eighteenth-Century France*. London: Longman, 1960.

 The Encyclopédie in Eighteenth-Century England and Other Studies. Newcastle-upon-Tyne: Oriel Press, 1970.

 The Encyclopédie. London: Longman, 1971.

 The Contributors to the Encyclopédie. London: Grant & Cutler, 1973.

 'Who Were the Philosophes?', in *Studies in Eighteenth-Century French Literature: Presented to Robert Niklaus*, ed. J. H. Fox, M. H. Waddicor and D. A. Watts. Exeter, England: University of Exeter Press, 1975, pp. 139–50.

Bibliography

MacCarthy, B. G. *Women Writers: Their Contribution to the English Novel, 1621–1744*. Cork, Eire: Cork University Press, 1944.

The Later Women Novelists, 1744–1818. Cork, Eire: Cork University Press, and Oxford: Blackwell, 1947.

McEwen, Gilbert D. *The Oracle of the Coffee House: John Dunton's Athenian Mercury*. San Marino, Calif.: The Huntington Library, 1972.

Macfarlane, Alan. *Witchcraft in Tudor and Stuart England: A Regional and Comparative Study*. London: Routledge & Kegan Paul, 1970.

Machin, Ivor W. J. 'Popular Religious Works of the Eighteenth Century: Their Vogue and Influence'. Diss. University of London, 1939.

McKillop, Alan Dugald. *Samuel Richardson: Printer and Novelist*. Chapel Hill, NC: University of North Carolina Press, 1936.

The Early Masters of English Fiction. Lawrence, Kansas: University of Kansas Press, 1956.

Maclean, Ian. *Woman Triumphant: Feminism in French Literature, 1610–1652*. Oxford: The Clarendon Press, 1977.

Marlowe, John. *The Puritan Tradition in English Life*. London: The Cresset Press, 1956.

Marshall, Dorothy. *English People in the Eighteenth Century*. London: Longman, Green & Co., 1956.

Dr Johnson's London. London, New York and Sydney: John Wiley & Sons Inc., 1968.

Mauzi, Robert. 'Les Rapports du bonheur et de la vertu dans l'oeuvre de Diderot', *Cahiers de l'Association Internationale des Études Françaises*, 12–13 (1960–1), 255–68.

May, Georges. *Diderot et 'La Religieuse': Étude historique et littéraire*. Paris: Presses Universitaires de France, and New Haven, Conn.: Yale University Press, 1954.

Le Dilemme du roman au dix-huitième siècle. Paris: Presses Universitaires de France, and New Haven, Conn.: Yale University Press, 1963.

'The Influences of English Fiction on the French Mid-Eighteenth Century Novel', in *Aspects of the Eighteenth Century*, ed. Earl Wasserman. Baltimore, Md: The Johns Hopkins University Press, 1965, pp. 265–80.

Mews, Hazel. *Frail Vessels: Woman's Role in Women's Novels from Fanny Burney to T. S. Eliot*. London: The Athlone Press, 1969.

Miller, Nancy K. *The Heroine's Text. Readings in the French and English Novel, 1722–1782*. New York: Columbia University Press, 1980.

Morton, R. S. *Venereal Diseases*. 2nd edn. London: Penguin Books, 1972.

Mortier, Roland. *Diderot en Allemagne (1750–1850)*. Paris: Presses Universitaires de France, 1954.

Mylne, Vivienne. 'Dialogue as Narrative in Eighteenth-Century French Fiction'. In *Studies in Eighteenth-Century French Literature: Presented to Robert Niklaus*, ed. J. H. Fox, M. H. Waddicor and D. A. Watts. Exeter, England: University of Exeter Press, 1975, pp. 173–92.

The Eighteenth-Century French Novel: Techniques of Illusion, 2nd edn. Cambridge, England: Cambridge University Press, 1981.

Bibliography

Napier, Elizabeth R. 'Tremble and Reform: The Inversion of Power in Richardson's *Clarissa*', *ELH*, 42, no. 2 (Summer 1975), 214–23.

Niklaus, Robert. *A Literary History of France: The Eighteenth Century, 1715–1789*. London: Ernest Benn, and New York: Barnes & Noble Inc., 1970.

Palache, John Garber. *Four Novelists of the Old Régime: Crébillon, Laclos, Diderot, Restif de la Bretonne*. London: Jonathan Cape, 1926.

Pappas, John. 'Le Moralisme des *Liaisons dangereuses*', *Dix-huitième siècle*, 2 (1970), 265–96.

Parnell, Paul E. 'The Sentimental Mask', *PMLA*, 78 (1963), 529–35.

Perkins, Jean A. 'Diderot's Concept of Virtue', *Studies in Voltaire and the Eighteenth Century*, 23 (1963), 77–91.

Picard, Roger. *Les Salons littéraires et la société française, 1610–1789*. New York: Brentano's, 1943.

Poetzsche, Erich. 'Samuel Richardsons Belesenheit: Eine literarische Untersuchung', *Kieler Studien zur englischen Philologie*, NF I–IV, 1908.

Politi, Jina. *The Novel and its Presuppositions: Changes in the Conceptual Structure of Novels in the Eighteenth and Nineteenth Centuries*. Amsterdam: Adolf M. Hakkert NV, 1976.

Pons, Christian. *Richardson et la littérature bourgeoise en Angleterre*. Aix-en-Provence: Publications des Annales de la Faculté des Lettres, 1968 (1969).

Powell, Chilton Latham. *English Domestic Relations, 1487–1653*. New York: Columbia University Studies in English and Comparative Literature, 1917.

Préclin, Edmond. *Les Jansénistes du XVIIIe siècle et la Constitution civile du Clergé*. Paris: Librairie universitaire J. Gamber, 1929.

Preston, John. *The Created Self: The Reader's Role in Eighteenth-Century Fiction*. London: Heinemann, 1970.

'Epistolary Narrative and Moral Discovery', *French Studies*, 24 (1970), 23–35.

Proust, Jacques. 'Le Paradoxe du *Fils naturel*', *Diderot Studies*, 4 (1963), 209–20.

Rabkin, Norman. '*Clarissa*: A Study in the Nature of Convention', *ELH*, 23 (1956), 204–17.

Ravenel, Florence Leftwich. *Women and the French Tradition*. New York: The Macmillan Company, 1918.

Reynolds, Myra. *The Learned Lady in England, 1650–1760*. New York: E. P. Dutton & Co., 1919.

Richetti, J. J. *Popular Fiction before Richardson: Narrative Patterns 1700–1739*. Oxford: The Clarendon Press, 1969.

Ricoeur, Paul. *De l'interprétation: essai sur Freud*. Paris: Éditions du Seuil, 1965.

Rodgers, Gary Bruce. 'Diderot and the Eighteenth-Century French Press', *Studies in Voltaire and the Eighteenth Century*, 107 (1973).

Rogers, Katherine M. 'Sensitive Feminism versus Conventional Sympathy: Richardson and Fielding on Women', *Novel* (Spring 1976).

Ruthven, K. K. *Myth*, no. 31 in the series *The Critical Idiom*. London: Methuen & Co., 1976.

Bibliography

Sale, William M. Jr. *Samuel Richardson: Master Printer*. Ithaca, NY: Cornell University Press, 1950.

Schmidt, Erich. *Richardson, Rousseau and Goethe*. Jena: Verlag von Eduard Fromman, 1875.

Schöffler, Herbert. *Protestantismus und Literatur: Neue Wege zur Englischen Literatur des 18. Jahrhunderts*. Göttingen: Vandenhoeck & Ruprecht, 1958.

Schücking, L. L. *The Puritan Family: A Social Study from the Literary Sources*, trans. Brian Battershaw, 1929; rpt London: Routledge & Kegan Paul, 1969.

Shepherd, T. B. *Methodism and the Literature of the Eighteenth Century*. London: The Epworth Press, 1970.

Siegel, June S. 'Diderot and Richardson: A Confluence of Opposites'. New York: Diss. Columbia University, 1963.

'Diderot and Richardson: Manuscripts, Missives, and Mysteries', *Diderot Studies*, 18 (1975), 145–67.

Sowell, William Marks. 'The Novel as Puritan Romance: A Comparative Study of Samuel Richardson, The Brontës, Thomas Hardy and D. H. Lawrence'. Diss. Stanford University, 1964.

Spacks, Patricia Meyer. 'Ev'ry Woman is at Heart a Rake', *Eighteenth-Century Studies*, 8 (Fall 1974), 27–46.

Spitzer, Leo. *Linguistics and Literary History: Essays in Stylistics*. Princeton, NJ: Princeton University Press, 1948.

Stearns, Bertha Monica. 'Early English Periodicals for Ladies (1700–1760)', *PMLA*, 48, no. 1 (1933), 38–60.

Stenton, Doris Mary. *The English Woman in History*. London: Allen & Unwin, New York: Macmillan, 1957.

Stephen, Leslie. *English Literature and Society in the Eighteenth Century*. London: Duckworth & Co., 1904.

Stone, Lawrence. *The Family, Sex and Marriage in England, 1500–1800*. London: Weidenfeld & Nicolson, 1977.

Tanner, Tony. *Adultery in the Novel: Contract and Transgression*. Baltimore, Md, and London: The Johns Hopkins University Press, 1979.

Taupin, René. 'Richardson, Diderot et l'art de conter', *French Review*, 12, no. 3 (1939), 181–94.

Taveneaux, René, ed. *Jansénisme et politique*. Paris: Armand Colin (La Collection U), 1965.

La Vie quotidienne des Jansénistes au XVIIe et XVIIIe siècles. Paris: Librairie Hachette, 1973.

Texte, Joseph. *Jean-Jacques Rousseau and the Cosmopolitan Spirit in Literature: A Study of the Literary Relations between France and England during the Eighteenth Century*. London: Duckworth & Co., and New York: The Macmillan Co., 1899.

Thelander, Dorothy Ramona. *Laclos and the Epistolary Novel*. Geneva: Droz, 1963.

Thomas, Keith. *Religion and the Decline of Magic: Studies in Popular Beliefs in Sixteenth- and Seventeenth-Century England*. London: Weidenfeld & Nicolson, 1971.

Bibliography

Thomas, Ruth P. '*Les Bijoux indiscrets* as a Laboratory for Diderot's later Novels', *Studies in Voltaire and the Eighteenth Century*, 135 (1975), 199–211.

Thompson, E. P. 'The Moral Economy of the English Crowd in the Eighteenth Century', *Past and Present*, 50 (1971), 76–136.

Tieje, Arthur Jerrold. 'A Peculiar Phase of the Theory of Realism in Pre-Richardsonian Fiction', *PMLA*, 28 (1913), 213–52.

Tinker, Chauncey Brewster. *The Salon and English Letters*. New York: The Macmillan Co., 1915.

Todd, Janet. *Women's Friendship in Literature*. New York: Columbia University Press, 1980.

Tompkins, J. M. S. *The Popular Novel in England 1770–1800*. London: Constable, 1932.

Traugott, John. '*Clarissa*'s Richardson: An Essay To Find the Reader', in *English Literature in the Age of Disguise*, ed. Maximilian Novak. Berkeley and Los Angeles: University of California Press, 1977, pp. 157–208.

Trevor-Roper, H. R. *The Crisis of the Seventeenth Century: Religion, the Reformation and Social Change*. New York: Harper & Row, 1968.

Trumbach, Randolph. *The Rise of the Egalitarian Family: Aristocratic Kinship and Domestic Relations in Eighteenth-Century England*. New York and London: Academic Press, 1978.

Turnell, Martin. *The Novel in France*. New York: Random House, 1951.

Utter, Robert Palfrey, and Gwendolyn Needham. *Pamela's Daughters*. New York: Macmillan, 1936.

Vaillant, Roger, ed. *Laclos par lui-même*. Paris: Éditions du Seuil, 1965.

Van Ghent, Dorothy. *The English Novel: Form and Function*. New York: Rinehart & Co. Inc., 1953.

Vartanian, Aram. 'Érotisme et philosophie chez Diderot', *Cahiers de l'Association Internationale des Études Françaises*, 12–13 (1961), 367–90.

Wagner, Geoffrey. *Five for Freedom: A Study of Feminism in Fiction*. London: Allen & Unwin, 1972.

Wagner, Roy. *Lethal Speech: Daribi Myth as Symbolic Obviation*. Ithaca and London: Cornell University Press, 1978.

   The Invention of Culture. Chicago and London: University of Chicago Press, 1981.

Wallas, Ada. *Before the Bluestockings*. London: Allen & Unwin, 1929.

Warner, William Beatty. *Reading Clarissa: The Struggles of Interpretation*. New Haven and London: Yale University Press, 1979.

Warnke, Frank J. *European Metaphysical Poetry*. New Haven and London: Yale University Press, 1961.

Wasserman, Earl R., ed. *Aspects of the Eighteenth Century*. Baltimore, Md: The Johns Hopkins University Press, 1965.

Watt, Ian. *The Rise of the Novel*. Berkeley and Los Angeles: University of California Press, 1967.

Wellek, René and Austin Warren. *Theory of Literature*. New York: Harcourt, Brace & World Inc., 1956.

Bibliography

Wendt, Alan. 'Clarissa's Coffin', *PQ,* 39 (1960), 481–95.

Whitney, Lois. *Primitivism and the Idea of Progress in English Popular Literature of the Eighteenth Century.* Baltimore, Md: The Johns Hopkins University Press, 1934.

Wilcox, Frank Howard. 'Prévost's Translations of Richardson's Novels', *University of California Publications in Modern Philology*, 12, no. 5 (1927), 341–411.

Wildeblood, Joan, and Peter Brinson. *The Polite World: A Guide to English Manners and Deportment from the Thirteenth to the Nineteenth Century.* London: Oxford University Press, 1965.

Wilkins, Kay S. 'Some Aspects of the Irrational in Eighteenth-Century France', *Studies on Voltaire and the Eighteenth Century*, 140 (1975), 107–202.

Willey, Basil. *The Eighteenth-Century Background: Studies on the Idea of Nature in the Thought of the Period.* London: Chatto & Windus, 1940.

Williams, David. 'The Politics of Feminism in the French Enlightenment', in *The Varied Pattern: Studies in the Eighteenth Century*, ed. Peter Hughes and David Williams. Toronto: A. M. Hakkert, 1971, pp. 333–51.

Williams, E. N. *Life in Georgian England.* London: Batsford, 1963.

Williams, Raymond. *Culture and Society: 1780–1950.* New York: Harper & Row, 1958.

The Country and the City. St Albans, Herts.: Paladin, 1975.

Wilson, Arthur M. *Diderot: The Testing Years, 1713–1759.* New York: Oxford University Press, 1957.

Diderot. New York: Oxford University Press, 1972.

Wilson, Stuart. 'Richardson's *Pamela*: An Interpretation', *PMLA*, 88, 1 (1973), 79–91.

Wilt, Judith, 'He Could Go No Farther: A Modest Proposal about Lovelace and Clarissa', *PMLA*, 92 (January 1977), 19–32.

Wokler, Robert. 'The Influence of Diderot on the Political Theory of Rousseau: Two Aspects of a Relationship', *Studies on Voltaire and the Eighteenth Century*, 132 (1975), 55–112.

Wolff, Cynthia Griffin. *Samuel Richardson and the Eighteenth-Century Puritan Character.* Hamden, Conn.: Archon Books, 1972.

233

INDEX

235

Index

Index

Index

Sade, Donatien, marquis de, 114, 119, 186
Salem witch trials, 87
Scudéry, Madeleine de, 150
Sedaine, Michel-Jean, 171, 175
Seneca, 187
'Sensibilité, Sentiment (Médicine)' – *Encyclopédie* article, 158
sexual ambiguity, homosexuality, 115–16, 160, 196, 198–204
sexuality, female, and smallpox, 153–6
sexuality, female, in *Clarissa*: 2, 3, 5, 9, 98, 113–16; and religion, 84–5, 91–3, 125–7, 205–6; related to paternal authority, 71 *passim*
sexuality in Diderot, 120–2, 151, 152–68, 186, 187, 188–204
Shaftesbury, Anthony Ashley, Third Earl of, 131, 134, 141, 143, 147, 152; *Essay Concerning Merit and Virtue*, 133
Shakespeare, William, 17, 64, 105, 115, 134, 135
Sir Charles Grandison, 1, 2, 6, 25, 27, 44, 56, 57, 128, 130, 132, 137, 139, 149, 204
Skelton, Philip, 28, 56
Spectator, The, 47, 50
Spitzer, Leo, 130
Steele, Sir Richard, 50
Stendhal (Henri Beyle), 5, 139
Stephen, Sir Leslie, 7
Sterne, Laurence, 133, 151, 175, 205
Stoker, Bram, 114
Stone, Lawrence, 52, 54, 59, 151, 186
Sturm und Drang, 131
Swift, Jonathan, 58, 153

Tanner, Tony, 5
Taylor, Jeremy: *Holy Living and Holy Dying*, 29–30, 32, 33, 36, 40–1, 49, 50, 54
Temple, Sir William, 53

Tencin, marquise de, 151
Thomas (writer attacked by Diderot), 157, 161
Thomas à Kempis: *The Christian's Exercise*, 28, 29
Tronchin, Dr, 174, 196
typology, biblical, 102–3, 117, 126

Urfé, Madame d', 154

vampirism, 114, 199
Vartanian, Aram, 152
Verdi, Giuseppe, 129
Vernet, Joseph, 186
Volland, Sophie, 133–4, 140, 149, 160, 168, 172–3, 183
Voltaire (François-Marie Arouet), 131, 134, 135, 136, 147, 149, 151; *Candide*, 134, 136; *Lettres angloises*, 134

Wagner, Richard, 129
Wagner, Roy, 19, 20
Warburton, William, 128
Warner, William Beatty, 9, 11–13, 18
Watt, Ian, 8, 45, 64, 99
Webster, John: *The Display of Witchcraft*, 87
Wilkes, John, 101
Williams, Raymond, 47
Wilt, Judith, 15
women: and religion in England, 36–7, 45–51, 60–5; and Richardson, 2, 3, 4, 76, 133, 205, 209 n. 13; in France, 5
women writers (eighteenth-century), 3, 5
Wolff, Cynthia Griffin, 68
Woolf, Virginia, 208
Wray, Lady Mary, 50, 51
Wuthering Heights, 206
Wycherley, William: *The Country-Wife*, 78

Young, Edward, 28, 56, 134, 135